INTERNAL CONTROL STRATEGIES

INTERNAL CONTROL STRATEGIES
A Mid to Small Business Guide

Julie Harrer

WILEY

John Wiley & Sons, Inc.

This book is printed on acid-free paper. ∞

Library of Congress Cataloging-in-Publication Data

Harrer, Julie, 1966–
    Internal control strategies : a mid to small business guide/Julie Harrer.
        p.   cm.
    Includes index.
    ISBN 978-0-470-37619-5 (cloth)
        1.   Auditing, Internal. 2.   Small business—Auditing. I. Title.
    HF5667.H338   2008
    657'.458—dc22
                                                                    2008011987

Printed in the United States of America

10 9 8 7 6 5 4 3 2 1

Contents

Preface

On February 2, 2004, I was hired by a consulting firm to begin working on a Sarbanes-Oxley (SOX) Section 404 project for a high-tech company with 8,000-plus employees and over $4 billion in revenues. At the time, the company was required to comply with Section 404 for its fiscal year ending September 24, 2004. The team that was already in place had been working on the project for over eight months with minimal progress. There was very little guidance published on SOX compliance, skilled resources were scarce, and the external auditors were stumbling through the project just as much as the company was.

At the end of February, the Securities and Exchange Commission (SEC) announced an extension for accelerated filers complying with Section 404. While most companies cheered the extension, our SOX team was disappointed. We had just started to turn the project around and set new goals, but now the company did not have to comply until the following year. Much to our delight, after a few days of deliberation, the company decided to comply early by filing its attestation for its current fiscal year.

The Public Company Accounting Oversight Board (PCAOB) issued Auditing Standard No. 2 (AS No. 2) in March 2004, and it immediately became our bible for compliance. Although helpful, the auditing standard only scratched the compliance surface and did not clarify the requirements or approach that was needed. In June 2004, the PCAOB issued a set of Staff Questions and Answers, and in July 2004, the Big Four firm that the company used for external audit issued a white paper with guidance for management. All three were instrumental in helping the project progress.

As the weeks passed, more information was published, but each time new information became available, we had to switch gears, causing inefficiencies and more work. There were power struggles and politics in the consulting firm I was working for and challenges with the original project manager, who stepped down but remained on the project.

The best way to describe the project was that it was tripping along, starting, stopping, readjusting then moving forward. Some days I thought we could complete the project on time; other days I thought the repeated setbacks would prevent us from reaching our goal.

As we approached our fiscal year-end with the project on schedule, it became apparent the external auditors did not want to take the risk of allowing the company to comply early. The concern was that new guidance might be issued after the company filed its attestation that would change the requirements. After several discussions, some fist pounding, and many days of waiting, the external auditors received approval from their national office that they could issue their opinions early on the company's internal controls as of September 24, 2004. We were back on track.

The next few months were a blur of testing, remediation, and rigid schedules. We had to pay a premium to the auditors for complying early in the form of impeccable process and testing documentation, extra analyses, and an ultra-conservative interpretation of AS No. 2. My manager told me we would never make it. On top of all the documentation, testing, and remediation challenges, the company's policy was to issue its earnings release on the same day it filed its 10-K, 40 days after the close of the fiscal year. At the time, the auditors had to file their opinions on the company's financial statements and internal controls with the 10-K, which meant the deadlines after the close of the year were remarkable.

But on November 2, 2004, the first company in the world to comply with Section 404 of the Sarbanes-Oxley Act filed its attestation with the SEC along with an unqualified opinion from its auditor. I was the project manager on the job.

Since then, I have managed or been a member of several other Section 404 teams, both internally working for management and as an external auditor. I have seen what works, what is expected, and what went wrong for these projects. The experience I gained over the last few years is the basis for this book.

Much like that first project, I have had to start, stop, and rewrite the information in this book several times because of the constant stream of new guidance. Most recently, the PCAOB published a new auditing standard to supersede AS No. 2 in an attempt to streamline and clarify compliance requirements. The SEC also published the first guidance for management. Now companies have a resource written for management instead of having to interpret guidance meant for their external auditors. Concepts from both of these documents have been incorporated throughout this book and are specifically addressed in Chapters 1 and 2.

While researching this book, I interviewed several people involved in SOX programs from both large and smaller companies and found many companies still struggling with Section 404 compliance. In addition, non-accelerated filers are now facing the SOX compliance challenge for the first time. This book is meant to be a resource for truly practical ideas that readers can implement into their own programs to cut costs and reduce time. Throughout the book, reference is made to PCAOB standards, the

SEC, and the Committee of Sponsoring Organizations' guidance and industry white papers to substantiate the suggested methods and point you in the right direction, should you need more information to create your own efficiencies.

"Think outside the box" has become a cliché in the business world today, but Section 404 programs can benefit from fresh, outside-the-box perspectives. The goal is to provide support for management's assessment of the company's internal controls, and management should be the one driving its program and approach. I sometimes hear comments such as "Our auditors told us we have to do it this way" or "Our auditors won't let us do that." These comments have no place in management's assessment and may be a sign that you need to rethink your approach or presentation to your auditors. Be innovative while still emphasizing quality and implement efficient methods that work for your company. An efficient method supported by guidance is the best defense against any possible argument.

The first company to comply with Section 404 never could have attested early without management's strong commitment to excellence and the high standards exemplified by its employees. Kudos to the company's external auditors, who were the front-runner in publishing white papers and guidance for their clients on complying with Section 404 and related topics such as fraud, spreadsheets, and mergers and acquisitions activities.

Since Section 404 is a requirement that all public companies must endure, I challenge you to strive for excellence and help your company get the most out of its internal control program. I hope this book can provide some out-of-the-box solutions for addressing the challenges associated with Section 404 compliance.

1

Understanding the SEC's Guidance for Management

Key Topics:
* The purpose of internal control over financial reporting

* The SEC's recommendations for internal control evaluations

* Guidance for management's reporting considerations

* Rule amendments and other SEC guidance related to internal control over financial reporting

PURPOSE OF INTERNAL CONTROL OVER FINANCIAL REPORTING

As most people involved with Section 404 already know, the overall purpose of internal controls over financial reporting is to prepare reliable, materially accurate financial statements. The rationale of Section 404 is to identify any material weaknesses that have more than a remote likelihood of leading to a material misstatement in a company's financial statements and ultimately to produce more reliable reporting. Since only material weaknesses need to be disclosed, the focus of Section 404 is on issues that could cause material errors in the financial statements.

Public companies have been required to establish and maintain internal accounting controls since the enactment of the Foreign Corrupt Practices Act of 1977. Now under Section 404 of the Sarbanes-Oxley Act (SOX), public companies must attest to the effectiveness of their internal controls over financial reporting when they file their annual report. Although laws on internal controls are not new, Section 404 was meant to spotlight the connection between strong internal controls and reliable financial statements.

Effective internal controls can also help to deter or detect fraudulent financial reporting practices and perhaps reduce any adverse effects. Internal controls are not meant to prevent or detect every instance of fraud,

1

especially when there is collusion of two or more people. However, Section 404 has increased awareness and put structures in place to help reduce the risk of fraud in financial reporting.

After the Sarbanes-Oxley Act (SOX), including the infamous Section 404, was enacted in 2002, the Securities and Exchange Commission (SEC) adopted final rules implementing the requirements of Section 404(a) in June 2003. The final rules did not prescribe any specific method or set of procedures for management to follow in performing its evaluation of internal control over financial reporting (ICFR). From an optimistic viewpoint, this gave public companies some flexibility for their assessment of internal control. In reality, the lack of guidance caused many companies confusion on what constituted "reasonable support" for their assessments. In the absence of specific guidance, management relied on Auditing Standard No. 2 (AS No. 2) and other guidance for auditors to help guide their own SOX programs.

Finally in June 2007, the SEC issued the first guidance for management in an attempt to enable public companies to conduct a more effective and efficient evaluation of ICFR. Further, under the SEC's rule amendments, auditors would express only a single opinion on the effectiveness of the company's internal controls in the attestation report rather than expressing separate opinions on the effectiveness of the company's ICFR and on management's assessment.

Also in 2007, the Public Company Accounting Oversight Board (PCAOB) issued a new auditing standard to supersede AS No. 2. Although much more robust, the PCAOB's new Auditing Standard No. 5 complements the SEC's guidance for management and supports the SEC amendments.

The SEC gives companies the option to follow its new guidance for compliance with Section 404. Managers may choose to rely on the interpretive guidance as an alternative to what is provided in existing auditing standards for two key reasons:

1. The rule would give managers who follow the interpretive guidance comfort that they have conducted a sufficient ICFR evaluation.

2. Elimination of the auditors' opinion on management's assessment in the auditors' attestation report should significantly lessen the pressures that managers have felt to look to auditing standards for guidance.

The SEC has high hopes for its guidance and rule amendments, believing they will promote competition and capital formation in the U.S. marketplace. The amendments should also increase efficiencies with the effort and resources associated with an evaluation of ICFR, facilitate more efficient allocation of resources within a company, and be scalable depending on the size of the company.

These claims may in fact be true. Although the information in the SEC's guidance for management is not novel, the SEC states, "The guidance sets forth an approach by which management can conduct a top-down, risk-based evaluation of internal control over financial reporting. An evaluation that complies with this interpretive guidance is one way to satisfy the evaluation requirements."[1] However, the SEC's guidance for management is very general and may create more confusion that efficiency.

The SEC believes it is impractical to prescribe a single methodology that meets the needs of every company and that management must bring its own experience and informed judgment to bear in order to design an evaluation process that meets company needs and provides reasonable assurance for its assessment. This guidance is intended to allow management the flexibility to design such an evaluation process.

Just as in the PCAOB's standards, the SEC identified the *Internal Control—Integrated Framework* created by the Committee of Sponsoring Organizations of the Treadway Commission (COSO) as an example of a suitable framework on which management can base its assessment of internal control. The SEC also states that while the COSO framework identifies the components and objectives of an effective system of internal control, it does not set forth an approach for management to follow in evaluating the effectiveness of a company's ICFR. It distinguishes between the COSO framework as a definition of what constitutes an effective system of internal control and guidance on how to evaluate ICFR.

The SEC points out the establishment and maintenance of internal accounting controls has been required of public companies since the enactment of the Foreign Corrupt Practices Act of 1977. Section 404 of SOX reemphasizes the important relationship between the maintenance of effective ICFR and the preparation of reliable financial statements.

The SEC and its staff issued guidance in May 2005 emphasizing that management, not the auditors, is responsible for determining the appropriate nature and form of internal controls for the company as well as their evaluation methods and procedures. Certain concepts from the May 2005 Staff Guidance have been incorporated into this new guidance for management, and the May 2005 Staff Guidance remains relevant. For more information on the May 2005 Guidance from the SEC, see Chapter 3.

The SEC advises management to conduct an evaluation of its internal controls that is sufficient to provide it with a reasonable basis for its annual assessment. Exchange Act Section 13(b)(7) defines "reasonable assurance" and "reasonable detail" as "such level of detail and degree of assurance as would satisfy prudent officials in the conduct of their own affairs." The SEC believes "reasonableness" is not an "absolute standard of exactitude for corporate records." In addition, the SEC recognizes that "reasonableness" is an objective standard, and there is a range of judgments that an issuer might make as to what is "reasonable" in implementing Section 404. Hence, the term "reasonable" in the context of Section 404 implementation does not imply a single conclusion or methodology, but a full range of appropriate conduct, conclusions, or methodologies upon which an issuer may reasonably base its decisions.

Keeping in line with the PCAOB's AS No. 5, the SEC's guidance for management is organized around two broad principles:

1. Management should evaluate the design of the controls that it has implemented to determine whether they adequately address the risk that a material misstatement in the financial statements would not be prevented or detected in a timely manner.

2. Management's evaluation of evidence about the operation of its controls should be based on its assessment of risk.

This guidance addresses a number of the common areas of concern that have been identified over the past two years by companies of all sizes. For example, the guidance:

- Explains how to vary approaches for gathering evidence to support the evaluation based on risk assessments

- Explains the use of "daily interaction," self-assessment, and other ongoing monitoring activities as evidence in the evaluation

- Explains the purpose of documentation and how management has flexibility in approaches to documenting support for its assessment

- Provides management significant flexibility in making judgments regarding what constitutes adequate evidence in low-risk areas

- Allows for management and auditors to have different testing approaches

To accomplish these goals, the SEC's guidance for management is broken into two sections:

1. **The Evaluation Process**
   - Identifying Financial Reporting Risks and Controls
   - Evaluating Evidence of the Operating Effectiveness of ICFR
   - Multiple Location Considerations

2. **Reporting Considerations**
   - Evaluation of Control Deficiencies
   - Expression of Assessment of Effectiveness of ICFR by Management
   - Disclosures about Material Weaknesses
   - Impact of a Restatement of Previously Issued Financial Statements on Management's Report on ICFR
   - Inability to Assess Certain Aspects of ICFR

EVALUATION PROCESS

The objective of an evaluation of ICFR is to provide management with a reasonable basis for its annual assessment of internal control as of the end of the fiscal year. To meet this objective, management should identify the risks to reliable financial reporting, evaluate whether the controls are designed with a reasonable possibility of addressing those risks, and evaluate evidence about the operation of the controls. The evaluation process will vary from company to company, but the SEC guidance uses the top-down, risk-based approach, which is widely regarded as the most efficient and effective.

Identifying Financial Reporting Risks and Controls

According to the SEC, the identification of financial reporting risks typically begins with evaluating how the requirements of generally accepted accounting principles (GAAP) apply to the company's business, operations, and transactions. Management should use its knowledge and understanding of the business and its processes to consider the sources and potential likelihood of errors in financial reporting and identify those errors that could result in a material misstatement to the financial statements. Risk factors to consider could include:

- Internal and external risks that impact the business, including the nature and extent of any changes in those risks

- Errors in the initiation, authorization, processing, and recording of transactions and other adjustments that are reflected in financial reporting elements

- The vulnerability of the entity to fraudulent activity (i.e., fraudulent financial reporting, misappropriation of assets, and corruption)

Identifying Controls that Adequately Address Financial Reporting Risks   The determination of whether an individual control, or a combination of controls, adequately addresses a financial reporting risk involves judgments about the likelihood and potential magnitude of misstatements that could arise from the risk. Controls are not adequate to address financial reporting risk if they are designed to allow a reasonable possibility that a material misstatement of the company's financial statements would not be prevented or detected on a timely basis. Judgments about the characteristics of controls, such as the level of expertise needed to operate them or their complexity, will affect the evaluation of risks that controls will fail to operate as designed.

Consideration of Entity-Level Controls   Some entity-level controls are designed to operate at the process, transaction, or application level and might adequately prevent or detect a material misstatement in the financial statements. However, some entity-level controls may be designed to identify possible breakdowns in lower-level controls but not in a manner that would, by itself, sufficiently address an identified financial reporting risk. The more indirect the relationship to a financial reporting element, the less effective a control may be in preventing or detecting a misstatement. It is unlikely that management would identify only indirect, entity-level controls as adequately addressing a financial reporting risk identified for a financial reporting element.

Role of General Information Technology Controls   Only those general information technology (IT) controls that are necessary to adequately address financial reporting risks should be evaluated for management's assessment of internal control. Although general IT controls usually would not directly prevent or detect a material misstatement in the financial statements, automated or IT-dependent controls rely on effective general IT controls to operate properly.

Evidential Matter to Support the Assessment   As part of its evaluation of ICFR, management is required to maintain reasonable support for its assessment. The form and extent of the documentation will vary depending on the size, nature, and complexity of the company, but should include documentation of the design of the controls management has placed in operation to adequately address the financial reporting risks. Documentation of the design of controls supports other objectives of an effective system of internal control, such as providing evidence that controls and changes to those controls have been identified, communicated to those responsible for their performance, and are capable of being monitored by the company.

Evaluating Evidence of the Operating Effectiveness of ICFR

The SEC states that evidence about the effective operation of controls may be obtained both from direct testing of controls and ongoing monitoring activities. The risk associated with a certain control should dictate the nature, timing, and extent of the evaluation procedures necessary for management to obtain sufficient evidence of the effective operation of that control. In determining whether the evidence obtained is sufficient to provide a reasonable basis for its evaluation of ICFR, management should consider not only the quantity of evidence (i.e., sample size) but also qualitative characteristics of the evidence. Qualitative characteristics of the evidence can include:

- The nature of the evaluation procedures performed
- The period of time to which the evidence relates
- The objectivity of those evaluating the controls

- For monitoring controls, the extent of validation through direct testing of the underlying controls

Different combinations of the nature, timing, and extent of evaluation procedures may provide sufficient evidence for any individual control.

Determining the Evidence Needed to Support the Assessment   Management should evaluate the ICFR risk for each control to determine the type of evidence needed to support its assessment. The risk assessment should consider the possibility of the control failing as well as the potential impact the failure could have on the company's financial statements. This concept is demonstrated in Exhibit 1.1.

As the risks surrounding a certain control increase, management should obtain more evidence that the control is effective. Financial reporting elements generally would have higher risks when they include transactions, account balances, or other supporting information that is prone to misstatement, such as elements that:

- Involve judgment in determining the recorded amounts

- Are susceptible to fraud

- Have complex accounting requirements

- Experience change in the nature or volume of the underlying transactions

- Are subject to environmental factors, such as technological and/or economic developments

Exhibit 1.1   SEC Grid for Determining the Sufficiency of Evidence Based on ICFR Risk

When considering the likelihood that a control might fail to operate effectively, management should consider:

- The type of control (i.e., manual or automated)
- The complexity of the control
- The risk of management override
- The judgment required to operate the control
- The competence of the personnel who performs or monitors the control
- Where there have been changes in key personnel who either perform or monitor the control
- The nature and materiality of misstatements that the control is intended to prevent or detect
- The degree to which the control relies on the effectiveness of other controls (i.e., general IT controls)
- Evidence of the operation of the control in the prior year

Certain financial reporting elements, such as those involving significant accounting estimates, related party transactions, or critical accounting policies, generally would be classified as high risk for both the risk of material misstatement and the risk of control failure. When the controls related to these financial reporting elements are subject to the risk of management override, involve significant judgment, or are complex, they generally should be assessed as having even a higher ICFR risk.

The existence of entity-level controls, such as controls within the control environment, may influence management's determination of the evidence needed to sufficiently support its assessment. Strong entity-level controls may reduce the sufficiency of evidence needed for a control that normally would be considered high risk. For example, management's judgment about the likelihood that a control could fail to operate effectively could be influenced by an effective control environment, which reduces the sufficiency of evidence needed for that control. However, a strong control environment would not eliminate the need for some type of testing to determine if the control was effective.

Implementing Procedures to Evaluate Evidence of the Operation of ICFR   The evidence management evaluates to determine if its ICFR are effective may come from a combination of ongoing monitoring and direct testing of controls.

Ongoing monitoring includes activities that provide information about the operation of controls and is commonly performed through self-assessment procedures or the analysis of performance measures designed to track the operation of controls. The SEC describes self-assessment procedures in this way:

> Self-assessment is a broad term that can refer to different types of procedures performed by individuals with varying degrees of objectivity. It includes assessments made by the personnel who operate the control as well as members of management who are not responsible for operating the control. The evidence provided by self-assessment activities depends on the personnel involved and the manner in which the activities are conducted. For example, evidence from self-assessments performed by personnel responsible for operating the control generally provides less evidence due to the evaluator's lower degree of objectivity.[2]

However, the SEC goes on to explain that for situations where a company's ongoing monitoring uses personnel who are not adequately objective, evidence obtained from the monitoring activities would normally be supplemented with direct control testing by people independent of the controls being tested.

Practice Tip

Although self-assessment procedures can be used as evidence for management to evaluate whether its ICFR controls are effective according to the SEC, the evidence provides low assurance and generally will not be relied on by your auditors. Self-assessment procedures can be time consuming and hard to document as well. Be sure to evaluate whether these types of procedures are truly efficient for your company.

Ongoing monitoring can also be achieved by the evaluation of key performance indicators (KPIs), where management reconciles operating and financial information with its knowledge of the business. If analyzing KPIs can indicate a potential misstatement in a financial reporting element, then the process is relevant for addressing financial reporting risks. However, if KPIs monitor operational results and do not address the effective operation of financial reporting controls, they may not be a useful tool for monitoring ICFR.

Direct tests of controls can be performed periodically to provide evidence as of a point in time and may provide information about the reliability of ongoing monitoring activities. Management can also vary the nature of evidence obtained by adjusting the period of time covered by direct testing. For high-risk areas, management's evaluation would ordinarily include evidence obtained from direct testing over a reasonable period of time during the year, including the fiscal year-end. For lower-risk areas, management may decide evidence from ongoing monitoring is sufficient and no direct testing is required.

In smaller companies, management's daily interaction with its financial reporting controls may provide it with sufficient knowledge about their effective operation. However, this can be a tricky situation because knowledge from daily interaction would have to be obtained by those people responsible for evaluating the effectiveness of ICFR (not process owners) through their ongoing direct knowledge and supervision of control operation. Also, management would have to have sufficient evidence of the daily interaction and monitoring to conclude that these controls were effective.

For example, daily interaction may be an effective control when the operation of controls is centralized and the number of personnel involved in their operation is limited. Companies with multiple management reporting layers or operating segments, however, may not be able to rely on daily interaction to provide sufficient evidence because those responsible for assessing the effectiveness of ICFR may not be sufficiently knowledgeable about the operation of the controls. In these situations, management may have to rely on direct testing or ongoing monitoring procedures.

Management should evaluate the evidence it gathers from ongoing monitoring or direct testing to determine whether the operation of a control is effective. This evaluation should consider:

- Whether the control operated as designed

- How the control was applied

- The consistency with which the control was applied

- Whether the person performing the control possesses the necessary authority and competence to perform the control effectively

Evidential Matter to Support the Assessment   The SEC believes the nature of the evidential matter that management uses to evaluate its internal controls will vary based on a company's assessed level of financial reporting risks and other circumstances unique to each company. A company's evidential matter to support its assessment should include documentation of the methods and procedures used to gather and evaluate evidence. For example, management could document its overall ICFR program in a comprehensive memo describing its evaluation approach, the evaluation procedures, and the basis for its conclusions for each financial reporting element.

The SEC states:

> If management determines that the evidential matter within the company's books and records is sufficient to provide reasonable support for its assessment, it may determine that it is not necessary to separately maintain copies of the evidence it evaluates.[3]

For example, at a small company where management is relying on its daily interaction with the operation of its controls to provide the basis for its assessment, there may be limited documentation created specifically for the evaluation of ICFR. Management needs to consider the type of reasonable support that would provide sufficient evidence for its assessment and whether reasonable support would include documentation of how its interaction provided it with sufficient evidence. This documentation might include memoranda, emails, and instructions or directions from management to company employees.

Practice Tip

Although the SEC's guidance on the matter of evidence for management's daily interactions with financial reporting controls strives to remain open and flexible, it does not imply that a company can have no evidence for these controls. If a company has no evidence that financial reporting controls are monitored daily by those responsible for assessing the company's internal control, the company may have to implement procedures to create the evidence, such as signoffs, emails, or meeting documentation.

According to the SEC, when management is evaluating the type of supporting evidential matter needed for the operation of controls, it should consider the degree of complexity of the control, the level of judgment required to operate the control, and the risk of material misstatement in the financial statements. As these factors increase, management may determine that it must maintain evidential matter supporting the assessment separately.

If management believes entity-level and other pervasive controls address the elements necessary for an effective system of ICFR, then the evidential matter for reasonable support of management's assessment should include documentation of how that belief was formed.

Multiple Location Considerations

A company's overall consideration of its financial reporting risks should include all of its locations or business units. In its evaluation of risks, management may decide that financial reporting risks are adequately addressed by controls operating at a central location. In this case, the company's approach to its ICFR program would be similar to a business with a single location or business unit. However, when the controls necessary to address financial reporting risks are in place at more than one location or business unit, management has to evaluate evidence of the operation of those controls at the individual locations or business units.

In situations where management determines that the financial reporting risks for controls that operate at individual locations or business units are low, it has more flexibility in its approach for documenting and testing controls at those locations. For example, management may determine that evidence gathered through self-assessment routines or other ongoing monitoring activities, when combined with the evidence derived from a centralized control that monitors the results of operations at individual locations, constitutes sufficient evidence for the evaluation.

When performing its risk evaluation of noncentral locations, management should consider whether location-specific risks may cause a control to not operate effectively. Additionally, there may be pervasive factors at a given location that cause some controls there to be considered higher risk.

When deciding whether the nature and extent of evidence that controls are operating effectively is sufficient, management should consider the risk for each financial reporting element rather than making a single judgment for all controls at a location.

REPORTING CONSIDERATIONS

The objective of the reporting process is to inform investors and other users of financial statements about the status of companies' internal control over financial reporting. In order to successfully communicate to the market, companies need a strong evaluation process for deficiencies and clear disclosures regarding management's assessment.

Evaluation of Control Deficiencies

The evaluation of a control deficiency should include both quantitative and qualitative factors. Management can evaluate a deficiency in ICFR by considering whether there is a reasonable possibility that the company's ICFR will fail to prevent or detect a misstatement of a financial statement amount or disclosure on a timely basis even though an actual misstatement may not have occurred. Management should also consider the magnitude of the potential misstatement that could result from the failed control(s).

Similar to the PCAOB's approach, the SEC mentions the "prudent official test" and states:

> If management determines that the deficiency, or combination of deficiencies, might prevent prudent officials in the conduct of their own affairs from concluding that they have reasonable assurance that transactions are recorded as necessary to permit the preparation of financial statements in conformity with generally accepted accounting principles, then management should treat the deficiency, or combination of deficiencies, as an indicator of a material weakness.

Similar again to the PCAOB's approach, the SEC advises management, when aggregating deficiencies, to evaluate individual control deficiencies that affect the same financial statement amount or disclosure to determine whether they collectively could result in a material weakness. An approach to aggregating individually insignificant control deficiencies was used by the American Institute of Certified Public Accountants (AICPA) in Statement on Auditing Standard No. 112, Communication of Internal Control Related Matters Identified in an Audit.

Management should also evaluate the effect of compensating controls when determining whether a control deficiency or combination of deficiencies is a material weakness. The SEC defines compensating controls as controls that serve to accomplish the objective of another control that did not function properly, helping to reduce risk to an acceptable level. To have a mitigating effect, the compensating control should operate at a level of precision that would prevent or detect a material misstatement.

The PCAOB and SEC list the same factors to help management (and auditors) evaluate if there is a reasonable possibility of a material misstatement and the potential magnitude of a misstatement for control deficiencies. Additionally, guidance from the PCAOB and SEC list the same four indicators of a material weakness. For more information on these topics, see Chapter 11 on evaluating deficiencies.

Expression of Assessment of Effectiveness of Internal Control over Financial Reporting by Management

Management should clearly disclose its assessment of the effectiveness of the company's ICFR and should not qualify its assessment by saying the company's ICFR is effective subject to certain qualifications. For example, management should not state that the company's controls are effective except for certain material weakness(es) that have been identified. However, management may state that controls are ineffective due solely to, and only to the extent of, the identified material weakness(es). However, management should consider the nature and pervasiveness of the material weakness prior to making this statement. Management may disclose any remediation efforts that it has made or plans to make to the identified material weakness(es) in Item 9A of Form 10-K, Item 15 of Form 20-F, or General Instruction B of Form 40-F.

Disclosures about Material Weaknesses

Disclosures about material weaknesses will be more useful to investors if management differentiates the potential impact and importance to the financial statements of the identified material weakness(es), including distinguishing those material weaknesses that may have a pervasive impact on ICFR from those that do not. According to the SEC, "The goal underlying all disclosure in this area is to provide an investor with disclosure and analysis beyond the mere existence of a material weakness." See Chapter 11 on evaluating deficiencies for specific recommendations for disclosing material weaknesses.

Impact of a Restatement of Previously Issued Financial Statements on Management's Report on Internal Control over Financial Reporting

When a material misstatement in previously issued financial statements is discovered, the SEC requires the company to restate those financial statements. However, the restatement of financial statements does not, by itself, necessitate management to consider the effect of the restatement on the company's prior conclusion on the effectiveness of its internal control.

While there is no requirement for management to revise its conclusion on the effectiveness of its internal control for the period of restatement, the SEC advises management to consider whether its original disclosures are still appropriate. Management may have to modify or supplement its original disclosures to include other material information that is necessary for the disclosures not to be misleading. For statements concerning ICFR and disclosure controls and procedures, the company may need to report in this context what impact, if any, the restatement has on its original conclusions regarding the effectiveness of ICFR and disclosure controls and procedures.

Inability to Assess Certain Aspects of Internal Control over Financial Reporting

There may be circumstances where management is unable to assess certain aspects of its ICFR. For example, management may outsource a significant process to a service organization and determine that the controls over that process should be evaluated. However, the service organization may be unwilling to provide a Type II Statement on Auditing Standard No. 70 report or provide management access to the controls in place at the service organization for management to assess their effectiveness. Additionally, management may not have compensating controls in place that allow it to conclude in an alternative manner that controls over the outsourced process are effective.

The SEC does not permit management to issue a report on ICFR with a scope limitation. Therefore, management must determine whether the inability to assess controls over a particular process is significant enough to conclude in its report that ICFR is not effective.

RULE AMENDMENTS AND OTHER SEC GUIDANCE RELATED TO INTERNAL CONTROL OVER FINANCIAL REPORTING

According to the SEC, the guidance for management and amendments related to internal control over financial reporting would not limit the ability of management to use its judgment to determine a method of evaluation that is appropriate for each company. The amendments would be similar to a nonexclusive safe harbor in that they would not require management to conduct the evaluation of internal control in accordance with the interpretive guidance but would provide certainty for management that chooses to follow the guidance that it has satisfied its obligation to conduct an evaluation for purposes of the requirements in Rules 13a-15(c) and 15d-15(c).

Newly Public Companies

The SEC's new rule, RELEASE NOS. 33-8760; 34-54942; File No. S7-06-03 provides a transition period for newly public companies before they become subject to the ICFR requirements. Under the new rule, a newly public company will not become subject to the ICFR requirements until it either had been required to file an annual report for the prior fiscal year with the SEC or had filed an annual report with the SEC for the prior fiscal year. See Release No. 33-8760 (December 15, 2006) available at www.sec.gov/rules/final/2006/33-8760.pdf.

Revision to the Auditor's Opinions on Internal Control over Financial Reporting

Because of the feedback the SEC received that auditors' opinions may not effectively communicate their responsibility in relation to management's evaluation process, auditors have to express only one opinion directly on the effectiveness of a company's ICFR.

Previous Staff Guidance and Staff Frequently Asked Questions

The SEC states that its May 2005 guidance remains relevant and has no plans to revise it. However, as of September 2007, the SEC staff reviewed its frequently asked questions as a result of the guidance for management and has updated them as appropriate. See Appendix E for a summary of the SEC's FAQs.

Cost-Benefit Analysis of the Rule Amendments and Guidance for Management

The SEC is very optimistic about its guidance for management and proposed rule amendments and believes that they will provide many benefits to investors as well as public companies in complying with Section 404. Although there are not many, if any, "new" ideas about complying with Section 404 in the guidance for management, the SEC believes the guidance and rule revisions will provide these benefits:

- Management can choose to follow guidance that is an efficient and effective means of satisfying the evaluation requirement.

- All public companies, especially smaller ones, that choose to follow the guidance would be afforded considerable flexibility to scale and tailor their evaluation methods and procedures to fit their own facts and circumstances.

- Management would have the comfort that an evaluation that complies with the SEC interpretive guidance is one way to satisfy the evaluation required by Exchange Act Rule 13a-15(c) and Exchange Act Rule 15d-15(c). This reduces any second-guessing as to whether management's process was adequate.

- There may be reduced risk of costly and time-consuming disagreement between auditors and management regarding the extent of documentation and testing needed to satisfy the ICFR evaluation requirement.

- Companies are likely to save money and reduce the amount of effort and resources associated with an evaluation by relying on a set of guidelines that clarifies the nature, timing, and extent of management's procedures and that recognizes the many different types of evidence-gathering methods available to management (such as direct interaction with control components).

- Management would have greater clarity regarding the SEC's expectations concerning an evaluation of ICFR.

Some larger public companies may face a transitory increase in compliance costs if they choose to follow the guidance. This is because many larger companies that have already evaluated their internal controls have reported cost reductions, or the anticipation of cost reductions, in the second and subsequent years of compliance with the internal control reporting provisions. The SEC believes that some accelerated and large accelerated filers that have completed one or more evaluations of their ICFR may adjust their evaluation procedures in order to take advantage of the proposed rule amendments, which could lead to an increase in compliance costs. This increase could happen if companies totally revamp their Section 404 programs, but it is unlikely since large companies already are using much of the SEC guidance for management.

In addition, the benefits of the SEC's guidance for management may be partially offset if the company's auditors obtain more audit evidence directly rather than using evidence generated by management's evaluation process; such direct evidence could lead to an increase in audit costs. This offset would certainly be expected if companies began using less sufficient testing methods and evidence for forming an opinion on their internal controls.

Although the methods are not new or innovative, the SEC guidance does reinforce a flexible, risk-based approach to compliance that is tailored to the unique circumstances of each company. Time will tell if the overly broad guidance will help management in their compliance programs. More likely, the SEC's guidance for management will have the most impact on compliance programs when it is applied in conjunction with the more robust PCAOB Auditing Standard No. 5.

NOTES

1. Commission Guidance Regarding Management's Report on Internal Control over Financial Reporting Under Section 13(a) or 15(d) of the Securities Exchange Act of 1934, by the security and Exchange Commission's RELEASE NOS. 33-8810; 34-55929; FR-77; File No. S7-24-06. Summary, p. 1.

2. Commission Guidance Regarding Management's Report on Internal Control Over Financial Reporting Under Section 13(a) or 15(d) of the Securities Exchange Act of 1934, by the Securities Exchange Commission, RELEASE NOS. 33-8810; 34-55929; FR-77; File No. S7-24-06, pages 28–29.

3. Commission Guidance Regarding Management's Report on Internal Control Over Financial Reporting Under Section 13(a) or 15(d) of the Securities Exchange Act of 1934, by the Securities Exchange Commission, RELEASE NOS. 33-8810; 34-55929; FR-77; File No. S7-24-06, page 31.

2

The PCAOB's Auditing Standard No. 5

Key Topics:
- Eight concepts for focusing your audit on the most important matters to internal control

- The new emphasis on entity-level controls

- The importance of a fraud risk assessment

- Tips to eliminate unnecessary procedures in an audit

- Scaling audits for smaller companies

In response to ongoing criticism in the business community that the requirements of Sarbanes-Oxley (SOX) Section 404 are too costly and time consuming and are driving businesses away to foreign markets, the Public Company Accounting Oversight Board (PCAOB) proposed a new auditing standard on internal control over financial reporting (ICFR) in December 2006 to supersede Auditing Standard No. 2 (AS No. 2). At the same time, the PCAOB proposed a new auditing standard on using the work of others, which was meant to supersede interim standard AU sec 322, *The Auditor's Consideration of the Internal Audit Function in an Audit of Financial Statements.* In May 2007, the PCAOB published the final version of AS No. 5 entitled An Audit of Internal Control over Financial Reporting that is Integrated with an Audit of Financial Statements. However, in the final version, the new, separate standard on using the work of others was abandoned and the information was incorporated into AS No. 5.

The PCAOB made a huge effort to avoid the mistakes it made with AS No. 2. It solicited and received many comment letters on the proposed guidance and coordinated its work with the Securities and Exchange Commission (SEC), which proposed its own guidance for management on evaluating internal control. In addition to its role of implementing Section 404, the SEC must approve new PCAOB auditing standards before they become effective. After analyzing the comments received on the new standard and coordinating the PCAOB's proposal with the SEC's own guidance, the SEC directed its staff to focus its remaining work in four areas:

1. Aligning the PCAOB's new auditing standard with the SEC's proposed new management guidance under Section 404, particularly with regard to prescriptive requirements, definitions, and terms

2. Scaling the 404 audit to account for the particular facts and circumstances of companies, particularly smaller companies

3. Encouraging auditors to use professional judgment in the Section 404 process, particularly in using risk assessment

4. Following a principles-based approach to determining when and to what extent the auditor can use the work of others

This direction from the SEC is good news for public companies and may cure the check-the-box approach that many auditors used in the past for Section 404 audits. Although the PCAOB's new standard is meant for external auditors, understanding it can help you develop your program to be compatible with that of your auditors. It can also help you know what your auditors will expect and help you keep their procedures (and costs) reasonable and in line with the standard.

The new standard is designed primarily to achieve these objectives:

- Focus the audit on the matters most important to internal control.

- Eliminate unnecessary procedures.

- Scale the audit for smaller companies.

- Make the text of the standard easier to understand.

Although there are many critics of Section 404 and the related regulation, many people believe there are benefits to the focus on internal controls. The challenge has been to increase the return on investment that companies have been required to make in complying with Section 404. As the title suggests, this new guidance is a call for integration, efficiency, and reasonableness. It appears to keep the law intact while still allowing companies the flexibility to implement the standard in a way that works for their own size, business structure, and corporate culture.

EIGHT CONCEPTS TO FOCUS THE AUDIT ON MATTERS MOST IMPORTANT TO INTERNAL CONTROL

The PCAOB believes it can help auditors focus their audits on matters most important to internal control by directing their attention to the critical controls using these eight concepts:

1. Integrating the internal control and financial statement audits

2. Emphasizing the importance of risk assessment

3. Clarifying the role of materiality

4. Using a top-down approach to direct auditors' attention toward the most important controls

5. Revising the definitions of significant deficiency and material weakness

6. Revising the definitions of the "strong indicators" of a material weakness

7. Clarifying the role of interim materiality in the audit

8. Introducing interim testing in an audit of internal control

Integrating the Internal Control and Financial Statement Audits

The main concept of an integrated audit is for auditors to design their testing of controls to accomplish the objectives of both financial and internal control audits simultaneously. These objectives are to obtain sufficient evidence to support the auditors' (1) opinion on the company's internal controls as of year-end and (2) control risk assessment for the financial statement audit.

In theory, if auditors can assess a company's control risk as below the maximum, they may be able to reduce the nature, timing, or extent of their substantive procedures for the financial statement audit. What better way to thoroughly assess control risk than through an audit of the company's internal control? Therefore, integrating the two audits should benefit companies by requiring less time to be spent overall, and ultimately should lower audit fees.

In Appendix B of AS No. 5, the PCAOB makes seven points for integrating the audits of internal control and the financial statements:

1. The auditor's opinion in an audit of internal control relates to the effectiveness of the company's ICFR as of a *point in time* and *taken as a whole.*

2. To express an opinion on ICFR as of a *point in time,* auditors should obtain evidence that ICFR has operated effectively for a sufficient period of time, which may be less than the entire period (ordinarily one year) covered by the company's financial statements.

3. The audit of ICFR requires auditors to test the design and operating effectiveness of controls they ordinarily would not test if expressing an opinion only on the financial statements.

4. To assess control risk for specific financial statement assertions at less than the maximum, auditors are required to obtain evidence that the relevant controls operated effectively during the *entire period* on which they plan to place reliance on those controls. However, auditors are

not required to assess control risk at less than the maximum for *all* relevant assertions. This fact suggests that auditors can rate different areas with different control risks (i.e., the accounts payable process has a low control risk but the inventory process has a high control risk) and different control risks for different aspects of the same area (i.e., the inventory existence controls related to cycle counts are considered low risk, but the inventory valuation controls related to allowances are considered high risk).

5. The results of auditors' tests of internal control obtained during the internal control audit may cause them to alter the nature, timing, and extent of substantive procedures and to perform further tests of controls, particularly in response to identified control deficiencies.

6. In an audit of ICFR, auditors should evaluate the effect of the findings of the substantive audit procedures performed in the audit of financial statements. This evaluation should include, at a minimum:

   • The auditors' risk assessments in connection with the selection of substantive procedures, especially those related to fraud.

   • Findings with respect to illegal acts and related party transactions.

   • Indications of management bias in making accounting estimates and in selecting accounting principles.

   • Misstatements detected by substantive procedures. These misstatements might alter auditors' judgment about the effectiveness of controls.

7. To obtain evidence about whether a selected control is effective, the control must be tested directly; the effectiveness of a control cannot be inferred from the absence of misstatements detected by substantive procedures.

Although PCAOB's May 2005 policy statement[1] introduced integrating the internal control and financial statement audits, the new standard gives specific direction that should help external auditors put the principles into practice. Be sure to ask your auditor about his or her specific steps for integrating the two audits.

Emphasizing the Importance of Risk Assessment

From the initial evaluation of the risk of material misstatement at the entity level, to the analysis of risk at the individual account, assertion, or control level, auditors should continuously adjust their procedures to reflect information learned from both the audits of internal control and financial statements. As a result, when auditors find an error or a proposed adjustment from their financial audit procedures, you can expect their focus to sharpen on controls in that area. They may even call the controls deficient or improperly designed because they did not catch the error.

Paragraph 11 of the standard specifically states: "It is not necessary to test controls that, even if deficient, would not present a reasonable possibility of material misstatement to the financial statements." The new standard makes clear that the evidence necessary to persuade auditors that a control is effective depends on the risk associated with the control. As the risk associated with a control being tested decreases, the evidence that auditors need to obtain also decreases.

Although auditors must obtain evidence about the effectiveness of controls for each relevant assertion, they are not responsible for obtaining sufficient evidence to support an opinion about the effectiveness of each *individual* control. Rather, the objective should be to express an opinion on a company's ICFR *overall*. This again allows auditors to vary the evidence obtained regarding the effectiveness of individual controls and presents more options for alternative testing methods based on the risk of individual controls.

When assessing risk and to further understand the likely sources of material misstatement, auditors will be trying to achieve these objectives:

- Understand the flow of transactions related to the relevant assertions, including how these transactions are initiated, authorized, processed, and recorded.

- Identify the points within the company's processes at which a misstatement—including a misstatement due to fraud—could arise that, individually or in combination with other misstatements, would be material.

- Identify the controls that management has implemented to address these potential misstatements.

- Identify the controls that management has implemented over the prevention or timely detection of unauthorized acquisition, use, or disposition of the company's assets that could result in a material misstatement of the financial statements.

- Understand how information technology (IT) affects the company's flow of transactions. The standard references AU sec 319, *Consideration of Internal Control in a Financial Statement Audit,* for a discussion of the risks and effect IT has on internal controls.

Performing walk-throughs is specifically encouraged in Paragraph 37 as the most effective means of achieving these objectives and obtaining a sufficient understanding of a process to be able to identify where controls are needed. In Paragraph 35, the new standard allows auditors to supervise the work of others who provide direct assistance to achieve these objectives.

By achieving the risk objectives just discussed, auditors will be better equipped to evaluate the risk associated with a particular control. In assess-

---

Practice Tip

Under AS No. 2, auditors were required to perform walk-throughs themselves, but walk-throughs can be one of the most time-consuming areas of an audit. Ask your auditors if they will allow company personnel or others working on behalf of management to provide direct assistance under the auditors' supervision for their walk-throughs.

---

ing control risk, AS No. 5 directs auditors to evaluate 10 factors:

1. The nature and materiality of misstatements that the control is intended to prevent or detect

2. The inherent risk associated with the related account(s) and assertion(s)

3. Whether there have been changes in the volume or nature of transactions that might adversely affect control design or operating effectiveness

4. Whether the account has a history of errors

5. The effectiveness of entity-level controls, especially controls that monitor other controls

6. The nature of the control and the frequency with which it operates

7. The degree to which the control relies on the effectiveness of other controls (i.e., the control environment or IT general controls)

8. The competence of the personnel who perform the control or monitor its performance and whether there have been changes in key personnel who perform the control or monitor its performance

9. Whether the control relies on performance by an individual or is automated (i.e., an automated control would generally be expected to be lower risk if relevant IT general controls are effective)

10. The complexity of the control

Clarifying the Role of Materiality in the Audit

AS No. 5 clarifies the role materiality should play in an internal control audit by advising auditors to plan and perform their audits of internal control using the same materiality measures used to plan and perform their financial statement audits. In addition, the significant accounts, disclosures and relevant assertions should be the same for both audits. The standard references AU sec 312, *Audit Risk and Materiality in Conducting an Audit* for additional information on materiality.

Using a Top-Down Approach   A top-down approach to an audit of internal control starts at the financial statement level with an understanding of overall risks of ICFR. The focus then moves to entity-level controls before moving to significant accounts and disclosures and their relevant assertions. Finally, the focus is on the processes and transactions that make up the significant accounts and the control activities that surround them.

Practice Tip

The terms "top-down" and "risk-based" are often used interchangeably. The "top-down" approach should lead you (and auditors) right into a risk-based approach because your attention is directed to the accounts, disclosures, and assertions that present a reasonable possibility of material misstatement to the financial statements.

Revising the Definitions of Significant Deficiency and Material Weakness   Since the concepts for SOX Section 404 and the related guidance center around the terms "significant deficiency" and "material weakness," the PCAOB refined and aligned the definition of these terms with the SEC in another attempt to clarify its guidance. AS No. 5 includes three changes to the definitions of significant deficiency and material weakness:

1. Replacement of the phrase "more than remote likelihood" with the phrase "reasonable possibility" in the definition of a material weakness

2. Rearticulation of the definition of "material weakness" to exclude significant deficiency

3. Replacement of the phrase "more than inconsequential" with the phrase "less severe than a material weakness, yet important enough to merit attention by those responsible for oversight of the company's financial reporting" in the definition of significant deficiency

Material Weakness   Reference within the definition of a material weakness in AS No. 2 to significant deficiencies raised concern that auditors may be performing their audits at a level of detail necessary to ensure their procedures identify all significant deficiencies, rather than only all material weaknesses. In an effort to bring the focus of audits of internal control back to the appropriate level, the PCAOB revised the definition of material weakness as shown below.

AS No. 2 Definition of Material Weakness	Revised Definition of Material Weakness
A significant deficiency, or combination of significant deficiencies, that results in a more than remote likelihood that a material misstatement of the annual or interim financial statements will not be prevented or detected.	A deficiency, or combination of deficiencies, in internal control over financial reporting, such that there is a reasonable possibility that a material misstatement of the company's annual or interim financial statements will not be prevented or detected on a timely basis.

There is a "reasonable possibility" of an event, as the term is used in the definitions of material weakness and significant deficiency, when the likelihood of the event is either "reasonably possible" or "probable," as those terms are used in Financial Accounting Standards Board Statement No. 5, *Accounting for Contingencies* (FAS No. 5).

Significant Deficiency   In its revised definition of significant deficiency, the new standard replaces the ambiguous phrase "more than inconsequential" and focuses the definition on the communication requirement. The differences in definitions of significant deficiencies are illustrated next.

AS No. 2 Definition of Significant Deficiency	Revised Definition of Significant Deficiency
A control deficiency, or combination of control deficiencies, that has a more than remote likelihood of resulting in a misstatement that is more than inconsequential.	A deficiency, or combination of deficiencies, in internal control over financial reporting that is less severe than a material weakness, yet important enough to merit attention by those responsible for oversight of the company's financial reporting.

Revising the Strong Indicators of a Material Weakness

AS No. 2 describes circumstances that should be regarded as at least significant deficiencies and as strong indicators of a material weakness in internal control. Examples of such circumstances include the restatement of previously issued financial statements and an ineffective control environment. Both of these situations can indicate issues in a company's internal control, but the conclusion as to the degree of the deficiency is not absolute because of unique circumstances for different companies. The new theory is that either of these indicators should bias auditors toward a conclusion that a material weakness exists, but they do not require auditors to reach that conclusion. Instead, auditors may determine that the circumstances do not rise to the level of a material weakness and that only a significant deficiency exists. In practice, however, auditors sometimes have determined that, in fact, no deficiency existed at all. As a result, to ensure that the requirement does not force auditors to conclude a deficiency exists when one does not, and to reaffirm the degree of judgment required to make these evaluations, the PCAOB removed the word "strong" for indicators of material weaknesses and removed the requirement to consider any circumstances as at least significant deficiencies.

AS No. 5 also removes from the list of indicators of material weaknesses uncorrected significant deficiencies. Under AS No. 2, significant deficiencies that were communicated to management and the audit committee and remained uncorrected after a reasonable period of time were a strong indicator of a material weakness. The modification recognizes that companies may have strong internal controls and be responsible but after evaluating their significant deficiencies may reasonably determine not to correct them. In such cases, they would not have a material weakness in their internal control. For the SEC and PCAOB's updated listing of indicators of a material weakness, see Chapter 11.

Clarifying the Role of Interim Materiality in the Audit

The PCAOB specifically references interim financial statements only as they relate to the evaluation of deficiencies, not to the scope of auditors' testing of internal controls. As described in the definition of a material weakness, when evaluating whether a control deficiency or combination of control deficiencies is a material weakness, the possibility of misstatement to both annual and interim financial statements must be considered.

Introducing the Concept of Interim Testing in an Audit of Internal Controls

The new standard discusses the possibility of interim testing for an audit of internal control; in practice, interim testing was a rare occurrence in the first few years of compliance. Interim control testing should allow companies (and auditors) more flexibility with schedules and timing, especially during the year-end crunch.

However, if evidence about the operating effectiveness of controls is obtained at an interim date, additional evidence concerning the operation of the controls for the remaining period, such as update or roll-forward procedures, may be necessary. The assessment of the risk associated with each control is essential to the decisions about what, if any, roll-forward procedures are necessary. These decisions should be part of determining the overall mix of the nature, timing, and extent of procedures that will provide sufficient evidence in relation to the risk associated with the control.

These factors should be evaluated when determining if additional evidence is necessary when interim testing of certain controls is performed prior to the company's year-end:

- The specific control tested prior to the as-of date and the results of those tests. Auditors should assess the risks associated with the control and the nature of the control.

- The sufficiency of the evidence of effectiveness obtained at an interim date.

- The length of the remaining period.

- The possibility that there have been any significant changes in ICFR subsequent to the interim date.

If after evaluating these criteria, auditors (or public companies) believe additional procedures are needed to update the results of testing performed at an interim date, update testing should be planned at or near the as-of date. However, if after evaluating these factors there is only a low risk that controls are no longer effective at year-end, the standard agrees that inquiry alone might be sufficient as a roll-forward procedure.

NEW EMPHASIS ON ENTITY-LEVEL CONTROLS

When discussing entity-level controls, the Committee of Sponsoring Organizations (COSO) components often come to mind. However, entity-level controls also include key financial reporting processes and certain policies. In the past, these controls were also referred to as company-level or entity-wide controls, but the PCAOB and SEC have now aligned their terminology and descriptions.

AS No. 5 tries to give more flexibility for using higher-level or entity-level testing. It omits the statement in Paragraph 54 of AS No. 2 that "testing company level controls alone is not sufficient for the purposes of expressing an opinion on the effectiveness of a company's internal control over financial reporting." Although testing entity-level controls alone will probably be rare in practice, the standard encourages auditors to test those entity-level controls that are important to their conclusion about whether the company has effective ICFR.

Controls Related to the Control Environment

Auditors are required to assess the company's control environment because of its importance to internal control. Auditors will have to evaluate if management's operating style promotes effective internal control, whether integrity and ethical values are understood, and whether the board or audit committee exercises responsibility over financial reporting and internal control. Unlike AS No. 2, the new standard does not mention any limitations for using the work of others when testing a company's control environment.

Controls over Management Override

Management override can be an issue at companies of every size and can be a difficult risk to mitigate. Controls over management override are particularly important at smaller companies because of the increased involvement of senior management in the financial reporting process. For smaller companies, the controls that address the risk of management override might be different from those at larger companies. For example, a smaller company might rely on more detailed oversight by the audit committee that focuses on the risk of management override.

For a complete listing and discussion of entity-level controls, see Chapter 5.

IMPORTANCE OF A FRAUD RISK ASSESSMENT

AS No. 5 has a distinct emphasis on fraud controls and risk assessment that was not seen in previous guidance. This seems appropriate since SOX was created in response to the biggest corporate fraud scandals in the new millennium.

Early in the new standard (Paragraph 11), the PCAOB gives the profound advice that "the risk a company's internal control over financial reporting will fail to prevent or detect misstatement caused by fraud usually is higher than the risk of failure to prevent or detect error." AS No. 5 also gives these examples of controls that may specifically address fraud:

- Controls over significant, unusual transactions, particularly those that result in late or unusual journal entries
- Controls over journal entries and adjustments made in the period-end financial reporting process
- Controls over related party transactions
- Controls related to significant management estimates

- Controls that mitigate incentives for, and pressures on, management to falsify or inappropriately manage financial results

Putting these controls into practice can be difficult, especially for small companies where proper segregation of duties over the accounting function may not exist. Some basic controls that most companies can implement to reduce the risk of fraud follow.

- Ensure your system will not allow the same person to enter and post journal entries. Even if you have a manual requirement for a second approver on all journal entries, restrict your system so that independent postings are not a possibility.

- Do not allow executives system access to post journal entries. In most companies, the chief financial officer has no business recording journal entries.

- Make sure the disclosure and/or audit committee is aware of all related parties and the type of transactions they are involved in with the company.

- Make sure the audit committee reviews the methodology of all reserves or other management estimates at least annually and any time there is a change.

- Have the controller send the financial package to the audit committee directly. This procedure may limit the opportunity for "management override" by executives after the accounting department has compiled the financial data.

- Ensure that incentives are not linked solely to earnings or revenue growth. Mix in other indicators, such as low employee turnover, community service, compliance, or ethics programs.

TIPS TO ELIMINATE UNNECESSARY PROCEDURES

AS No. 5 strives for a more efficient approach by removing certain requirements that critics viewed as redundant or unnecessary. This economical approach includes:

- Removing the requirement to evaluate management's process

- Permitting consideration of knowledge obtained during previous audits

- Benchmarking automated controls

- Refocusing the multilocation testing requirements on risk rather than coverage

- Removing barriers to using the work of others
- Recalibrating the walk-through requirement

Removing the Requirement to Evaluate Management's Process

Many comment letters to the PCAOB stated that under AS No. 2, auditors performed work unnecessary to achieve the intended benefits of Section 404 by directly testing controls *and* evaluating management's evaluation process. Commenters believed that, as a result of these provisions in AS No. 2, auditors were inappropriately dictating how management should perform its evaluation, which in some cases may have resulted in unnecessary cost and effort by management.

To attest to and report on management's assessment, auditors must test controls directly to determine whether they are effective. For that reason, the PCAOB now believes that auditors can perform effective audits of internal control without evaluating the adequacy of management's evaluation process.

As a result, AS No. 5 eliminates the requirements in AS No. 2, Paragraphs 40 to 46, to evaluate management's annual evaluation process and requires auditors to express only one opinion on internal control—a statement of the auditors' opinion on the effectiveness of the company's internal control over financial reporting. It eliminates the separate opinion on management's assessment because it is redundant and because the sole audit opinion of a company's internal control more clearly conveys the auditors' opinion on whether the company's internal control is effective.

Practice Tip

Although the removal of the evaluation requirement should eliminate unnecessary work by your external auditors, the quality of your program is inherently linked to the amount of work your auditors will need to do. The removal of this requirement should not affect your procedures. Management still should carry out strong documentation, testing, and analysis processes.

Under AS No. 5, auditors still need to obtain an understanding of management's own process for assessing internal control as a starting point to understanding the company's internal control, assessing risk, and determining the extent to which they will use the work of others. The extent of work necessary for these purposes, however, should be limited.

The extent of your auditors' ability to use the work of others will depend on the quality of the company's annual evaluation process and its ongoing monitoring activities as well as on the competence and objectivity of those performing the work. For these reasons, auditors and management still must coordinate their respective efforts.

Permitting Consideration of Knowledge Obtained during Previous Audits

AS No. 5 encourages auditors to incorporate knowledge obtained during past audits of the company's internal control over financial reporting into the decision-making process for determining the nature, timing, and extent of testing necessary in the current year. As one step to facilitating this change, the new standard deliberately omits the statement in Paragraph E120 of AS No. 2 that "each year's audit must stand on its own."

Knowledge obtained in previous years' audits should also affect auditors' assessment of risk. Factors that specifically affect the risk associated with a control in subsequent years' audits include:

- The nature, timing, and extent of procedures performed in previous audits

- The results of the previous years' testing of the control

- Whether there have been changes in the control or the process in which it operates since the previous audit

After taking into account all the risk factors, the additional information available in subsequent years' audits might permit auditors to assess the risk as lower than in the initial year. This could permit auditors to reduce their testing in subsequent years. The lower the risk associated with a control, the less evidence auditors need to obtain in subsequent years' audits.

For example, an auditor considers the risk factors for a certain control and determines the control presents a low risk overall because there

---

Practice Tip

Management can use the same idea of using results from a prior year's assessment. If a control was successfully tested in a prior year using a method that provides strong evidence of effectiveness, and there were no changes to that control since the last test, a less persuasive form of testing could be used in the current period. See Chapter 8 for more information on testing effective controls in subsequent years.

---

is low inherent risk, is a low degree of complexity, were no changes to the control since the previous audit, and the previous years' testing revealed no deficiencies. The auditor may determine that sufficient evidence of operating effectiveness could be obtained by performing a walk-through only.

Benchmarking Automated Controls

According to AS No. 5, auditors may use a benchmarking strategy for automated application controls in subsequent years' audits because entirely automated application controls generally are not subject to breakdowns due to human failure. If general IT controls over program changes, access to programs, and computer operations are effective and continue to be tested, and if auditors verify that certain automated application control have not changed since they last tested the application control, auditors may conclude those automated application controls continue to be effective without repeating the prior year's specific tests of the operation. Keep in mind that the nature and extent of the evidence auditors may obtain to verify that the control has not changed will vary and may include depending on the strength of the company's program change controls.

Three risk factors should be assessed when determining whether to use a benchmarking strategy. If these factors indicate lower risk, the control being evaluated could be viewed as well suited for benchmarking.

1. The extent to which the application control can be matched to a defined program within an application

2. The extent to which the application is stable (i.e., there are few changes from period to period)

Practice Tip

Benchmarking automated application controls can be especially effective for companies using purchased software when the possibility of program changes is minuscule because access or modification to the source code is not allowed.

---

3. The availability and reliability of a report of the compilation dates of the programs placed in production. (This information may be used as evidence that controls within the program have not changed.)

After a period of time, the baseline of the operation of application controls should be reestablished. Evaluating these factors can help determine when to reestablish a performance baseline for automated application controls:

- The effectiveness of the IT control environment, including controls over application and system software acquisition and maintenance, access controls, and computer operations.

- The understanding of the nature of changes, if any, on the specific programs that contain the controls.

- The nature and timing of other related tests.

- The consequences of errors associated with the application control that was benchmarked.

- Whether the control is sensitive to other business factors that may have changed. For example, an automated control may have been designed with the assumption that only positive amounts will exist in a file. Such a control would no longer be effective if negative amounts (credits) begin to be posted to the account.

Refocusing the Multilocation Testing Requirements on Risk Rather than Coverage

AS No. 2 describes an approach to multilocation scoping that identifies three categories of locations: locations that are individually significant or involve specific risk; locations that are significant only when aggregated with others; and locations that are insignificant individually and in the aggregate. Additionally, AS No. 2 directs auditors to evaluate whether their testing strategy results in performing tests of controls over a "large portion" of the company.

Critics of the "large portion" approach believe that it did not allow the flexibility necessary to efficiently address the specific risks of certain companies. The PCAOB agreed and omitted the provision requiring testing of controls over a large portion of the company in AS No. 5. Instead, it directs auditors to use a risk-based approach to determine the proper strategy for auditing multiple locations. For additional information on the new standard's approach for multilocation testing, see Chapter 6.

Removing Barriers to Using the Work of Others

When auditors duplicate high-quality, relevant work that already has been performed by competent and objective individuals, they risk increasing effort and cost without enhancing quality.

AS No. 5 gives external auditors permission to use the work of or receive direct assistance from internal auditors, other company personnel, and third parties working under the direction of management or the audit committee "to provide evidence about the effectiveness of internal control over financial reporting." Thus, in an integrated audit of internal control and the financial statements, auditors can use the work of others to support their assessment of control risk in the financial statement audit. The standard refers to AU sec 322, *The Auditor's Consideration of the Internal Audit Function in an Audit of Financial Statements.*

Competency and Objectivity   In order to determine the extent to which they can use the work of others, external auditors will have to assess the competence and objectivity of the people they plan to use in their audits. Of course, the more competent and objective those people are, the greater the use auditors may make of their work. For details on how auditors will evaluate the degree of competence and objectivity of your personnel, see Chapter 9.

Relevant Activities   AS No. 5 omits two provisions on using the work of others contained in AS No. 2. The new standard eliminates the "principal evidence" provision, which requires auditors' own work to provide the principal evidence for their opinions on companies' internal control. Instead, auditors can determine how much of the work of others can be used by evaluating the nature of the subject matter tested by others and the competence and objectivity of those who performed the work.

AS No. 5 also omits the specific restriction on using the work of others for testing controls in the control environment. Instead, the extent to which others can be used depends on the risk associated with the control being tested. As the risk increases, so does the need for auditors to perform their own work.

For example, certain aspects of the control environment could be tested by others when the competence and objectivity of the people performing the work are sufficiently high. Auditors could use the work of others for determining that a written code of conduct exists and that employees have received and confirmed their understanding of it. However, evaluating whether a company's code of conduct is actually being followed requires more judgment. Auditors may determine that they would need to perform more of the testing themselves, just as they may conclude in other high-risk areas regardless of the objectivity or competence of others.

Recalibrating the Walk-through Requirements

Under AS No. 2, auditors had to complete walk-throughs of all major classes of transactions. In many cases, management followed this requirement and performed its own walk-throughs of all transactions in significant processes. There is little debate that walk-throughs are one of the best ways to gain an understanding of a process and understand where misstatements could occur. However, walk-throughs can be tedious and time consuming.

AS No. 5 removes the requirement for auditors to perform walk-throughs but focuses on the objectives that walk-throughs usually fulfill. These objectives are described in AS No. 5 in this way:

- Understand the flow of transactions related to the relevant assertions, including how these transactions are initiated, authorized, processed, and recorded.

- Verify that the auditor has identified the points within the company's processes at which a misstatement—including a misstatement due to fraud—could arise that, individually or in combination with other misstatements, would be material.

- Identify the controls that management has implemented to address these potential misstatements.

- Identify the controls that management has implemented over the prevention or timely detection of unauthorized acquisition, use, or disposition of the company's assets that could result in a material misstatement of the financial statements.

In an effective walk-through, auditors (and company personnel) are encouraged to use a combination of probing inquiries and observation and examine the same documents and IT used by company personnel to understand how transactions recorded in the general ledger are ultimately reflected in the company's financial statements and related disclosures. AS No. 5 points out that performing a walk-through often is the most effective way of achieving the listed objectives.

Since walk-throughs can be so time consuming and disruptive to process owners, it is important to plan these procedures for maximum effectiveness. A retail company, for example, could put the objectives into practice by performing a walk-through of at least one retail sales transaction. If the company generates revenue from both store and Internet sales, it would not, however, be necessary to walk through both types of retail transactions as long as both were handled by the same significant process and did not have significantly different risks. During the walk-through, it would be helpful to ask probing questions to gain a sufficient understanding of the process, but it would not required to follow a separate transaction through each minor variance in the process.

Unlike AS No. 2, the new standard allows auditors to utilize the direct assistance of others when performing walk-throughs. The difference between an audit staff member and another sufficiently competent and objective individual providing direct assistance in a walk-through is judged as minimal and should not affect audit quality.

SCALING AUDITS FOR SMALLER COMPANIES

In considering how to minimize the costs of an audit of internal control while preserving its benefits, the PCAOB recognized that smaller companies often present different financial reporting risks than larger and more complex ones, and that their internal control systems often appropriately address those risks in different ways. Scaling audits to fit the specific sizes and complexities of companies is a natural extension of the risk-based approach. AS No. 5 recognizes that the size and complexity of companies are important and the planning process and procedures auditors perform should depend on where along the size and complexity continuum companies fall.

The broad changes in the new standard that are designed to eliminate unnecessary audit work for all companies will affect smaller company audits in particular. Most important, AS No. 5 gives auditors more flexibility for relying on strong entity-level controls and financial statement audit procedures to reduce the level of testing.

The final report of the SEC Advisory Committee on Smaller Public Companies indicated that market capitalization and annual revenue are useful indicators of a company's size. AS No. 5 does not provide such specific criteria but lists attributes common to smaller and less-complex companies that affect the risks of misstatement and the controls necessary to address those risks These attributes include:

- Fewer business lines

- Less complex business processes and financial reporting systems

- More centralized accounting functions

- Extensive involvement by senior management in the day-to-day activities of the business

- Fewer levels of management, each with a wide span of control

Throughout, AS No. 5 refers to audits of smaller and less-complex companies. Specific comments addressed to smaller public companies include:

- **Obtaining sufficient audit evidence with limited company documentation.** Auditors have the option to conclude a control is operating effectively even in the absence of documentation evidencing the operation of the control. In smaller and less-complex companies with less formal documentation, testing controls through inquiry combined with observation or other procedures could provide sufficient evidence about whether the control is effective, even in the absence of documentation.

- **Evaluating the risk of management override and mitigating actions.** Because of the extensive involvement of senior management in performing controls and the period-end financial reporting process, controls to prevent management override are particularly important in smaller and less-complex companies. However, controls to address the risk of management override at these smaller companies may be different from those at larger companies. For example, a smaller and less-complex company may rely on more detailed oversight by the audit committee that focuses on the risk of management override.

- **Evaluating controls implemented in lieu of segregation of duties.** Smaller and less-complex companies might have few employees in the accounting function, limiting opportunities to segregate duties. This may lead companies to implement alternative controls to achieve their control objectives.

- **Evaluating financial reporting competencies.** Auditors are instructed to take into account the combined competence of company personnel and other parties who assist with the financial reporting function when assessing the company's financial reporting and associated controls.

These examples of audit procedures described in the new standard give auditors permission to use alternative audit procedures based on their professional judgments about a company's internal control and may be applied to both smaller- and large-company audits of internal control.

As part of a four-point plan to improve implementation of the internal control requirements, the PCAOB determined to amend AS No. 2. Other aspects of the plan were to develop or facilitate development of implementation guidance for auditors of smaller public companies, continue PCAOB Forums on Auditing in the Small Business Environment, and reinforce auditor efficiency through PCAOB inspections. The PCAOB is continuing to work on its plan with several forums on auditing in the small business environment scheduled throughout 2008.

For a comprehensive listing of changes to AS No. 2, see Appendix F.

NOTE

1. Policy Statement Regarding Implementation of Auditing Standard No. 2, an Audit of Internal Control over Financial Reporting Performed in Conjunction with an Audit of Financial Statements, issued May 16, 2005.

3

SEC's Guidance on a Risk-Based Approach

Key Topics:
- Reasonable assurance, a risk-based approach, and scope of testing and assessment

- Evaluating internal control deficiencies: qualitative factors to consider and how financial statement restatements affect the evaluation

- Disclosures about material weaknesses

- Information technology scoping and system implementations or upgrades

- External auditor communications, independence, and prohibited services

- Issues related to small businesses and foreign private issuers

It is apparent in its May 2005 guidance that the Securities and Exchange Commission (SEC) does not want to give specifics on the scope of Section 404 assessments or the amount of documentation and testing required by management. The SEC believes the scope and process of management's assessment should be supported by some type of evidential matter that fits each company's own operations, risks, and procedures. It calls for a customized assessment process where companies use their own experience and informed judgment. Unfortunately, many public companies and external auditors are looking for specifics and practical steps for compliance.

The SEC's view is supported in instruction 1 to item 308 of Regulation S-K, which states: "The registrant must maintain evidential matter, including documentation, to provide reasonable support for management's assessment of the effectiveness of the registrant's internal control over financial reporting." The point is also made by the Committee of Sponsoring Organizations of the Treadway Commission (COSO) in the third volume of its *Internal Control—Integrated Framework: Evaluation Tools.* COSO states: "Because facts and circumstances vary between entities and industries, evaluation methodologies and documentation will also vary." These comments are not the only reference in the May 2005 guidance that advises against a one-size-fits-all approach to compliance.

SEC Roundtable Discussion

The SEC hosted its first roundtable discussion in April 2005 to actively seek input for assessing the impact of its new reporting requirements under Section 404. Representatives of public companies (domestic and foreign), auditors, investors, members of the legal community, and the board members of the Public Company Accounting Oversight Board (PCAOB) sent a message of general support for the objectives of Section 404, but they expressed concern over the cost of compliance. As a result of the discussion, the SEC and PCAOB concurrently published additional guidance for issuers and auditors on May 16, 2005.

Many were surprised at the speed of the SEC and PCAOB's responsiveness and thought the new guidance was a call for reasonableness. Others thought the guidance suggested more leniency without specific instruction, leaving many external auditors' procedures unchanged for internal control audits.

SEC Commission Statement

In May 2005, the SEC issued a Commission Statement, the SEC staff issued a Staff Statement, and the PCAOB issued a Policy Statement and Staff Questions and Answers. Each issuance complemented the others. The Commission Statement was the briefest of all the May 2005 guidance and generally summarized the Staff Statement issued that same day. There were no changes to information previously published in Auditing Standard No. 2 (AS No. 2), but the emphasis was shifted to a more practical approach using the "top-down" and "risk-based" concepts.

Since that time, the SEC has issued its guidance for management,[1] which reiterates many concepts in its May 2005 guidance. Although the SEC plans to revisit previous guidance published in its Staff's Frequently Asked Questions, it indicates that the May 2005 guidance remains relevant. Additionally, in 2007, the PCAOB issued Auditing Standard No. 5 (AS No. 5), which is meant to supersede AS No. 2.

HIGHLIGHTS OF THE SEC STAFF STATEMENT

The SEC sought feedback on the first-year implementation of Section 404 from a panel of representatives from domestic and foreign public companies, auditors, investors, members of the legal community, and board members of the PCAOB. It also solicited written submissions from the public. Comments from the panel and submissions from the public that were sent in were the reason the Staff Statement was created.

The message at their first roundtable discussion on Section 404 was that companies have realized improvements to their internal controls as a result of implementing the requirements of Section 404 and that the requirements have led to an improved focus on internal controls throughout the organizations. However, the feedback also identified implementation areas that needed further clarification to reduce unnecessary costs without jeopardizing the benefits of the new requirements.

The Staff Statement addresses these areas:

- The purpose of internal control over financial reporting
- Reasonable assurance, risk-based approach, and scope of testing and assessment
- Evaluating internal control deficiencies
- Disclosures about material weaknesses
- Information technology issues
- Communications with auditors
- Issues related to small business and foreign private issuers

The main theme of the guidance is that management is responsible for determining the form and level of controls appropriate for its own organization and to scope the assessment and testing accordingly. The statement notes that one size does not fit all and that control effectiveness is affected by many factors.

STAFF'S EMPHASIS ON REASONABLE ASSURANCE

Though not a new concept, the staff describes the idea of reasonable assurance as a high level of assurance but not absolute assurance. It refers to the Foreign Corrupt Practices Act (FCPA) Section 13(b)(7), which defines "reasonable assurance" and "reasonable detail" as "such level of detail and degree of assurance as would satisfy prudent officials in the conduct of their own affairs."

Footnote 12 in the Staff Statement makes an interesting point: The conference committee report on amendments to the FCPA also noted that the standard "does not connote an unrealistic degree of exactitude or precision. The concept of reasonableness of necessity contemplates the weighing of a number of relevant factors including the *costs of compliance*."

During the first year of compliance, some companies believed the concept of reasonableness was forgotten. The staff addresses reasonableness in a specific section in its guidance to emphasize the idea. Reasonableness in the context of Section 404 does not imply a single conclusion or methodology, but takes into account a full range of potential conduct and conclusions.

> This also suggests that registered public accounting firms should recognize that there is a zone of reasonable conduct by issuers that should be recognized as acceptable in the implementation of Section 404. While that zone is not unlimited, the staff expects that it will be rare when there is only one acceptable choice in implementing Section 404 in any given situation.

If this has been an area of concern for you in the past, you may consider framing this quote so you can easily point to it if your auditor becomes unreasonable.

Keep in mind that AU sec. 230, *Due Professional Care in the Performance of Work,*[2] defines reasonable assurance as high assurance, and that is what external auditors will expect to achieve. Companies making the attestation need their own "high assurance," as they cannot rely on audit procedures for their assessment.

Using a Top-Down and Risk-Based Approach to Narrow Scope

A common problem area cited by issuers was the determination of scope. Many believe that the requirements of Section 404 were too conservatively interpreted and auditors did not use professional judgment, causing too many controls to be identified, documented, and tested.

The staff supports addressing both qualitative and quantitative factors when identifying significant accounts and processes in order to determine the scope of your assessment:

> The use of a percentage as a minimum threshold may provide a reasonable starting point for evaluating the significance of an account or process; however, judgment, including a review of qualitative factors, must be exercised to determine if amounts above or below that threshold must be evaluated.

Pointers on Qualitative and Quantitative Factors Involved in Scoping

- Keep in mind that your auditor should have no differences in the significant (i.e., material) accounts for your internal control and financial statement audits.

- The PCAOB agreed at its June 2005 Standing Advisory Group meeting that it would be rare for an account that is above the quantitative threshold to be considered insignificant.

- Generally, qualitative factors will pull an account into scope but will not allow a quantitatively significant account to be excluded from scope even if it is considered low risk.

- Control risk should not come into play when you are evaluating the risk of a specific account or process. You should look at inherent risk.

- Significant accounts can be divided into pieces for scoping purposes, with certain pieces remaining out of scope (i.e., petty cash can be separated from cash as a whole and excluded from scope if not material).

The result of a top-down approach is that management would devote greater attention and resources to the areas of greater risk. The SEC staff points to a mechanistic, check-the-box exercise as one of the reasons too many controls and processes were identified, documented, and tested in year one. It cautions that a formulaic and/or too detailed assessment of internal control may not allow for a focus on risk or fulfill the underlying purpose of Section 404 requirements:

> The desired approach should devote resources to the areas of greatest risk and avoid giving all significant accounts and related controls equal attention without regard to risk.

An internal control assessment will be more effective if the company first focuses on the significant accounts and disclosures that are likely to be materially misstated in its financial statements. Then the nature, timing, and extent of control testing can be planned based on the financial statement risk assessment. This is what is meant by a top-down approach. Hence, a low-risk account would be tested using a different testing method at a different point during the year than a high-risk account.

> Employing such a top-down approach requires that management apply in a reasonable manner its cumulative knowledge, experience and judgment to identify the areas of the financial statements that present significant risk that the financial statements could be materially misstated and then proceed to identify relevant controls and design appropriate procedures for documentation and testing of those controls.

Staff's Ideas on Efficiency

One way to increase efficiency is to make sure your company has the right number of key controls. For most accelerated filers, this means a reduction in the number of key controls. The staff believes that too many controls were documented and tested during the first year of implementation because too many individual steps within a broader control were considered key. The recommendation is to step back from the detail to determine if "combinations of controls previously identified individually constitute the actual control that contributes to financial statement assurance." Focus on the broader objective of controls instead of testing each individual step involved.

This would be the most obvious approach to reducing the number of controls that are not really key. Focus on the one or two controls that you cannot live without, directly address the risk, and cover the relevant financial assertion(s).

The staff believes efficiencies eventually will come through the natural learning process, a risk-based approach, and using the reasonable assurance concept. These encouraging words throw a bit of hope into the SOX environment, suggesting that efficiencies are imminent.

The staff suggests that internal auditors, company personnel, and external auditors who are "on the ground" and closest to the assessment will be the ones to drive efficiency and effectiveness. These are the people who will see the unique circumstances in an organization and should be able to customize the approach, so they must be properly trained and have the requisite skills to make reasonable assessments.

The staff's statements on the natural learning process and skilled auditors come from a multitude of issues raised by panelists at the round-table and public comments. These issues include:

- Auditor preparedness (or lack of) for first-time implementation
- Shortages of qualified resources at the auditor, consultant, and preparer level
- Indecision by management and auditors about acceptable levels of control documentation and testing
- Shifts in direction after work had started
- Pressures on companies to commit firmly to the precise timing of work because auditor resources were limited
- Inexperienced staff
- Auditors reluctant to make decisions without national office support
- Pressures and long hours expended by auditors and companies to complete the control evaluation
- Communication difficulties between auditors and management
- Auditors' concerns over the PCAOB inspection process impacting their decisions for the appropriate level of documentation and testing

Experience and time has diminished some of these concerns. As the experience base increases, management and external auditors should gain confidence in their Section 404 judgments. Surprisingly, the lateness of the standards and ineffective guidance and interpretation mechanisms (questions and answers) is hardly mentioned. Only recently, years after accelerated filers began attesting to their internal controls and just before nonaccelerated filers and foreign private issuers are required to comply with Section 404, was guidance for management published. For the time being, management may continue to rely to some degree on the more comprehensive auditor standards because there is so little guidance specifically for management, even though it is required to make its own assessment.

Although not explicitly stated, the staff implies that the issues noted are nonrecurring or first-time implementation issues, and most are. However, the concern over the auditors' lack of decision making, the PCAOB inspection process, the shortage of qualified resources, and the related issues of long hours and commitment to precise timing of work are proving to be longer-term compliance issues.

When to Use Annual or Quarterly Financial Periods in Analyses

Although it generally is not an area of confusion, the staff states that a top-down approach entails using annual and entity-level measures to identify significant accounts and plan the scope of the assessment. As most already know, this means the annual, consolidated financial statements would be used for scoping. However, as a qualitative item, companies with key segments or seasonal transactions should also take these factors into account in their scoping exercise.

Deficiencies, though, should be evaluated using quarterly and annual measures, and could include analysis at the segment level if applicable. These statements necessitate the unpopular practice of analyzing the potential magnitude of a deficiency on a quarterly basis using a lower, quarterly threshold for materiality.

Timing of Tests of Control

Much to everyone's relief, the staff confirmed that not all testing had to be performed around the as-of date. The staff states: "In fact, we believe that effective testing and assessment may, and in most cases preferably would, be accomplished over a longer period of time. In its adopting release, the SEC expressly noted that testing may be done over a period of time." Spreading control tests throughout the year will relieve some of the bottleneck and panic that occurred in the past at year-end, but many external auditors require some type of testing near the end of the year, at least within the fourth quarter. Fourth-quarter testing may include update tests, newly remediated control tests, and tests of year-end controls. Even if testing is spread throughout the year, there is still plenty to test near year-end.

COMMENTS ON EVALUATING INTERNAL CONTROL DEFICIENCIES

Companies are encouraged to consider the significance of deficiencies encountered in their internal control assessments by "exercising judgment in a reasonable manner." Although auditors have striven to quantify the severity of deficiencies, both quantitative and qualitative factors should be used to evaluate deficiencies.

Qualitative Factors to Consider in Evaluating Deficiencies

Qualitative factors by their nature are subjective and can cause debate because they require you to consider issues that are not black and white. Issues that are open to interpretation allow room for negotiation and persuasion, which can be a benefit in some cases. These factors can help evaluate the qualitative aspects of deficiencies:

- The nature of the deficiency

- The cause of the deficiency

- The relevant financial statement assertion the control was designed to support

- Its effect on the broader control environment

- Whether compensating controls are effective

How Financial Statement Restatements Affect an Evaluation of Deficiencies

Nowhere in Section 404 or any of the SEC guidance does it require that a material weakness in internal control exists if a company restates its financial statements because of an error. However, in AS No. 5, the PCAOB states that a restatement of previously issued financial statements to reflect the correction of a misstatement is an "indicator" that a material weakness exists. The staff suggests that management and the auditor use professional judgment to determine why the error occurred and if the restatement resulted from a material weakness in internal control.

Although a company's internal controls are supposed to provide reasonable, not absolute, assurance that the financial statements will not contain a material misstatement, it will be difficult for you to argue that a material weakness in internal controls does not exist if a restatement occurs due to an error. Financial statements are restated only for significant and/or material errors. If this type of error went through all the checks and controls at a company without being caught, there is little chance you could argue that the likelihood and magnitude of the control deficiency were low enough to fall below the material weakness threshold. Auditors tend to be very cautious in this area. Although judgment will come into play, generally a restatement will result in a material weakness in internal control.

DISCLOSURES ABOUT MATERIAL WEAKNESSES

Part of the SEC's rule on implementing Section 404 was to bring to the public's attention material weaknesses in internal controls at public companies. As such, the staff believes disclosures of material weaknesses should include:

- The nature of any material weakness
- The impact on financial reporting and the control environment
- Management's current plans for remediating the weakness

The staff "strongly encourages" companies to provide information in their material weakness disclosure that allows investors to assess the impact of each material weakness. Companies also are encouraged to include information on whether the weakness may have a pervasive effect on internal control over financial reporting. The goal of such a disclosure is to provide improved investor information as the starting point, not the only point, for analysis.

INFORMATION TECHNOLOGY COMMENTS FROM THE STAFF

The appropriate level of information technology (IT) documentation and testing needed for an assessment of internal control was also a topic for discussion at the roundtable. The staff encourages companies to use judgment in determining which application and general IT controls (controls over program development, program changes, computer operations, and access to programs and data) are relevant to their Section 404 assessment. The staff points out that for Section 404 purposes, it "would not expect testing of general IT controls that do not pertain to financial reporting."

In discussing possible separate, specific IT frameworks as a guide for the IT portion of a Section 404 assessment, the staff states that using a separate IT framework is not required. Some companies have found parts of these frameworks to be useful for their individual approach. "However, the staff does not believe it necessary for purposes of Section 404 for management to assess all general IT controls, and especially not those that primarily pertain to the efficiency or effectiveness of the operations of the organization but are not relevant to financial reporting."

The footnote to this section specifically names Control Objectives for Information and Related Technology (COBIT) as an alternate IT framework. COBIT was often referred to by external auditors in year one as an appropriate IT standard for Section 404 compliance. While the standards in COBIT are exemplary, the staff implies that you can use the parts that are relevant to financial reporting, but other parts of the framework may have a more operational purpose. Many auditors today believe the COBIT framework as a whole is over and above what is needed for Section 404 compliance.

IT Systems Implementations and Upgrades

Considerable feedback was sent to the SEC regarding companies that delayed system updates or changes in the first year of compliance for fear they would not be able to fully implement, document, and successfully test the system before year-end. Some of the feedback requested that management be allowed to exclude new IT systems and upgrades implemented late in the year, similar to the exclusion given to new business acquisitions (refer to Staff FAQ in Appendix E). Although a practical suggestion, it does not seem feasible given the pervasive effect financial IT systems have on companies' financial reporting. The staff held firm on its belief that new IT systems must remain under management's existing responsibilities in regard to internal control assessment and did not provide an exclusion.

COMMUNICATIONS WITH AUDITORS: AN UNINTENDED CONSEQUENCE

Both auditors and registrants noted a "chilled effect in the level and extent of communication between auditors and management" due to implementing Section 404. In the past, a company's external auditors often provided technical advice in accounting, auditing, and/or financial reporting matters. As a result of the SOX, both parties have been unsure of the type of communications and advice allowed. Management is concerned about providing draft copies of financial statements to the auditor because they may not be complete or may contain errors, and fear that the auditor could identify supposed internal control deficiencies because of the draft quality of the financials. However, external auditors are concerned that providing technical advice to management may impinge on their independence.

As will be discussed, the SEC has clear guidelines for maintaining auditor independence and does not preclude auditors from giving advice and approval. It does, however, prohibit auditors from making decisions for management. As a result of the controversy, roles and responsibilities are more defined. Instead of management asking its auditor how to handle a certain issue or transaction, companies are now submitting plans or journal entries to their auditors, then asking for advice. Semantics? Maybe, but this approach requires companies to take more responsibility for coming up with solutions instead of waiting for auditors to tell them the path to take.

Four Principles of the SEC's Auditor Independence Requirements

The SEC's auditor independence requirements are based on these four principles:

1. Auditors cannot function in the role of management.

2. Auditors cannot audit their own work.

3. Auditors cannot serve in an advocacy role for their client.

4. Auditors and audit clients cannot have a relationship that creates a mutual or conflicting interest.

These principles are consistent with guidance in the Independence Standard Board's Interpretation 99-1, *Impact on Auditor Independence of Assisting Clients in the Implementation of FAS 133* on derivatives, which was adopted by the PCAOB.

SEC's Nine Categories of Prohibited Services

In addition to the SEC's independence principles, nine different categories of services that auditors were prohibited from providing to their audit clients were established.

1. Bookkeeping or other services related to the accounting records or financial statements

2. Financial information system design and implementation

3. Appraisal of valuation services, fairness opinions, or contribution-in-kind reports

4. Actuarial services

5. Internal audit outsourcing

6. Management functions or human resources

7. Broker/dealer, investment advisor, or investment banking services

8. Legal services and expert service unrelated to the audit

9. Any other service that the SEC or PCAOB determines, by regulation, is impermissible

The staff's stance is that discussions and exchanging views with management does not in itself cross the independence line or fall into any of the nine prohibited services categories. It believes that investors benefit when auditors discuss such issues as new accounting standards and the appropriate treatment of complex or unusual transactions with management. As long as management makes the final decision for the accounting treatment and the auditor does not design or implement accounting policies, auditor involvement would be appropriate. Technical discussions between companies and their auditors can be necessary to increase the quality of financial reporting.

In addition to technical discussions, management should not be discouraged from providing its auditors with draft financial statements.

In the staff's view, errors in draft financial statements in and of themselves should not be the basis for the determination by a company or an auditor of a deficiency in internal controls. Rather. . .management and auditors should determine whether a deficiency exists in the processes of financial statement preparation. That identification is essentially independent of whether an error exists in draft financial statements and who found it.

The PCAOB also comments on this issue in its May 16, 2005, guidance and gives specific examples (see Chapter 4).

MESSAGE FOR SMALL BUSINESS ISSUERS AND FOREIGN PRIVATE ISSUERS

On a last note, the staff commented on the concerns of small businesses and foreign private issuers that have not yet had to comply with Section 404. Its words of encouragement state that it has developed an Advisory Committee on Smaller Public Companies and that a COSO task force has been established to create guidance on applying the COSO framework to smaller companies.

Since the SEC's Staff Statement in May 2005, new guidance published from COSO for smaller companies gives illustrative tools and attributes for evaluating internal controls (see Chapter 5). In addition, the SEC has issued the first guidance specifically geared toward management (see Chapter 1), and the PCAOB has issued AS No. 5 (see Chapter 2). Although extensions for Section 404 implementation have been common, the SEC has made it clear that it will ultimately enforce Section 404 on companies of all sizes. In the staff's own words, it will, "continue to assess the effects of the internal control reporting rules on smaller public companies and foreign private issuers."

NOTES

1. Commission Guidance Regarding Management's Report on Internal Control over Financial Reporting Under Section 13(a) or 15(d) of the Securities Exchange Act of 1934, published in June 2007.
2. www.pcaob.org/Standards/Interim_Standards/Auditing_Standards/index.aspx.

4

Highlights of the PCAOB's May 2005 Policy Statement

Key Topics:

- Policy statement highlights

- Integrating the financial and internal control audits

- Importance of professional judgment

- Using a top-down approach and the role of risk assessment

- When external auditors can use the work of others

- Auditors' ability to provide advice to audit clients

- How the PCAOB inspections help drive improvements

Even back in 2005, the guidance issued by the Securities and Exchange Commission (SEC) and Public Company Accounting Oversight Board (PCAOB) was using more of a principles-based method, and the risk-based approach with an emphasis on professional judgment was coming into style. In addition to the guidance issued by the SEC, the PCAOB's Policy Statement and related Staff Questions and Answers were also published on May 16, 2005, based on comments received at the SEC Roundtable on Implementation of Internal Control Reporting Provisions and on other occasions. The PCAOB Policy Statement confirmed that many participants generally supported the objectives of Sarbanes-Oxley (SOX) Section 404; the primary concern was the cost of compliance.

Although based on Auditing Standard No. 2 (AS No. 2), the points made in the PCAOB's Policy Statement are still pertinent and represent the direction that regulators were headed when creating Auditing Standard No. 5 (AS No. 5). Even though the PCAOB guidance is geared toward external auditors, information and advice from the Policy Statement can be beneficial for management's own assessment and for financial managers dealing with their auditors.

POLICY STATEMENT HIGHLIGHTS

The PCAOB's Policy Statement focuses on efficiency by using a risk-based approach. This concept is exemplified in the statement that "failure to apply the concepts discussed in this Policy Statement may reflect poor audit planning and result in unnecessary cost." The PCAOB agrees that the cost of compliance in year one was too high and that costs must be reduced to ensure sustainability. As a means to reduce costs without sacrificing quality, the PCAOB encourages auditors to use these five concepts:

1. Integrate the audits of internal control with the audit of the client's financial statements so that evidence gathered and tests conducted in the context of either audit contribute to the completion of both.

2. Exercise judgment to tailor the audit plans to the risks facing individual audit clients instead of using standardized checklists that may not reflect an allocation of audit work weighted toward high-risk areas (and weighted against unnecessary audit focus in low-risk areas).

3. Use a top-down approach that begins with company-level controls, to identify for further testing only those accounts and processes that are, in fact, relevant to internal control over financial reporting, and use the risk assessment required by the standard to eliminate from further consideration those accounts that have only a remote likelihood of containing a material misstatement.

4. Take advantage of the significant flexibility that the standard allows to use the work of others.

5. Engage in direct and timely communication with audit clients when those clients seek auditors' views on accounting or internal control issues before those clients make their own decisions on such issues, implement internal control processes under consideration, or finalize financial reports.

INTEGRATING THE FINANCIAL AND INTERNAL CONTROL AUDITS

In the past, it was common practice for auditors to rely on less costly and time-consuming procedures for a financial statement audit if they determined a company's internal controls were adequately designed and operating effectively. If auditors determined that internal controls were not adequate or chose not to rely on them, auditors would conduct more detailed tests during the financial audit. This long-standing auditing approach is described in Chapter 5 of the American Institute of Certified Public Accountants's (AICPA's) Statements on Standards for Attestation

Engagements (SSAE) No. 10, *Reporting on an Entity's Internal Control over Financial Reporting* (AT 501) and the PCAOB's interim auditing standard AU Sec. 319.03, *Consideration of Internal Control in a Financial Statement Audit.*

However, SOX Sections 103 and 404 have created a new requirement. Now auditors are required to obtain an understanding of a company's internal controls and render an opinion on them, not as part of a financial audit but as its own audit. The PCAOB states that AS No. 2 was designed as an integrated audit model to make the overall audit process as efficient as possible. The concept of integrating the financial and internal controls audits also has been carried forward to AS No. 5.

By an integrated approach, the PCAOB means to combine the audit of internal control and the audit of the financial statements so auditors achieve the objectives of the two audits simultaneously through a single coordinated process. Evidence and tests performed for the internal control audit can be used to better plan and reduce the number of procedures needed to come to an opinion for the financial audit. "The two processes are mutually reinforcing." This coordinated process could have cost-reduction benefits for management under the belief that an integrated audit is more cost-effective than two separate audits. More planning would have to be performed in the beginning to integrate the two audits, but it seems logical that there could be efficiencies.

Although this step is clearly for the benefit of external auditors, management will benefit from efficiencies gained in auditor testing by a reduced number of test samples requested and fewer actual tests. In reviewing the process documentation in Section 404 audits, external auditors will gain a better sense of the businesses they are auditing, producing better audit procedures and, it is hoped, results.

An exception to the integrated audit cost-saving theory may occur if certain controls were not effective throughout the year but were remediated and effective at year-end. Auditors may be unable to reduce the procedures needed for their financial audit, and cost savings due to integration of the two audits will be lower. Overall, if auditors spend fewer hours on the two audits, the time savings should be reflected in the company's audit bill.

Cost of Compliance Data

The PCAOB cites a survey commissioned by the largest U.S. accounting firms that states auditors believed the total cost of compliance for Section 404 would be reduced by 46% in year two.[1] Among the reasons for the cost reduction were auditors' expectations that audit integration will be improved.

Now that actual cost data is available, it seems the PCAOB's cost reduction estimates were a bit optimistic. According to a survey of second-year Section 404 costs by CRA International, total Section 404 costs for smaller companies (market capitalization between $75 and $700 million)

Exhibit 4.1   Summary of CRA International's Spring 2006 Section 404 Cost Survey

Smaller Company Cost Summary

404 Cost Summary:	Year 2 in 000s ($)	Year 1 in 000s ($)	% change
Internal Issuer 404 Costs	301	355	−15.2%
Third Party Costs for 404	223	463	−51.8%
Total 404 Issuer Costs	**524**	**818**	**−36.0%**
404 Audit Fees	336	423	−20.6%
Total 404 Costs	**860**	**1,241**	**−30.7%**
Proxy Audit Fee Component Summary:			
404 Audit Fees	336	423	−20.6%
Other (non-404) Audit Fees	477	423	12.8%
Total Proxy Audit Fees	**813**	**846**	**−3.9%**

Larger Company Cost Summary

404 Cost Summary:	Year 2 in 000s ($)	Year 1 in 000s ($)	% change
Internal Issuer 404 Costs	2,220	4,260	−47.9%
Third Party Costs for 404	980	2,230	−56.1%
Total 404 Issuer Costs	**3,200**	**6,490**	**−50.7%**
404 Audit Fees	1,570	2,020	−22.3%
Total 404 Costs	**4,770**	**8,510**	**−43.9%**
Proxy Audit Fee Component Summary:			
404 Audit Fees	1,570	2,020	−22.3%
Other (non-404) Audit Fees	3,540	3,080	14.9%
Total Proxy Audit Fees	**5,110**	**5,100**	**0.2%**

were reduced by 30.7% in their second year of compliance.[2] Total Section 404 costs for larger companies (market capitalization over $700 million) were reduced by 43.9%. The study takes its data from proxy materials and distinguishes Section 404 costs from total audit fees, which includes Section 404, financial statement, and other audit services costs. Exhibit 4.1 summarizes the findings of the survey.

Controversy on the Integrated Audit Theory

If the "two processes are mutually reinforcing" and "the auditor's examination of internal control is validated by the findings in the audit of the financial statements," it seems illogical that the two audit opinions could differ. If the quality of financial reporting depends on internal controls, and those internal controls are not adequate or reliable, how can the product of those processes and controls be materially correct?

There may be some leeway because of the two different reporting dates, "as of" for internal control audits and "over the period" for financial audits. However, it still seems illogical for companies to receive an adverse or qualified opinion for their internal control audit and an unqualified opinion for their financial audit. If internal controls were not effective "as of" the end of the year, how can anyone be sure there was not a material misstatement "over the period"? It seems the opinions would make sense only if they were reversed.

IMPORTANCE OF PROFESSIONAL JUDGMENT

Like the SEC staff, the PCAOB also emphasizes professional judgment in its May 16, 2005, guidance. Just as auditors are leery of transactions that require management's judgment, auditors appear to be leery of the PCAOB's recommendation. In both cases, the auditors are the ones who could lose. If they concur with management's judgment or use their own judgment to test management's controls and either subjective decision is scrutinized and deemed a bad judgment, they may have trouble. The PCAOB's investigations of accounting firms seem to have done little to give firms confidence in this area. In the post–Enron and Arthur Andersen world, professional judgment can be a scary concept.

The PCAOB (as well as the SEC staff) cautions auditors against using a "one-size-fits-all" approach or standardized checklists to address the unique risks for each company's internal control audit. The PCAOB even chastises auditors who have used this approach by saying "This is a disappointing development indicative of poor training and audit planning." The standardized approach is also blamed for increased costs and a decrease in audit quality. Professional judgment is needed to focus audit work on high-risk areas and tailor auditors' approaches for clients in different industries or of different size.

While most would agree that a one-size-fits-all approach is not optimal and that attention should be focused on the high-risk areas, the theory does not always translate into practice. Although the SEC and PCAOB have made strides with their most recent Guidance for Management and AS No. 5, guidelines for auditors still may not be clear enough for some to substantially change their approach for Section 404 audits. After all, what if a material misstatement squeaks by because of a material weakness in internal control in a low-risk area? In a PCAOB investigation, could the audit firm use as a defense the fact that they did not find the material weakness because it existed in a low-risk area and their professional judgment caused them to perform only limited audit procedures?

Although you may understand your auditor's cautious approach, it still does not mean that every traditional internal control will apply to your company. For example, a company that works with distributors to sell its products may not need controls around customer credit checks if its distributors are contractually responsible for any unpaid customer accounts and the company does not have a history of material bad debt write-offs. Although your auditor may have these types of controls on its "checklist," and controls around granting customer credit typically are significant for many companies, they would not be relevant for this situation.

Practice Tip

Auditors may expect to see all traditional key controls in your Section 404 program. If you believe a certain control does not apply to your circumstances, document the control and the reasons you believe it does not mitigate a key financial risk for your company. Be sure to include both quantitative and qualitative reasons to support your argument.

Just as in financial statement audits, auditors will have programs or checklists to follow to ensure they have not forgotten to consider any significant controls. The message from the SEC staff and PCAOB is that there has to be room for customization depending on a company's unique circumstances.

TOP-DOWN APPROACH AND ROLE OF RISK ASSESSMENT

The PCAOB states that its original approach in AS No. 2 was designed to be applied from the top down, meaning focusing first on company-level controls and then on significant accounts, significant processes, and then individual controls at the process, transaction, or application level. Now the top-down approach is widely used in practice because it helps auditors (and management) naturally to lean toward the areas of higher risk. The top-down approach should provide a "road map through the control system" to ensure individual controls selected as key are relevant to financial reporting. Again, the guidance states that the threat of increased costs and lack of quality is the result if another approach is followed.

A top-down approach does not mean you should start at the top, get to a certain point, and then stop. In other words, the guidance does not encourage companies to document and test entity-level controls and then come to conclusions on their internal control assessments.

However, in an effort to alter the nature, timing, and extent of their testing, auditors should consider, as part of the risk assessment, how strong the entity-level controls are. "Although the auditor may not rely solely on testing entity-level controls, strong entity-level controls should lead the auditor to do less work than he or she otherwise would have performed or rely to a greater degree on the work of others." This means you should match the type of test, when the test is performed, and the number of sample sizes to the level of risk. For example, nonroutine, high-risk controls that require judgment might be tested at year-end, using reperformance and a large sample size. Conversely, auditors may be able to rely on the work of others for low-risk controls.

WHEN AUDITORS CAN USE THE WORK OF OTHERS

Using a top-down approach and properly assessing risk may lead auditors to identify areas where they could use the work of others to perform their audit in the most efficient way. Redoing work in low-risk areas may increase costs without increasing the quality of the audit and may be indicative of poor audit planning.

Originally AS No. 2 and now AS No. 5 give external auditors considerable flexibility to use the work of others, a practice that has long been accepted in financial statement audits. AS No. 5 allows the work of competent and objective internal auditors and others to affect the nature, timing, and extent of procedures in both financial statement and internal control audits. For example, personnel can be used to test less material financial statement amounts where the risk of material misstatement or degree of subjectivity involved in evaluating the audit evidence is low. Auditors will be more likely to rely on the work of others if the testers are independent and competent. In addition, the standard allows personnel to work under the direct supervision of the external auditor.

The reluctance of auditors to use the work of others may have stemmed from the AS No. 2 requirement that external auditors obtain the principal evidence in support of their opinion from their own work. This "principal evidence" language has been removed in AS No. 5. See Chapter 9 for more detailed information on using the work of others.

AUDITORS' ABILITY TO PROVIDE ADVICE
TO AUDIT CLIENTS

The PCAOB mirrors the SEC staff's advice on communication among auditors and their clients. The PCAOB advises auditors to not provide accounting advice to their audit clients and to ask their clients to finish their internal control assessments and financial statements before they begin their own audit work.

Fears of a PCAOB inspection have led some auditors to take a hard stance on independence rules, not allowing their clients to consult with them on accounting issues or not reviewing draft financial statements for fear of finding an error. "When auditors are unwilling, or believe that they are unable, to provide advice on accounting or internal control, management may be forced to retain other accounting experts, or to make accounting decisions without the benefit of access to the auditor's technical knowledge."

Draft Financial Statements

As originally stated in AS No. 2 and carried over into AS No. 5, an auditor's detection of a material misstatement in financial statements is an indication of a material weakness in internal control. Both the PCAOB's May 2005 guidance and its Staff Question and Answer No. 7 (revised July 27, 2004) discuss the difference between draft financials and completed financials:

> The auditor should be concerned primarily about instances in which the company completed its financial statements and disclosures without recognizing a potential material misstatement. If it is clear that all applicable controls have not yet operated, then a conclusion as to whether a material misstatement in draft financial statements demonstrates a control deficiency would be premature.

Staff Q&A No. 7 gives the example of a company giving to its auditor draft financial statements that lack two required disclosures according to generally accepted accounting principles (GAAP). Without the communication from management that the two required disclosures were missing, the auditor might conclude there is a material weakness in controls surrounding the preparation of financial statement disclosures. However, because management communicated that the financials were missing two required disclosures, the auditor should not conclude that a deficiency exists.

Practice Tip

Whether you give your auditor a paper or an electronic copy of your financial statements, make sure they are stamped or marked "draft" until finalized.

Accounting Advice

Rules on auditor independence prohibit auditors from preparing management's financial statements or from making financial reporting decisions on behalf of management. Auditors still are allowed to provide technical advice to clients on the proper application of GAAP or on recent accounting standards. The PCAOB gives its blessing for management to provide and discuss with the auditor preliminary drafts of accounting research memos, spreadsheets and other working papers in order to obtain the auditor's views on the assumptions and methods selected by management.

Giving technical advice when requested for a consultation is different from auditors finding a potential misapplication of accounting principles during a quarterly review or after management's financial statements and disclosures are complete. In the latter circumstance, auditors may determine that a misapplication of accounting principles constitutes a significant deficiency or material weakness.

HOW THE PCAOB INSPECTIONS HELP DRIVE IMPROVEMENTS

The PCAOB believes its inspections will help with Section 404 audit effectiveness and efficiency in registered audit firms in two ways. First, it plans to look for audits

> that suffer from poor planning and risk assessment, such as by using standardized checklists without appropriately tailoring the procedures to the circumstances of focusing the audit on areas that are unlikely to lead to the discovery of material weaknesses in internal control.

The PCAOB will demand improvements when it encounters "such shortcomings."

Second, it will look for audits that apply the approaches described in its May 2005 guidance and Staff Q&A because it believes those approaches promote effectiveness and efficiencies. Auditors who do not follow PCAOB guidelines will have to justify their decisions and explain how their audit plan met the objectives of the standard.

The PCAOB specifically states it does not intend to second-guess good-faith audit judgments and that it is looking for a thoughtful, risk-focused approach to internal control audits. The May 2005 guidance closes with a remark that the PCAOB "will not hesitate to demand changes to the auditor's approach to implementing Auditing Standard No. 2" if the auditor has approached the audit in a mechanistic way or did not use professional judgment.

A FINAL COMMENT

The resounding criticism of the SEC and PCAOB May 2005 guidance is that it calls for more judgment and reasonableness but does not give any practical steps to implement a more reasonable approach. What are the audit firms, still quaking from the Arthur Andersen fiasco, to do with this guidance? The staff calls for professional judgment and reasonable assurance but ultimately will investigate firms' methods for auditing their clients' internal controls. Without definitive guidance from the SEC or PCAOB, external auditors have little reason to take anything but the most conservative approach to an internal control audit.

However, recent changes and guidance may have a positive bearing on auditors' approaches to Section 404 audits. Perhaps AS No. 5 along with the SEC's Guidance for Management will help auditors use more reasonableness and professional judgment in their audits. As part of the SEC's oversight of the PCAOB, SEC staff reviews aspects of the PCAOB's operations, including its inspection program. Among other things, SEC staff promises to examine whether PCAOB inspections of audit firms have been effective in encouraging cost-saving efficiencies for audits of internal control.

NOTES

1. See Charles River Associates, "Sarbanes-Oxley Section 404 Costs and Remediation of Deficiencies: Estimates from a Sample of Fortune 1000 Companies" (April 2005).
2. CRA International, *Sarbanes-Oxley Section 404 Costs and Implementation Issues: Spring 2006 Survey Update* A copy of the full survey is available at www.crai.com/publications/listingdetails.aspx?id=6928&terms=sarbanes

5

Starting at the Top: Using Entity-Level Controls to Create Efficiencies

Key Topics:
- How strong entity-level controls can reduce the scope of your program
- How to apply COSO's recent internal control guidance
- How to create a winning control environment
- Steps for creating a useful risk assessment process
- Creating an effective information and communication program
- How to implement successful monitoring controls
- How to assign roles and responsibilities to enhance internal controls
- Small-company issues for implementing entity-level controls
- A summary of COSO's Guidance for Smaller Public Companies

WHAT ARE ENTITY-LEVEL CONTROLS?

First emphasized in the Public Company Accounting Oversight Board's (PCAOB's) May 2005 guidance and reinforced in most Section 404 guidance since then, the top-down approach is one of the concepts used to control costs without sacrificing quality in an internal control audit. Evaluating entity-level controls at the beginning of your program will promote a top-down approach and provide a road map to ensure your program focuses only on significant financial reporting controls.

Entity-level controls as described in Auditing Standard No. 5 (AS No. 5) have changed slightly from their description in Auditing Standards No. 2 (AS No. 2) but still generally encompass the Committee of Sponsoring

Organizations (COSO) components and key financial reporting processes. In the Securities and Exchange Commission's (SEC's) Guidance for Management, these controls are defined as "aspects of a system of internal control that have a pervasive effect on the entity's system of internal control." The terms "company-level" and "entity-wide" controls were commonly used in past guidance to describe these controls.

Entity-level controls as described by the SEC and PCAOB include:

- Controls related to the control environment, such as management's philosophy and operating style, integrity, and ethical values; board or audit committee oversight; and assignment of authority and responsibility

- Controls over management override

- Company's risk assessment process

- Centralized processing and controls, including shared service environments such as human resources, stock administration, payroll, or accounting

- Controls to monitor results of operations

- Controls to monitor other controls, including activities of the internal audit function, the audit committee, and self-assessment programs

- Controls over the period-end financial reporting process—as part of the period-end financial reporting process, inputs; the extent of IT, management participation, different locations, and the consolidating process; and the extent of oversight by management and the audit committee should all be evaluated

- Policies that address significant business control and risk management practices

This is not an all-inclusive list, and not all companies will have all of these entity-level controls.

HOW STRONG ENTITY-LEVEL CONTROLS CAN
REDUCE THE SCOPE OF YOUR PROGRAM

Using the top-down approach and evaluating entity-level controls at the beginning of your Section 404 program every year will cause you naturally to lean toward the areas of higher risk. According to the PCAOB's May 2005 guidance, auditors may use strong entity-level controls to alter the nature, timing, and extent of testing. This idea is reinforced again in AS No. 5, which states in Paragraph 1: "The auditor's evaluation of entity-level controls can result in increasing or decreasing the testing that the auditor otherwise would have performed on other controls."

On a practical level, management's assessment of risk performed at the beginning of the year should consider the impact of entity-level controls such as the relative strengths and weaknesses of the control environment. According to the SEC in its Guidance for Management:

> Management's assessment of internal control over financial reporting risk also considers the impact of entity-level controls, such as the relative strengths and weaknesses of the control environment, which may influence management's judgments about the risks of failure for particular controls.[1]

Based on the company's risk assessment, documenting and testing entity-level controls early in the year could cause the company to select different testing methods, periods, and sample sizes when testing other controls. If entity-level controls are strong, less persuasive testing methods, smaller sample sizes, and earlier testing could be used in other areas. However, compromised entity-level controls or the control environment could negate all other control testing.

The evaluation of entity-level controls could cause an increase or decrease in the testing of other controls at the process, transaction, or application levels. Three types of entity-level controls listed could affect your control testing:

1. **Indirect.** Certain entity-level controls have an indirect effect on the likelihood that a misstatement will be prevented or detected in a timely manner (i.e., control environment controls). These controls may affect the nature, timing, or extent of testing performed on other controls.

2. **Monitoring.** Certain entity-level controls may monitor the effectiveness of other controls and identify possible breakdowns in lower-level controls, but not at a level of precision that would sufficiently address the risk that misstatements would be prevented or detected in a timely manner. However, these monitoring controls may help to reduce the testing of other controls.

3. **Direct.** Certain entity-level controls are designed to operate at a level of precision that would prevent or detect a potential misstatement to the financial statements in a timely manner. The SEC states, "If management determines that a risk of a material misstatement is adequately addressed by an entity-level control, no further evaluation of other controls is required."

Possibilities for Reducing the Nature, Timing, and Extent of Testing

Entity-level control testing requires sufficient documentation and strong testing techniques, just as transaction-level testing would. However, once

---

Practice Tip

Focus on whether selected controls sufficiently address the risk of misstatement of a given relevant assertion rather than whether the controls are called entity-level or control activities.

Although the concept of using entity-level controls at the control activity level is spelled out in AS No. 5, auditors may be reluctant to alter their own testing procedures if a company has strong entity-level controls. They may also be slow to accept their clients' Sarbanes-Oxley (SOX) programs that use this method for their own testing.

---

you are confident that entity-level controls are effective, you have these options for reducing your transaction-level testing methods:

- Use more observation and inquiry instead of reperformance and examination in less risky areas.

- If you perform annual walk-throughs, combine them with examination testing. You can update your documentation and examine a sample at the same time.

- Plan to test controls earlier during the year. Low- and medium-risk controls could be tested during the second or third quarters.

- Mix various testing methods to reduce the number of samples selected for examination and reperformance testing. For example, you could use inquiry plus 10 examination samples to satisfy testing of certain controls.

Practice Tip

Test entity-level controls at the beginning of the year using methods with a high degree of assurance, such as reperformance and examination. If you can prove that your entity-level controls are effective, present the results along with your reduced scoping and testing plans for the remaining controls to your auditor for their input. Be armed with paragraphs 22 and 23 of AS No. 5 to support your approach.

In addition to testing entity-level controls at the beginning of the year to prove your case for reduced testing, be sure that your program includes updating the testing of entity-level controls again near the end of the year to ensure they are still effective.

Refer to Chapter 9 for more ideas on how to reduce the scope of your testing. Keep in mind that if you are attempting to "right-size" the nature, timing, and/or extent of testing due to strong entity-level controls, the results, timing, and testing methods used for entity-level control testing must be impeccable.

HOW TO APPLY COSO'S RECENT INTERNAL CONTROL GUIDANCE

Although COSO's *Internal Control over Financial Report—Guidance for Smaller Public Companies* issued in July 2006 was developed for the benefit of small companies, it is more of a practical approach to its original internal control guidance with examples that can be followed for companies of any size. Small companies may have felt that risk assessments, the internal audit function, and audit committees referred to in the *Internal Control— Integrated Framework* were reserved for larger organizations. The Guidance for Smaller Public Companies gives options for smaller companies, with or without internal audit departments and audit committees, to apply the COSO concepts to their organizations. It also reiterates that informal entity-wide controls can be effective and appropriate for some companies.

According to Scott Taub, Acting Chief Accountant of the U.S. Securities and Exchange Commission:

> This guidance will help smaller companies more efficiently and effectively implement the Section 404 internal control requirements. It will also help companies of all sizes understand and apply the fundamental concepts of COSO's internal control framework. The comments received during the exposure period added significantly to the development of the guidance. I am grateful to COSO and their Advisory Task Force for all of their efforts to develop this guidance.[2]

Effectiveness of Internal Controls

Management and the board of directors can conclude that internal controls are effective if there is reasonable assurance that:

- Operational objectives are achieved.
- Published financial statements are reliable.
- The company is complying with applicable laws and regulations.

COSO describes internal control as consisting of five interrelated components. Although the five components relate to all companies, large and small companies may implement them differently yet still have effective internal control. The five components are:

1. **Control environment** sets the tone of an organization, influencing the control consciousness of its people.

2. **Risk assessments** help companies identify and plan for specific risks the business may encounter from internal and external sources.

3. **Control activities** are the policies and procedures that help ensure management's directives are followed out.

4. **Information and communication** is how information is identified, captured, and communicated throughout an organization.

5. **Monitoring** is a process that assesses the quality of performance over time.

Each of the five components must exist in some form and function in an entity to be able to conclude that internal controls are effective.

Although all five criteria must be satisfied, there may be some trade-off between components. Because controls can serve a variety of purposes, controls in one component can serve the same purpose of controls that are typically found in another component. For example, an effective audit committee and board of directors can address risks in the control environment and information and communication components, but these controls are typically seen in the monitoring component. Although there may be some crossover between components, keep in mind that an unmitigated material weakness in any component will result in a conclusion that internal control is not effective.

Implementing the COSO Guidance

In the guidance for smaller public companies issued in 2006, the COSO Task Force examined ways to simplify implementation of the control concepts published in the original internal control framework. As a result, 20 fundamental principles were highlighted from the original guidance to clarify and streamline the implementation process. If the 20 principles are achieved, a company can conclude that financial reporting controls are in place throughout the company.

HOW TO CREATE A WINNING CONTROL ENVIRONMENT

The control environment lays the groundwork for all other components of internal control and is a company's first line of defense against financial reporting errors and fraud. A company with a strong control environment is committed to competence, instills an enterprise-wide attitude of integrity and control consciousness, and sets a positive "tone at the top." These factors should be demonstrated by all levels of management, appropriate policies and procedures, and a well-established code of conduct.

COSO has identified seven principles related to an effective control environment. These principles are described next.

1. **Integrity and ethical values.** Sound integrity and ethical values, particularly of top management, are developed and understood and set the standard of conduct for financial reporting.

2. **Board of directors.** The board of directors understands and exercises oversight responsibility related to financial reporting and related internal controls.

3. **Management's philosophy and operating style.** Management's philosophy and operating style support achieving effective internal control over financial reporting.

4. **Organizational structure.** The company's organizational structure supports effective internal control over financial reporting.

5. **Financial reporting competencies.** The company retains individuals competent in financial reporting and related oversight roles.

6. **Authority and responsibility.** Management and employees are assigned appropriate levels of authority and responsibility to facilitate effective internal control over financial reporting.

7. **Human resources.** Human resource polices and practices are designed to facilitate effective internal control over financial reporting.

Integrity and Ethical Values

Integrity and ethics lay the groundwork for all the other control environment controls. Without them, none of the others matter.

Integrity and Ethical Values Principle Example   The examples that follow describe activities that management can perform to help achieve an effective control environment.

Communicating Integrity and Ethics through a Company Newsletter   A company can communicate the importance of sound integrity and ethical values to its employees, customers, and suppliers with specific articles in its newsletter. A section related to ethical decision making with examples of ethical dilemmas and resolutions or recognition of an employee that "did the right thing" could be included.

Evidence;   Company newsletter with ethics articles.

Ethical Behavior Awareness in Meetings and Emails   Senior management can promote awareness of ethical behavior through company-wide emails or regularly scheduled employee meetings. Emails and company meetings could include discussions on ethical responsibilities and competence expectations for all employees. Key components of the code of conduct could be discussed as well as examples of employees that acted exceptionally.

Evidence;   Evidence of the meetings includes meeting notifications, agendas, or session presentations.

Aligning Incentives with Ethics and Values   A percentage of the potential incentive award in employee bonuses could be directly related to how employees demonstrate the company's ethical values. Supervisors and subordinates could be surveyed for their feedback on whether an employee adheres to the company's values for sound integrity and ethics.

Evidence;   Employee reviews.

Code of Conduct   Most public companies have a code of conduct by now that is published on the company's Web site. One way to show that the code is communicated effectively throughout the organization is for each employee to have a signed confirmation retained in their personnel file. Take it one step further, and retain a signed confirmation of the code for all contractors and temporary employees.

Evidence;   Signed code of conduct document in employee files or printout from the company's Web site.

Hotline   SOX Section 301 specifically states that the audit committee is responsible for establishing procedures for the confidential anonymous submission by employees of concerns regarding questionable accounting or auditing matters. As a result, hotlines have been created for employees to discuss potential fraud occurrences and other ethical concerns without fear of reprisal. Potential illegal acts or financial reporting improprieties called in on the hotline are reported directly to the audit committee and general counsel.

Practice Tip

Be sure your hotline number is well published in company break-rooms and the company Web site. Zero calls during the year can be a sign that your hotline number does not have enough visibility.

Taking Action When Violations Occur   Telling employees that management supports a strong ethical environment is not enough. Actions and follow-through should reflect the seriousness of management's conviction of integrity. Appropriate disciplinary actions must be taken when there is a violation against the company's code of conduct, whether the code is formally documented or not.

For example, a company's no-tolerance attitude for expense report fraud is clearly and regularly communicated to all employees via semi-annual emails. When a mortgage company learned that a salesperson was including his spouse's airfare in his expense reports, he was immediately suspended pending an investigation. Once the impropriety was confirmed, the company terminated the salesperson, permanently revoked all access and privileges, and billed him for his spouse's reimbursed airfare.

Evidence;   Documented investigations and resolutions of misconduct and company-wide emails explaining any occurrences of fraud and the outcome.

Board of Directors

An active and involved audit committee, board of directors, or board of trustees is vital for effective internal controls. The board(s) should possess some degree of management, technical, and financial expertise so that it can adequately perform the necessary governance, guidance, and oversight responsibilities. Board members should be independent and active so they can scrutinize management's activities, present alternative views, and proactively respond to any wrongdoing.

According to SOX Section 407, each issuer must disclose whether the audit committee contains a "financial expert." If the audit committee does not include at least one financial expert, the issuer must explain why not. A "financial expert" is defined as a person who has

> through education and experience as a public accountant or auditor or a principal financial officer, comptroller, or principal accounting officer of an issuer, or from a position involving the performance of similar functions:

- An understanding of generally accepted accounting principles (GAAP) and financial statements;
- Experience in the preparation or auditing of financial statements of generally comparable issuers and the application of such principles in connection with the accounting for estimates, accruals, and reserves;
- Experience with internal accounting controls;
- An understanding of audit committee functions.

Effective Board of Directors Examples

Board Review of Key Management Decisions   To aid in effective financial oversight, the board of directors should approve all major business decisions having material financial reporting implications, such as acquisitions or major capital expenditures, and approve all bonus and incentive plans for executives. To stay in touch with major expenditures and bonuses, the board should also review and approve budgets and require management to explain significant variances.

Evidence;   Corporate bylaws, meeting minutes, and committee charters that are updated annually or as needed.

Independence and Financial Expertise for the Audit Committee   The company's audit committee (or board of directors) should not include any members of management and should include at least one financial expert (as defined above). Audit committee members can sign statements of independence to confirm they do not have any related party transactions or immediate family in management.

Evidence;   Audit committee statements of independence and financial expert resume.

Active Participation of the Audit Committee and Management   Management and the audit committee meet regularly to discuss key financial statement accounts, estimates, disclosures, and the company's approach for adopting new accounting guidance. The audit committee reviews management's assumptions used to develop significant estimates, the quarterly and annual financial statements before filing, and management's assessment of internal control over financial reporting.

Evidence;   Audit committee meeting minutes or board presentation.

Audit Committee Interacting with External Auditors   The audit committee meets with the external auditors privately at least once a year to discuss issues such as internal control over financial reporting, significant adjustments to the financial statements, and the quality of financial reporting. In addition, the audit committee engages the external auditors, reviews their audit plans and fees, and terminates their services if needed.

Evidence;   Note of an executive session in the audit committee meeting minutes.

Audit Committee Fraud Risk Assessment   At least annually, the audit committee discusses the possibility of financial reporting fraud and management override and discusses why management might override controls and how it would conceal its activities.

The audit committee also receives input from the controller or second-level management as a means to prevent executive override. Audit committee members occasionally make inquiries of members of management not responsible for financial reporting (such as sales managers, procurement managers, human resource managers, etc.) to ask about any ethical concerns.

Evidence;   Audit committee fraud risk assessment or meeting minutes; emails or questionnaires between audit committee members and nonfinancial management.

Changing the Board Composition of Closely Held Companies   A company is registered with the SEC and trades on the over-the-counter (OTC) exchange. The company has always maintained a board of directors that includes two directors from management, two members of the chief executive officer (CEO) and founder's family, and three outside directors that are not independent (including the company's outside counsel, a representative from the company's bank, and a personal friend of the CEO).

In order to improve the independence and expertise of the board, the two family members and personal friend of the CEO were replaced by three independent directors. One of the independent directors is a certified public accountant (CPA) and qualifies as a financial expert.

Evidence;   Board member resumes and statements of independence.

Management's Philosophy and Operating Style

The way the business is run and its risk tolerance is greatly affected by management's philosophy and operating style. The attitudes toward financial reporting, how conservative or aggressive management is when making estimates and interpreting accounting principles, and attitudes toward information systems, accounting functions, and accounting personnel are all dictated by management's philosophy and operating style.

Management's Philosophy and Operating Style Principle Examples

Reinforcing an Ethical Tone at the Top   A high-growth company's operating style matches its aggressive short-term goals. Senior management and the audit committee actively monitor the actions of operating managers in order to maintain the integrity of its financial reporting. Management uses an outsourced internal audit group to investigate irregularities and randomly tests areas that are significant for financial reporting. In addition, management continually reminds employees of its lack of tolerance for unethical behavior through its words and behavior in meetings, business dealings, and emails.

Evidence;   Internal audit reports, ethics topics in meeting agendas, presentations, and emails.

Soliciting Suggestions during Performance Reviews   During each employee's annual performance review, the company solicits suggestions on improving internal controls for financial reporting. Employees receive a reward if their suggestion for improving internal controls is implemented.

Evidence; Employee review forms.

External Party Contracts In all its contracts with customers, suppliers, and consultants, the company emphasizes its commitment to excellence and ethical conduct. It encourages external parties to notify the company through its anonymous hotline if suspicions arise about questionable employee actions.

Evidence; Copies of customer, supplier, and consultant contracts.

Organizational Structure

The company's organizational structure should establish responsibility for effective financial reporting and maintain structures and processes that facilitate effective internal controls.

Effective Organizational Structures Examples

Establishing Job Descriptions and Responsibilities Each manager is responsible for maintaining documented job descriptions and reporting responsibilities for each position that he or she manages. Organization charts are established for each business unit with clear lines of authority for each position. New positions are not filled until a job description and updated organization chart is completed explaining where the new employee will fit into the organization. All job descriptions and organizational charts are reviewed and updated at least once a year.

Evidence; Job description and organizational charts.

Reorganizing to Support Control Structure When a certain manufacturer was a small company, most of the employees reported directly to the owner manager. As the number of employees grew, the company added layers of management. The new layers provided more accountability and better supervision. Separate business units were created based on three different product lines. Each business unit had a general manager to manage the operations, a controller to oversee the finance and accounting functions, and a vice president of sales to oversee sales, marketing, and customer service. All employees in a business unit reported directly to one of these three managers.

Formal job descriptions were created to enable a full understanding of each person's role within the organization. Internal controls at each business unit were documented to highlight key controls and each person's responsibility in the key processes.

Evidence;   Job descriptions and organizational charts.

Financial Reporting Competency

Financial reporting personnel should be qualified and possess the experience and competencies needed to ensure the financial statements are of a high quality. Specific skills and experience needed to prepare reliable financial statements should be identified and regularly evaluated, and accounting, tax, and IT personnel should have training to keep their skills current.

Financial Reporting Competency Principle Examples

Key Financial Reporting Personnel Assessment   On an annual basis, the chief financial officer (CFO) assesses the competencies and skill sets of the key financial reporting personnel and solicits feedback from the external auditor. The evaluation is reported to the audit committee, and management uses the input to plan staffing changes and additions for the following year.

Evidence;   Written evaluation from the external auditor or audit committee meeting minutes.

Advice for Complex Technical Matters   A small high-tech company issues stock options to all of its employees. The company has an employee that acts as both a CFO and controller and is generally knowledgeable with GAAP. However, the individual is not familiar with the recently issued, complex technical pronouncements for stock options. The CFO discusses the issues with the external auditors to gain a basic understanding of the requirements of the new pronouncements. The company does not want to hire a new employee with stock option experience, so it outsources the calculation of the quarterly stock option expense to a subject matter expert. The CFO is comfortable with the expert's credentials and reputation.

Evidence;   Third-party resume, stock option reports, calculations, or memos.

Adequate Technical Training   The company regularly sends its accounting, tax, and IT personnel to external specialized training to stay current on immerging issues and industry guidance in their respective areas. Keep in mind that significant audit adjustments in accounting and tax areas could negate apparent training evidence.

Evidence;   Training certificates and documentation retained in employee files.

Authority and Responsibility

The company should assign appropriate limits of authority, establish appropriate reporting relationships, and assign responsibility-based employees' positions. This is especially true for employees involved in the financial reporting process to help prevent misstatements and fraud. In addition, the board of directors should oversee management's process for defining responsibilities for key financial reporting roles.

Authority and Responsibility Principle Examples

Board or Audit Committee Review of Key Financial Roles   The audit committee bylaws include a provision to oversee and evaluate the principal roles and responsibilities of key financial reporting management. A member of the audit committee meets with the head of human resources, internal audit, general counsel, and the external auditors to review the roles and responsibilities of key members of financial management. As a result of the meetings, the audit committee discusses and recommends to management any needed changes to the roles and responsibilities of key financial reporting management.

Assigning Responsibilities and Levels of Authority   Each finance and accounting position is assigned clear responsibilities and levels of authority that are outlined in written job descriptions and a formal organizational chart. Employees are evaluated annually based on their specific responsibilities and authority.

Evidence;   Written job descriptions, organizational chart, annual evaluations.

Properly Authorizing Material Transactions   A company created a signature authorization policy that clearly defines the level of authority and dollar limits for purchasing, check signing, and contracts. As dollar thresholds increase, additional approvals are required from senior management. The policy states that approvals must be documented in writing or email.

Evidence;   Approved signature authorization policy.

Human Resources

The company's human resource (HR) policies and practices should encourage integrity, ethical behavior, and competence, and promote a strong financial reporting function. The focus should be on recruiting and retaining competent accounting and finance employees with integrity. Management should support its employees with the proper tools and training to succeed. In addition, performance evaluations and compensation practices should be based largely on financial reporting objectives.

Successful Human Resource Principles Examples

Developing Human Resource Policies   Because of its small size, a company is not able to hire a full-time HR person. Instead, an HR committee comprised of management from each department documents various HR practices and policies. The policies are reviewed and approved by the board of directors and are implemented by all department managers. The committee updates the policies if needed in the beginning of each year.

Evidence;   Signed HR policies and board meeting minutes for approval.

Communication of Policies to New and Existing Personnel   Human resource policies are communicated to newly hired employees, temporary employees, and contractors on their first day of employment. They are required to sign a confirmation that they have received and understand all of the policies, and a copy is retained in their personnel file. Existing employees receive updated policies via email once policies are approved by the board of directors.

Evidence;   Signed new-hire policy confirmation pages and emails of updated policies sent to employees.

Periodically Assessing Objectives   Employees responsible for performing or testing financial reporting and disclosure controls are routinely evaluated on their performance compared with objectives established at the beginning of the year. The evaluations can be formal, annual reviews or more informal quarterly progress reports.

Evidence;   Formal or informal employee evaluations retained by the HR department.

Using a Questionnaire to Test Control Environment   One way to test the control environment is with an employee questionnaire. Questioning a broad cross-section of employees can provide strong evidence of the attitudes and culture at an organization. However, what if the results of the questionnaires are not what you expected? For example, an employee may not remember discussing the company's sexual harassment policy and signing a statement that he received a copy on his first day of employment. In a questionnaire, the employee may mistakenly report that the policy was not communicated to him.

Practice Tip

It is difficult to remediate flawed results from employee questionnaires. Before you embark on a lengthy interview or questionnaire process, be sure the method will work for your purposes.

STEPS FOR CREATING A USEFUL RISK ASSESSMENT PROCESS

It is common for companies to set goals or long-term strategic plans as part of their annual planning process. What most companies do not realize is that they have taken the first step in the risk assessment process by planning and setting goals. Risk assessment simply brings planning to the next level. Companies first set objectives and goals, and then management identifies the risks to the achievement of those objectives. Controls are then put in place to mitigate those risks.

Risk assessments can be performed for a variety of issues, such as fraud, IT, or financial reporting. A financial reporting risk assessment involves the identification and analysis of the risks that could cause a material misstatement in the financial statements. Specific transactions and economic events that impact financial reporting are identified, and then they are related to specific processes and controls that can reduce the risk of errors and misstatement.

COSO has identified three principles related to financial reporting risk assessments:

1. **Financial reporting objectives.** Management specifies financial reporting objectives with sufficient clarity and criteria to enable the identification of risks to reliable financial reporting.

2. **Financial reporting risks.** The company then identifies and analyzes risks to the achievement of financial reporting objectives as a basis for determining how the risks can be managed.

3. **Fraud risk.** The potential for material misstatement due to fraud is explicitly considered in assessing risks to the achievement of financial reporting objectives.

Small-Company Risk Assessment

Risk assessment in smaller companies can be particularly effective because the CEO and other key managers often are more involved in day-to-day activities. This means that risks are assessed by management with hands-on knowledge of the business and a good understanding of the implications of the risks to the business.

Smaller businesses may have fewer business units and processes, which allows for the identification of more specific risks. More specific risks may produce more precise control activities. The clarity can provide efficiencies and reduce the number of unnecessary or redundant controls.

Typical Financial Reporting Risks

For both small and large companies, the risk of financial misstatement could be caused by one or more of these errors:

- Not capturing all transactions
- Losing or altering transactions once recorded
- Improperly accounting for transactions or estimates
- Recording inappropriate journal entries
- Misclassifying transactions
- Recording transactions in the wrong period or at the wrong amount
- Failing to gather pertinent information to make reliable estimates
- Inappropriately applying formulas or calculations, specifically in spreadsheets
- Recording assets that do not exist
- Recording transactions that did not occur

A financial reporting risk assessment identifies which one of these errors is mostly likely to occur at a particular company based on its unique business. The analysis that follows leads the way for strong processes and controls to be implemented to prevent or detect these types of errors.

Step One: Establish Financial Reporting Objectives

The first step for a financial reporting risk assessment is to establish objectives. Objectives for reliable financial reporting usually follow three principles:

1. Comply with GAAP.
2. Identify significant accounts and disclosures based on quantitative and qualitative materiality and risk factors.
3. Address the relevant financial statement assertions for all significant accounts and disclosures.

Establishing Financial Reporting Objectives Example

Financial Statement Account Analysis Management begins its risk assessment process by analyzing the accounts at the financial statement level to determine which accounts are quantitatively significant and pose specific risks. Additional analysis at the consolidated general ledger level is performed if needed. Financial reporting objectives are established based on the financial assertions that underlie the company's significant accounts and all disclosures. The significant accounts and disclosures and the relevant assertions are linked to specific business units, functional departments, and processes. This approach is shown in Exhibit 5.1.

Evidence;   Documented account analysis and objectives.

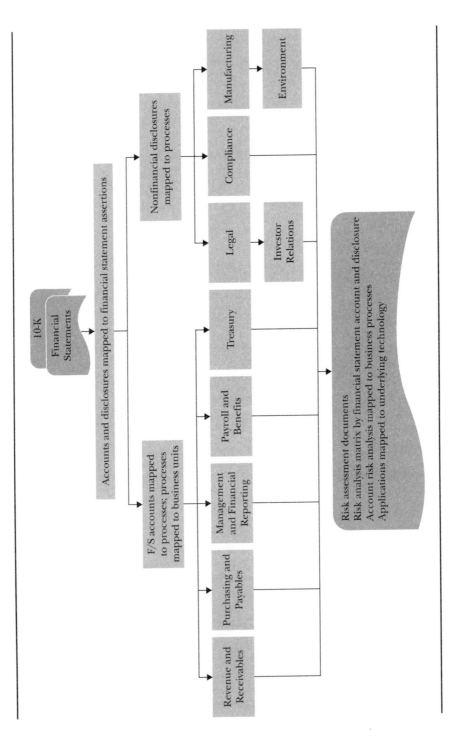

Exhibit 5.1 COSO's Guidance for Smaller Public Companies: Linking Accounts, Assertions, and Risks

The risk assessment process follows a similar pattern to the creation of a control matrix. Combine the creation or update of the company's control matrices with the risk assessment process for added efficiency.

Step Two: Identify and Analyze Financial Reporting Risks

The second step is to identify and analyze the financial reporting risks that specifically apply to the organization. Identifying and analyzing risk is the basis for determining how to manage the risks. Be sure to:

- **Consider potential risks.** These are risks that could possibly stop the company from achieving its financial reporting objectives.

- **Consider all business processes.** Consider all of the business processes that could impact the financial statement accounts and disclosures.

- **Consider information technology.** Include IT risks that could affect financial reporting objectives.

- **Consider personnel.** Consider the competency of personnel that support your financial reporting objectives.

- **Consider internal and external factors.** Identify the risks from both internal and external factors and their impact on financial reporting objectives.

- **Involve management from different functions.** Nonfinance managers, such as legal, IT, inventory, and HR, should contribute to the risk assessment to create a well-rounded analysis.

- **Estimate impact and likelihood.** Consider the potential impact of the risk and the likelihood of the risk occurring.

- **Establish triggers for reassessment.** Establish triggers for management to reassess risks as changes occur that might affect financial reporting.

Identifying and Analyzing Risks Examples

Third-Party Service Provider Risks   A company's payroll is processed by an outside service provider. The company identifies potential external risks related to the completeness and accuracy of employee data maintained by its payroll service provider. Internal risks include incomplete or inaccurate data being submitted to the payroll service provider by employees due to ineffective review and authorization controls. Each risk factor could lead to errors in the financial reporting of compensation and benefit expenses.

Additionally, the company identifies an internal IT risk around access to the payroll application. The lack of security could result in the setup of fictitious employees or unauthorized pay rate changes and further risks of fraudulent financial reporting.

Evidence;   Documented third-party risk assessment and results of management's inquiries and any related tests.

Analyzing Information Technology Risk   The IT group at a manufacturing company begins its risk assessment by meeting with a group of middle managers for each significant business process to identify applications that support the financial reporting process. Middle managers are the target group because they are high enough to understand the financial reporting implications of their department, but still play a somewhat active role in the transactions and processes of their department or business unit.

Based on the meetings, the IT group creates a list of key applications that affect financial reporting. The IT group maps the key applications to the operating systems, databases, and IT processes that support those applications. Their documentation includes "packaged software box" applications and third-party Web sites that play a role in the financial reporting process.

Evidence;   Documented IT risk assessment or IT scoping analysis.

Risk Assessment with Various Functional Managers   ABC biotech company, with revenues of $80 million and 170 employees, gathers the department heads from finance, HR, operations, IT, and internal audit to discuss fraud and other risks that affect the company's financial reporting. The internal auditor has already analyzed the financial statements for significant accounts and disclosures, and leads the group in a discussion of risks by business process.

Risks are rated as high, medium, or low based on both the impact to the business and the likelihood of occurrence. The analysis is discussed in a working session format, and the results are documented in a table that outlines the specific risk, the rating, and the factors that contribute to the rating. Two of the risks identified are shown:

Business Process	Risk	Impact	Reason	Likelihood	Reason
Revenue to Cash	Revenue is not recorded according to GAAP	High	Could cause a material misstatement in financial statements causing a restatement	High	Sales contracts and revenue recognition rules are complex; bonus structure and sales targets are aggressive
Fixed Assets	Misappropriation of company computers	Low	Most laptop computers are expensed when purchased or are almost fully depreciated	High	Since there are no formal termination procedures, employees who leave often do not return their laptops

Setting Triggers to Reassess Financial Reporting Risk   Management at a national restaurant company established several criteria that would trigger a new risk assessment for financial reporting. The criteria established by management includes:

- Significant IT changes made within the company's systems (such as an enterprise resource planning [ERP] conversion)

- Unusual variances in revenue, gross margin, or other key financial indicators

- Changes to key functional manager positions

- New accounting or reporting pronouncements that impact the company's financial reporting

- The company engaging in new transactions that involve complex accounting issues (merger, acquisition, derivatives)

- New regulatory requirements that affect the company's industry

Evidence;   The company's documented triggers and any new risk assessment that occurred as a result of a trigger being activated.

Step Three: Consider the Risk of Material Misstatements Due to Fraud

Considering the potential for a material misstatement in the company's financial statements due to fraud is an integral part of a robust risk assessment. Factors to consider when developing a fraud risk assessment include:

- **Incentives and pressures.** What are the incentives and pressures, attitudes, rationalizations, and opportunities to commit fraud?

- **Industry and geography.** What are the specific risks relevant to the company's industry and geographic regions where it does business?

- **High-risk areas.** What are the high-risk areas? What risks surround revenue recognition, management override, significant unusual accounts, significant intercompany accounts, and vulnerabilities related to misappropriation of assets?

- **High-risk transactions.** Which transactions are subject to management influence and judgment or involve estimates? Which transactions are complex, unusual, or recorded at the last minute?

- **Audit committee oversight.** Does the audit committee play an active role in evaluating and monitoring risks affecting the reliability of financial reporting, including the risk of management override?

Fraud Risk Assessment Examples   ABC biotech company performs and documents its fraud risk assessment in the same manner as its financial reporting risk assessment. Management from significant business units come together to discuss fraud risk based on the type of fraud. Risks are rated as high, medium, or low based on the impact and likelihood and are documented in a table. The audit committee performs a review of management's assessment to determine the adequacy of antifraud controls. Fraud risks assessed by type are documented as shown below.

Type of Fraud	Risk	Impact	Reason	Likelihood	Reason
Financial fraud	Executive override of financial data	High	Executive fraud is always noteworthy and probably material in amount	Medium	Executive override is inherently high risk; executives have no access to IT systems, and financials are sent to the audit committee directly from the controller
Misrepresentation	Fictitious employees on payroll	Low	Fraudulent payroll amounts would have to be small to go unnoticed	Medium	Proper segregation of duties and review of payroll records exist

Practice Tip

1. In addition to the types of fraud that directly affect financial reporting, consider including violations of laws or other compliance in your fraud risk assessment. Violations of laws could be considered fraud and may have financial implications that should be disclosed in your financial statements even though they do not have a direct impact.

2. When discussing sensitive topics such as fraud and violations of laws with outsiders, consider inviting the company's attorney. Since accountants do not have a right to privileged communications, having a lawyer in the room may provide some benefit.

Step Four: Identify Controls to Mitigate the Risks

Although not included in COSO's risk assessment principles, the final step in the risk assessment process is to identify specific controls that mitigate the financial reporting and fraud risks identified during your assessments. The company may decide to accept some low or medium risks if the costs to mitigate them outweigh the potential benefit. Generally some type of control should be put in place to mitigate or reduce the severity of high risks.

Effective Ways to Mitigate the Risks Examples   ABC biotech company identified these controls to mitigate risks:

- **Revenue is not recorded according to GAAP.** Standardized sales contracts (with standard terms) are used for customer contracts. Revenue for standard sales contracts is recognized according to the revenue recognition policy, which has been reviewed and agreed to by the company's external auditors.

- **Misappropriation of company computers.** When employees leave the company, the director of human resources completes and signs a termination checklist to ensure that all company assets have been returned and computer access is revoked in a timely manner.

- **Executive override of financial data.** Executives are granted read-only access to the company's ERP system and/or financial data for the quarterly audit committee meeting is sent to the members via email directly from the controller to prevent executive editing of financial data.

- **Fictitious employees on payroll.** New employees, rate changes, and terminations are communicated in writing to the payroll processor by the director of human resources. The payroll manager reviews and initials the payroll change report from the outside payroll company, verifying that each change in payroll is authorized.

Circumstances Demanding Special Attention

Managing change plays a large role in the risk assessment process. The changes listed next demand special attention because of their direct relationship to financial reporting.

- **Changed operating environment.** Regulatory or economic changes can result in operational changes that produce significantly different risks. For example, divestiture in the telecommunications industry and deregulation of commission rates in the brokerage industry caused significant change in those companies' competitive environments.

- **New personnel.** New employees are not familiar with a company's controls and processes and cause errors if not properly monitored. In addition, high turnover of personnel without the proper training and supervision can result in breakdowns.

- **New or updated information systems.** Data may not be reliable when new systems are implemented, particularly when done under unusually tight time constraints.

- **Rapid growth.** When organizations grow quickly, resources such as staff and systems may not be able to keep pace. Existing systems may be strained to the point where controls break down, and departments may be understaffed, causing delays and errors.

- **New technology.** New technologies that are incorporated into an organization's operations usually create the need for controls to be modified. For example, just-in-time inventory manufacturing technologies commonly require changes in cost systems and related controls to ensure reporting of meaningful information.

- **New lines, products, or activities.** Existing controls may not be adequate to deal with new product lines or services. For example, when savings and loan organizations ventured into investment and lending arenas, they had little or no previous experience dealing with the new risks involved.

- **Corporate restructuring.** Downsizing, buyouts, and other restructurings may be accompanied by staff reductions, inadequate supervision, and segregation of duties issues. Positions that were responsible for certain key controls may be eliminated without a replacement. In the first year of compliance, many companies learned too late that they made rapid, large-scale cutbacks in personnel without considering the possible control implications.

- **Foreign operations.** Expanding or acquiring foreign operations often creates new risks for management. For instance, the foreign organization may be unfamiliar with U.S. GAAP and SOX regulatory requirements. Their control environment will most likely be driven by the culture and customs of the local economy and regulatory environment. Channels of communication and information systems may not be well established or available to all individuals.

Conclusion

Risk assessment is often an area that is neglected by small- and medium-size companies because it is viewed as a large, bureaucratic activity. However, even an informal risk assessment can give enormous benefits for planning and goal setting. Risk assessments can give smaller companies a competitive edge, allowing them to be more proactive in their business approach instead of merely reactive.

CONTROL ACTIVITIES

Control activities mitigate the risks associated with the company's objectives. Although control activities is one of the five components of COSO, the bulk of the work in SOX Section 404 projects is devoted to it. Your control matrix identifies and documents the company's key control activities, and your tests of the controls ensure they are operating effectively.

According to COSO's *Internal Control—Integrated Framework*:

> The concepts underlying control activities in smaller organizations are not likely to differ significantly from those in larger entities, but the formality with which they operated will vary. Further, smaller entities may find that certain types of control activities are not always relevant because of highly effective controls applied by management of the small or mid-size entity.

CREATING AN EFFECTIVE INFORMATION AND COMMUNICATION PROGRAM

Businesses require relevant information to be communicated in a timely manner so that people can carry out their responsibilities. Information systems produce financial and compliance-related reports that are necessary to run and control businesses. The information must be communicated throughout the organization, flowing down, across, and up the ranks. Effective communication is also essential with external parties such as customers, suppliers, regulators, and shareholders.

COSO's *Guidance for Smaller Public Companies* has identified four principles for the information and communication function.

1. **Financial reporting information.** Pertinent information is identified, captured, used at all levels of the company, and distributed in a form and time frame that supports the achievement of financial reporting objectives.

2. **Internal control information.** Information needed to facilitate the functioning of other control components is identified, captured, used, and distributed in a form and time frame that enables personnel to carry out their internal control responsibilities.

3. **Internal communication.** Communication enables and supports understanding and execution of internal control objectives, processes, and individual responsibilities at all levels of the organization.

4. **External communication.** Matters affecting the achievement of financial reporting objectives are communicated with outside parties.

Financial Reporting Information

Information to record financial transactions must be captured completely, accurately, and in a timely manner and made accessible to accounting personnel. However, information from operational, internal, and external sources is also needed to produce reliable financial reporting. Information from these sources can be used for accounting estimates and adjustments as well as a reasonableness check for other financial data.

Financial Reporting Information Principle Example

Using Management Meetings to Discuss Key Assumptions   The CEO and CFO of a small manufacturer hold quarterly meetings with all the department heads to discuss and document the key assumptions used in the company's reserves and accruals. Reserves and accruals for inventory, legal, bonuses, and contracting are validated.

Evidence;   Meeting minutes, agendas, or follow-up emails.

Identifying Key Indicators to Improve Performance Monitoring   The CFO of a consulting firm determined that managers should watch continually five key performance/control indicators for the company. Indicators for the management of receivables, expenses, pricing, engagement staffing, and staff productivity all had a high correlation with financial reporting. The monitoring of the five indicators led to improved controls and business performance. Internal management reports now stress these five indicators.

Evidence;   Management reports and analysis.

Internal Control Information

Data required to execute controls must be captured accurately and completely. The quality of system-generated information can be monitored regularly with exception reports to ensure financial data are reliable and controls can be updated if needed. System updates and upgrades can be used to improve the timeliness and reliability of data.

The quality of information is crucial for management to make the best decisions and control the business. The quality of information will be determined by the these attributes:

- **Content is appropriate.** Is the needed information available?
- **Information is timely.** Is it there when it is needed?
- **Information is current.** Is the information the latest?
- **Information is accurate.** Are the data correct?
- **Information is accessible.** Can the data be obtained by the people who need it?

Information Control Principle Examples

Updating IT Information When Performing Risk Assessments A risk manager at a retailer continually reviews risks to the company. As part of the reviews, she asks the IT manager for input on any changes in systems use, personnel, or infrastructure. She also asks other managers if any changes in their processes and activities may have an effect on IT systems.

Evidence;   Emails, memos, and reports from the risk assessment process.

Analyzing an Information System Upgrade A midsize automotive parts manufacturer is scheduling a major financial software upgrade. The company performs a risk assessment of the upgrade using a what-could-go-wrong approach, paying particular attention to the impact the system changes could have on other financial applications and internal controls. Based on this analysis, the company creates a plan for preproduction system testing and a reassessment of procedures and controls that will be affected by the system change.

Evidence;   Documented what-could-go-wrong analysis.

Internal Communication

Management should develop a communication system so that all employees, especially those involved with financial reporting, understand the company's internal control objectives and their roles in achieving those objectives. There should be multiple lines of communication in place as a fail-safe in case certain channels are not operating effectively.

Open and regular communication should exist between management and the board of directors so that the board can carry out its oversight and advisory duties. In turn, the board should tell management what information it needs and provide direction and feedback. The board should also have access to information outside of management through sources such as the external auditors, regulatory authorities, and internal auditors.

Internal Communication Programs Examples

Executive Communications Programs The CEO of a software company has a communications program that includes a quarterly newsletter, personal visits to each location, and participation in department meetings and training programs. In these meetings, the CEO discusses the importance of internal control over financial reporting, how it relates to laws and regulations, and what is expected of all employees in the organization.

Evidence;   CEO's communications in the newsletter, emails, or meeting agendas.

New Employee Orientation Programs A company requires all new personnel to attend an orientation session given weekly for new employees. Each new employee is presented with an employee handbook describing various company policies, including the company's code of conduct and responsibility for internal controls policy. Each employee is required to sign a statement documenting that the individual has read, understands, and will comply with the company's behavioral expectations. The company retains this signed statement in each employee's personnel file as evidence.

Evidence;   New employee orientation presentation slides and agenda.

Communicating through an Intranet Site A professional services firm with multiple locations worldwide maintains current documentation related to internal control objectives on its intranet. The documentation includes flowcharts that depict the company's main processes and internal control system, control matrices, the company's code of ethics, and a section on fraud. The intranet provides a resource for ethical behavior and allows each employee to identify how his or her role impacts internal control for the company.

Evidence;   "Print screens" from the company's intranet site listing internal control objectives.

Using a Finance Conference to Communicate the Importance of Internal Control A company holds a semiannual finance conference that is led by the CFO and attended by all of the individual location controllers and finance managers. The CFO uses the conference as a forum to provide an update of the business, discuss key objectives for the next six months, reinforce the company's expectations of integrity, and emphasize internal control objectives.

Evidence;   Meeting agendas, presentation slides, and a list of attendees.

Holding Monthly Lunch Meetings to Facilitate Upstream Communication A high-tech company with multiple business units holds monthly lunch meetings with a rotating group of employees representing each of the departments and the president, vice president of operations, and controller of each business unit. The meetings are kept informal to foster open communication. The group meets to discuss hot topics affecting the company.

Senior management uses these meetings to emphasize its commitment to ethics and integrity, to provide a brief business update, and to solicit feedback on policy changes that are being considered. The employees use the meetings to voice any questions or concerns they have in their departments and to provide suggestions to improve processes.

Evidence;   Meeting agendas and attendance listings.

Establishing a Mentoring Program A smaller professional services company established a mentoring program where each staff employee is assigned a senior manager; they meet monthly or as needed to discuss the employee's performance, goals, and any questions or problems the employee is experiencing.

Evidence;   Documented mentoring policy and mentor/staff interviews.

Practice Tip

Mentoring programs can help employee loyalty and boost morale. Consider assigning mentors who are outside of the employees' direct chain of command so there is a free flow of conversation and concerns, and employees have a link to diverse groups within the organization.

CEO and Board Communication   The CEO and the chair of the board of a small pharmaceutical company talk at least weekly or more frequently if needed. The chair organizes questions raised by other board members and presents them to the CEO. The CEO often has members of senior management respond directly to the chair while copying the CEO in the response, to get to the root of the issue and to give members of the management team more exposure to the board and the governance processes.

Evidence;   Management's response as part of the board minutes.

Teleconference Board Meetings   The corporate secretary retains emails and the attached documents and presentations that were sent to board members for teleconference meetings, identifying who was invited and who attended. Official minutes document items discussed during the meeting.

Evidence;   Emails with attachments of financial reports and meeting minutes.

External Communication

Internal parties are not the only source of valuable communication. Useful information can come from outside parties such as customers, suppliers, regulators, and shareholders. The whistleblower process or hotline should also be available to these parties. Expectations for dealing with outside parties and the company's values and ethics should be shared with employees at all levels.

Effective External Communication Examples
Communicating with Customers   A small manufacturing company with a single location developed a policy where a member of management, independent of the customer's primary contact, communicates with each of the

company's customers as necessary but at least annually. These discussions help build a strong, loyal relationship with the company's customers and also enable the company to better understand the customer's business. In addition to strengthening customer relationships, this practice has led to more accurate sales information and reduced the days outstanding for receivables.

Evidence;   Documentation by management of each customer conversation, including the customer name, the date of the conversation, individual topics discussed, and any action items and their resolution.

Communication from External Parties through the Company's Hotline   On the store Web site, a small retail chain provides its hotline number to its customers and suppliers. The number can be called with questions, concerns, and complaints. Matters that are reported using the hotline are recorded and addressed, and a log is presented to the board at least quarterly. Hotline logs are attached to the board minutes as part of the internal control review.

Evidence;   Communication to customers and suppliers of the hotline number in contracts or letters.

Conclusion

An entity with a strong control environment and a history of integrity already has a successful communication program if the company's values are well understood by its employees. Such a company probably will not have problems communicating its objectives and message to external parties, its board, or shareholders. In any case, communication in all companies takes constant effort and monitoring.

HOW TO IMPLEMENT SUCCESSFUL MONITORING CONTROLS

Companies require monitoring processes to be in place to assess the quality and effectiveness of its internal controls over time. Internal controls can become ineffective or irrelevant as processes change or may no longer be performed in a way they were originally intended to be performed. Accordingly, management needs to determine whether internal controls continue to be effective, are still relevant for current processes, and are able to address new risks.

COSO has identified two principles related to monitoring:

1. **Ongoing and separate evaluations.** Ongoing and separate evaluations enable management to determine whether the other components of internal control over financial reporting continue to function over time.

2. **Reporting deficiencies.** Internal control deficiencies are identified and communicated in a timely manner to those parties responsible for taking corrective action and to management and the board as appropriate.

Ongoing and Separate Evaluations

Ongoing monitoring activities are performed by managers and supervisors in the course of everyday business and include specific identification of variances from the norm that prompt them to investigate potential issues. Ongoing monitoring provides continual feedback of the effectiveness of controls by people who are familiar with the controls and knowledgeable of the process.

Separate evaluations of processes and controls generally provide a more in-depth analysis by an independent party. Separate evaluations can be especially helpful for areas with control weaknesses, new departments, or when there is suspected fraud. Large companies usually have an internal audit function to perform these functions, but small companies can benefit from outsourced resources to keep costs variable. The scope and frequency of separate evaluations will be determined by the amount of risk associated with an activity.

Ongoing and Separate Evaluations Examples

Using Key Control Indicators to Monitor Performance   A CFO uses key indicators for all accounting and financial processes that present material risks to the reliability of the financial statements. For example, the key control indicators in the accounts receivable function focus on the accuracy of sales and invoicing by monitoring the amounts of credits and returns. The credit department's effectiveness is monitored by the amount of bad debt that is actually written off from the reserve, and both are rated by the day's sales outstanding number. Targets consistent with the company's history have been set, and performance is tracked to target. Results are shared with the relevant management team and also are used for performance appraisals and development programs. Key indicators for the account payable, treasury, payroll, purchasing, inventory, and financial reporting functions are also monitored by the CFO and reported to the respective managers monthly.

Evidence;   Monthly key indicator reports for all departments.

Using Operating Information to Monitor   The sales team for a hotel chain uses its centralized accounting group to maintain a sales target report that is published to the sales team weekly. The report compares daily room sales by property to forecasted amounts to track performance. The controller reconciles actual sales from this report to the company's general ledger system, researches and resolves all discrepancies, and emails the report and reconciliation to the vice president of finance. The vice president of finance emails the weekly report and a short sales summary to the sales team.

Evidence;   The vice president of finance sign off on the reconciliation or the controller and vice president of finance emails.

Firsthand Knowledge of the Business   A manufacturer with approximately 100 employees has three different warehouses that run two shifts per day each. Each location has approximately the same number of employees, and the accounting is centralized at the corporate office. The CFO has been with the company for eight years and thoroughly understands each business process. The CFO reviews weekly payroll summary reports by location for reasonableness. Based on his years and background with the company, the CFO understands the seasons, cycles, and workflow of the operation and can easily determine the cause of a change in payroll dollars. Whether the increase or decrease is due to a particular project, expected overtime, hiring, or layoffs, the CFO can take corrective action if necessary to address the change. The small size of the company and the CFO's knowledge and experience allows for effective monitoring of one of the company's largest expenses. Although CFOs at many small companies may monitor payroll expenses, it is important that there is evidence to confirm this kind of review.

Evidence;   The CFO's initials on the payroll reports or biweekly emails to the warehouse managers, informing them of their labor expense for the period.

Using an Independent Party to Perform Separate Evaluations   The CFO of a small construction firm has suspicions that one of his buyers is receiving kickbacks from a supplier. The company does not have an internal audit department, so the CFO hires an independent consultant to test the procurement controls as well as investigate all transactions with the supplier in question. The results from the investigation are summarized for the CFO in a report to provide feedback on the effectiveness of the procurement controls and report evidence that the buyer did not have fair dealings with several suppliers. Because of the evidence of fraud, the results are reported to the board of directors.

Evidence;   Audit report from the independent consultant and board minutes.

Determining the Scope and Frequency of Separate Evaluations   At the beginning of the year, the director of internal audit compiles a schedule of tests and investigations that will be performed during the year by the internal audit department. The scope and frequency are agreed to by senior management and members of the board and include areas that were determined to be high risk during the company's risk assessment, had a significant deficiency or material weakness in the prior year's internal control assessment, or were mentioned in the external auditors' management letter.

While planning for the year, the director determines that the staff scheduled to perform the reviews can be objective, has a general understanding of the processes and controls involved, and understands the objectives of the review.

Upon completion of each review, the director communicates the findings to senior management and the board of directors in a report that contains this information:

- The scope of the work performed, including a description of the process being reviewed

- Identification of the controls over the process and any controls that are not in place

- Opinion on the effectiveness of the controls, management's response, and plans for remediation if needed

Evidence;   Audit report and board minutes.

Internal Auditor's Tests of Standardized Procedures and Controls   A retail company has a number of stores that are relatively similar in nature, operations, and structure. An operating manual is provided to each location covering instructions for certain operational and financial tasks. The audit committee instructs its internal audit group to test internal controls in these areas to determine whether the stores are following the procedures and controls outlined in the operations manual.

Evidence;   The internal audit group's findings reported to the audit committee.

Outsourcing the Internal Audit Function   A small pharmaceutical company outsources its internal audit activity. The CFO and the audit committee meet with the project manager every quarter to monitor findings, plan additional work, and review any issues encountered.

Evidence;   Audit committee minutes and any internal audit reports.

Reporting Deficiencies

Once a deficiency has been identified by ongoing monitoring or a separate evaluation, it must be reported in a timely manner so that corrective action can be taken. The deficiency should be reported to the person who owns the process or a person in a position to take corrective action. In addition, the deficiency should be reported to a person at least one level of management above the process owner to ensure the proper oversight is achieved. Significant deficiencies or material weaknesses that affect any internal controls over financial reporting should be reported to senior management and the audit committee or board of directors. Corrective actions should be taken for any significant or material deficiencies.

Effective Ways to Report Deficiencies Examples

Reporting Control Deficiencies to Management   At a small travel agency with one location and 50 employees, each functional department is led by a member of management. Department managers discuss ways to improve the internal control structure and address control deficiencies at their weekly department meeting. Depending on the nature and materiality of matters raised by the team, the managers deal with the reported deficiencies as appropriate.

Evidence;   One person from each department prepares minutes for each meeting and distributes them to the entire department via email.

Reporting Control Deficiencies to the Board   Management of a midsize software company notifies process owners and relevant supervisors of deficiencies found during internal control testing and requests a plan for corrective action. Management reports all deficiencies to the board quarterly. The board monitors all deficiencies and their resolution by creating a log of all deficiencies, their owner, and the planned remediation.

Evidence;   Board log of deficiencies.

HOW TO ASSIGN ROLES AND RESPONSIBILITIES TO ENHANCE INTERNAL CONTROLS

The draft COSO *Guidance for Smaller Public Companies* included a section on roles and responsibilities that was introduced in COSO's Internal Control Framework. The section was incorporated within the 20 principles in the final publication, but because of its importance (especially for first-time compliance) it is segregated here. The section discussed the many players that affect internal controls, including management, the audit committee, internal audit, and other employees, and the responsibilities of each.

Management is ultimately responsible for a company's internal control, but process owners should feel a sense of ownership for processes and controls that they perform. The performance and review of all internal controls rolls up to the audit committee in their oversight role over financial reporting.

The three major roles affecting financial reporting are:

1. **Management roles.** Management is ultimately responsible for internal control over financial reporting.

2. **Board and audit committees.** The board of directors and/or audit committee has oversight responsibilities for effective internal control over financial reporting.

3. **Other personnel.** All company staff should accept responsibility for their part in internal controls over financial reporting.

Management Roles

The CEO and senior management set the tone for sound internal controls throughout the company. The attitudes of senior management should trickle down the ranks to emphasize the importance of compliance with financial controls and policies. Finance and accounting officers are primarily responsible for the design, implementation, and monitoring of the company's financial reporting system and play a major role in preventing and detecting fraud.

Effective Management Roles Examples

CEO and Board Input to Developing Roles   Due to significant growth and changes occurring within the company, the CEO, working directly with the board of directors, updated and developed new roles for each level of the company's management team. Once the new roles were refined or created, the CEO held a meeting with the senior and middle managers where the goals of the business, along with specific responsibilities and roles, were communicated. The CEO sent a consistent message about how the managers would interact with one another and expectations for adequate controls within the organization.

Evidence;   New policies and procedures established to define and communicate key roles and responsibilities, new organizational charts, or an agenda or presentation from relevant meetings.

Top Management Certification of Roles and Responsibilities   Senior management at a medium-size services firm reinforces the roles and responsibilities for internal control over financial reporting by having all directors and above sign certifications similar to the Section 302 certifications required by the SEC. The internal certifications provide accountability for company-wide controls and responsibilities.

Evidence;   Signed quarterly certification letters.

Board and Audit Committee

The audit committee's primary function (or the board in the absence of the audit committee) is to govern, guide, and oversee the financial reporting process and the related internal controls. The audit committee along with strong internal controls is one of the best defenses against management override and misrepresentation of financial results. The SOX has caused increased scrutiny on the independence of board members, allowing them to better balance their roles as advisors and overseers.

Effective Boards and Audit Committees Examples

Board Bylaws and Committee Charters   The responsibilities of the company's board of directors are defined in the corporate bylaws, and the audit committee's responsibilities are defined in its charter. The audit committee's charter requires an annual review to confirm the charter reflects current activities of the committee and is consistent with the committee's objectives.

Evidence;   Minutes of the board of directors and audit committee meetings documenting the annual review and approval of their bylaws and charter.

Audit Committee Governance, Guidance, and Oversight   The audit committee at a midsize pharmaceutical company reports matters related to the financial reporting process to the board of directors quarterly. Reported topics include any deficiencies identified in the company's internal controls, instances of executive fraud, financial reporting issues, and the IT environment.

Evidence;   The board of directors' meeting minutes and/or the meeting agenda and presentation package.

Audit Committee Independence   The members of the audit committee sign a questionnaire and certification of their independence annually. The certification states that the member has no related party transactions with the company, is not involved in managing the business, and does not have any immediate family members in management.

Evidence;   Signed annual certifications of independence for all audit committee members.

Other Personnel

Management cannot perform and monitor all of the company's internal controls alone. Virtually all employees have some role in financial reporting controls and should know the impact of their daily activities on the financial statements.

Management should send the message that employees are responsible to report operational problems, noncompliance with the company's code of conduct, violations of policies, or illegal acts to senior management when they occur. Internal controls are everyone's business, and the roles and responsibilities of all employees should be well communicated and included in their job descriptions.

Internal auditors are responsible for examining operations, policies, and procedures to ensure they are being carried out as planned. They also provide objective assessments about the design and operating effectiveness of an organization's internal controls and recommend improvements. Typically internal auditors report directly to the audit committee or board of directors but may have a dual reporting responsibility to someone in management. However the organizational chart is structured, the head of internal audit should have direct access to the audit committee or board of directors, can be dismissed only with the audit committee's concurrence, and should have the authority to follow up on findings and recommendations.

In smaller companies, the role of internal audit often is not as traditional or structured as in larger companies. Internal audit often is combined with compliance (e.g., SOX) work and can include process improvement and policy creation. For companies with limited resources, this blended role can be more practical and easier to sell to management. A person who facilitates process improvement could ultimately pay for him- or herself by improving billings, collections, the sales or shipping processes, or other efficiencies. A large disadvantage to this approach is the loss of independence that you would have with a traditional internal auditor.

Other Personnel's Roles and Responsibilities Examples

Reviews across Business Units   A company with no internal audit function uses one financial employee with an audit background from each business unit to monitor the internal controls over financial reporting of another business unit. These employees report their findings and recommendations quarterly to management and the audit committee.

Evidence;   The employees' documented findings and recommendations.

Cosourcing Internal Audit   The director of internal audit at a smaller retail outlet supplements the internal audit function with qualified audit consultants to add needed skills and expertise in specific audit areas. The director oversees the work of the consultants, reviews all of their findings and reports, and communicates the outcome of all projects to the audit committee.

Evidence;   Audit reports provided by third party and audit committee meeting minutes.

Outsourcing Internal Audit   A small manufacturer outsources its internal audit activity to a third party that specializes in internal audit services. The CFO monitors and controls the third party and meets quarterly with the

CEO and audit committee chair to discuss the work that the internal audit outsourcer has performed, findings from all investigations, planned work, and any other concerns the CFO may have.

Evidence;   The quarterly written report provided by the third party to the company explaining current results, recommendations with management responses, and future audit plans.

SMALL-COMPANY ISSUES FOR IMPLEMENTING ENTITY-LEVEL CONTROLS

In its *Guidance for Smaller Public Companies*, COSO did not use specific revenue figures, number of employees, or other quantitative tests to determine whether a company should be considered small. Instead, COSO chose to describe smaller businesses in terms of their characteristics, which include one or more of these:

- Fewer lines of business and fewer products within lines

- Concentration of marketing focus, by channel or geography

- Leadership by management with significant ownership interest or rights

- Fewer levels of management, with wider spans of control

- Less complex transaction processing systems

- Fewer personnel, many having a wider range of duties

- Limited ability to maintain deep resources in line as well as support staff positions such as legal, human resources, accounting, and internal auditing

None of these characteristics by itself would cause a company to consider itself small. In fact, many companies that already consider themselves small because of revenues, number of locations, and employees would not be considered small according to these criteria. However, as companies' revenues and assets begin to grow, management will be able to take advantage of more economies of scale and will have narrower spans of control.

Challenges for Implementing Internal Control in Smaller Businesses

Smaller businesses face certain challenges in implementing effective internal control systems, particularly if the business views controls as something to be added on rather than integrated with core processes. These challenges often include:

- Segregation of duties issues because of a small staff.

- Potential for management override because of management's ability to dominate activities.

- Attracting board of directors and audit committee members that are independent and have the expertise of the industry, operational, and financial matters.

- Recruiting qualified accounting personnel for reliable financial reporting.

- Diverting a portion of management's attention away from running the business to provide adequate management focus on accounting and financial reporting.

- Keeping up to date with IT; small companies often do not have the budget or expertise in-house to manage information systems effectively.

Ideas for Addressing Segregation of Duties Issues

Segregation of duties is one of the biggest control problems that small companies face. How can a company have adequate segregation of duties with three people in the accounting department? A few ideas for compensating controls to address limited segregation of duties issues follow.

- **Increase detection controls and monitoring.** Management may consider reviewing reports of detailed transactions that are recorded by staff that perform key activities with limited segregation of duties. The reviews should occur regularly on a timely basis, and questionable transactions should be investigated and corrected. If the accounts payable clerk sets up and maintains all vendor master files, a manager could review a report of all changes and additions made to the master files monthly. The report could be electronic or paper copy, signed off and retained for evidence of review.

- **Examine random transactions.** A manager could review a small sample of supporting documents daily for a few select transactions. The sample could be generated with a listing of all transactions during the day. Transactions reviewed could be noted on the report and initialed by the manager as evidence.

- **Outsource activities when possible.** Using a third-party provider, such as a payroll service or lockbox bank account, can reduce the number of conflicting activities performed by one employee.

- **Use nonaccounting personnel when possible.** Transactions can be initiated or processed by employees who do not have a traditional accounting function. For example, a receptionist can open and log incoming customer checks, an office manager can manage petty cash, and an operational department head such as the vice president of research and development or operations manager can act as an additional check signer.

- **Take periodic counts of assets and compare them with accounting records.** When there is limited segregation of duties over transactions involving inventory, equipment, or other tangible assets, periodic counts and the comparison to the inventory records ensures assets recorded in the books are on hand.

- **Review analytics.** Although less effective, the review of budget and trend analyses of costs can be another compensating control. While this does not provide a detailed review, it can be a way to identify problem areas where further investigation is needed.

Dealing with Management Override

Smaller businesses often are run by a hands-on founder or small group of managers who have the opportunity to override financial reporting controls. Management override may be one of the most difficult control issues to overcome for any business but is best mitigated by the company's commitment to competence and ethical behavior. Independent board members who are inquisitive and know the business can provide effective oversight to further enhance outside control. Finally, an internal audit function and whistleblower program have been shown to effectively combat management override.

Finding Eligible Board and Audit Committee Members

The pool of eligible board and audit committee members has diminished since SOX went into effect. Members have more responsibility and may feel the potential legal issues do not justify the time and energy required to fulfill the duties. In the past, small companies may have used representatives from law firms, bankers, investors, or other partners who did business with the company. Now that independence is an issue, these partners may not always be the best choice. However, these partners are a good source for referrals.

Recruiting Qualified Accounting Personnel

It can be a challenge for smaller companies to recruit qualified personnel at higher levels where a greater understanding of accounting principles is required. Unlike larger companies, which may have entire departments of technical accounting personnel to research and study complex accounting issues, smaller companies may only have one or two high-level accounting people. Many smaller businesses have historically discussed appropriate accounting practices and guidance with their external auditor. The PCAOB and SEC both confirmed that companies can and should continue to have discussions with their external auditors to help them deal with complex accounting issues. However, smaller companies need enough expertise in house for management to make its own decisions based on the advice they receive.

Practice Tip

Since smaller companies do not always have the prestige or resources of larger companies, they offer other benefits to attract quality employees. Often employees are more interested in flexible work schedules, extra time off, educational assistance, regular training, and opportunities to perform untraditional responsibilities than a big salary.

Maintaining Focus on Accounting and Financial Reporting

Strategic initiatives, sales, and running the business often take up the bulk of management's time at start-up or in smaller companies. Since they do not directly generate revenues, accounting and financial reporting functions often do not get the attention and resources they need.

Try to leverage monitoring activities that are already in place to increase management's focus on financial matters. For example, the CFO may monitor payroll or travel costs closely in a monthly report or daily sales figures may be reported to the vice president of sales to track performance. These types of procedures can also serve as valuable monitoring and financial reporting controls.

Maintaining Up-to-Date IT Systems

Just as in the accounting arena, small companies do not always have the resources or expertise to maintain adequate and up-to-date IT systems. In addition, non-IT employees may not have the computer skills, or the company may not to be able to provide training so that systems are used to their fullest potential. Outsourcing implementations, maintenance, and training can keep costs variable allowing smaller companies to obtain quality IT services without the fixed costs.

Conclusion

Many of the issues in internal controls that small companies face can be overcome in unconventional ways. Traditional controls available to larger companies are not the only answer for effective internal controls. If your

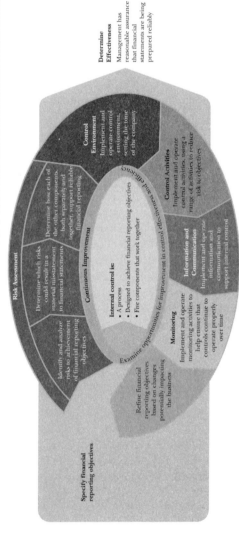

Specify financial reporting objectives

Risk Assessment

Determine which risks could result in a material misstatement to financial statements

Determine how each of the other components, both separately and together, support reliable financial reporting

Control Environment
Implement and operate control environment, setting the tone of the company

Control Activities
Implement and operate control activities, using a range of activities to reduce risk to objectives

Information and Communication
Implement and operate information and communication to support internal control

Monitoring
Implement and operate monitoring activities to help ensure that controls continue to operate properly over time

Identify and analyze risks to achievement of financial reporting objectives

Refine financial reporting objectives based on changes potentially impacting the business

Internal control is:
• A process
• Designed to achieve financial reporting objectives
• Five components that work together

Continuous Improvement

Examine opportunities for improvement in control effectiveness and efficiency

Determine Effectiveness
Management has reasonable assurance that financial statements are being prepared reliably

Risk Assessment

- **Identify financial reporting objectives**
  Complies with GAAP, supports information disclosures, reflects company activities, is supported by relevant financial statement assertions and considers materiality
- **Identify and analyze financial reporting risks**
  Includes business processes, personnel and information technology, involves appropriate levels of management, considers both internal and external factors, estimates likelihood and impact, and triggers reassessment
- **Identify and assess the risk of fraud as it affects the company**
  Considers incentives and pressures, risk factors, and establishes responsibilities and accountability

Control Environment

- **Integrity and ethical values are developed and understood**
  Articulates values, monitors adherence, addresses deviations
- **Board of directors understand and exercise oversight**
  Defines authorities, operates independently, monitors risk, retains financial reporting expertise, oversees quality and reliability and oversees audit activities
- **Management philosophy and operating style support internal control**
  Sets the tone, influences attitudes towards accounting principles and estimates and articulates objectives
- **Organizational structure supports internal control**
  Establishes lines of financial reporting and establishes structure
- **Financial reporting competencies are retained**
  Identifies competencies, retains individuals and evaluates competencies
- **Authority and responsibility are assigned**
  Defines responsibilities and limits authority
- **Human resource policies and practices facilitate internal control**
  Establishes human resource practices, recruits and retains, adequately trains, and evaluates performance and compensates

Control Activities

- **Control activities integrate with risk assessment**
  Mitigates risk, considers all significant points of entry into the company's G/L and information technology
- **Control activities are selected and developed**
  Considers range of activities, includes preventive and detective controls, segregates duties, and considers cost vs. benefit
- **Policies are established and communicated and result in management directives being carried out**
  Integrates into business processes, establishes responsibility and authority occurs on a timely basis, thoughtfully implements, investigates exceptions, and periodically reassesses
- **Information technology controls are designed and implemented**
  Includes application controls, considers general computer operations, and includes end-user computing

Information and Communication

- **Financial reporting information is identified, captured, used and distributed**
  Captures data, includes financial information, uses internal and external sources, includes operating information, and maintains quality
- **Internal control information is identified, captured, used and distributed**
  Captures data, triggers resolution and update, and maintains quality
- **Internal communication supports execution of internal control**
  Communicates with personnel and board, includes separate communication lines, and accesses information
- **Matters affecting achievement of objectives are communicated**
  Provides input and independently assesses

Monitoring

- **Ongoing and/or separate evaluations enable management to determine function of internal control**
  Integrates with operations, provides objective assessment, uses knowledgeable personnel, considers feedback and adjusts scope and frequency
- **Internal control deficiencies are identified and communicated**
  Reports findings and deficiencies, and corrects on a timely basis

Exhibit 5.2 COSO's Navigating *Internal Control over Financial Reporting—Guidance for Smaller Public Companies*

company does not have traditional entity-wide controls in place, think outside the box and consider creative ways to monitor, communicate, plan, and test controls. Be sure to see Appendix A for a simplified sample entity-level control matrix and Appendix B for an internal control checklist for entity-level controls.

SUMMARY OF COSO'S GUIDANCE FOR SMALLER PUBLIC COMPANIES

COSO provides a road map for navigating internal control over financial reporting that summarizes its methodology and the five components. (See Exhibit 5.2.)

NOTES

1. Commission Guidance Regarding Management's Report on Internal Control over Financial Reporting under Section 13(a) or 15(d) of the Securities Exchange Act of 1934, p. 22.
2. July 11, 2006, SEC press release.

6

Minimizing Excess through Proper Scoping and Planning Practices

Key Topics:
- How to determine materiality for scoping purposes

- How to use a top-down, risk-based approach to reduce the scope of your program

- Methods for determining significant locations

- Specific areas included and excluded from the scope of your assessment

- PCAOB and SEC guidance on other common scoping issues

- Tips for resource planning and developing useful timelines

A crucial element for making any Sarbanes-Oxley (SOX) Section 404 program a success is meticulous planning, risk assessment, and scoping. Resource needs, deadlines, and an overall plan for every step of the program should be established at the beginning of each year after a thorough scoping analysis has been performed. Properly scoping your project can reduce the number of significant accounts, disclosures, processes and locations, and ultimately the number of key controls that need to be documented. Not only will it focus your program on the key risk areas that are specific to your organization, it will help determine the nature, timing, and extent of testing necessary throughout the year.

Practice Tip

The scoping process sets the tone for the project and ultimately dictates the number of key controls an organization will have. Scoping requires audit savvy. Be sure someone with an audit background is closely involved.

SCOPING ANALYSIS: EVENT OR PROCESS?

You can use an initial scoping exercise at the beginning of the year using prior-year numbers or a forecast to plan your annual Section 404 program. However, the initial scoping assessment may change substantially during the year, depending on the organization's activities, accuracy of forecasts, or relevance of prior-year financial data. Because your initial scoping analysis may not reflect the significant risks, accounts, or locations of the business at year-end, scoping should be considered a process rather than an annual event.

It is a good idea to reassess your scoping decisions using actual figures at least once closer to the end of the year to avoid surprises. This ensures the project's coverage of the financial statements is still adequate and that unusual or unanticipated events that occurred during the year are taken into account. In addition, you may have to rescope your project when major transactions occur that affect the business, such as a merger or acquisition, introducing a new product, or opening a new location.

Practice Tip

Consider performing a new scoping analysis, including risk assessment, whenever there is a significant change to the budget or forecast during the year.

HOW TO DETERMINE MATERIALITY FOR
SCOPING PURPOSES

The Securities and Exchange Commission (SEC) in its Guidance for Management states that management's consideration of the misstatement risk of a financial reporting element includes both the materiality of the financial reporting element (quantitative factors) and the susceptibility of the underlying account balances, transactions, or other supporting information to a misstatement that could be material to the financial statements (qualitative factors). As the materiality of the financial reporting element increases in relation to the amount of misstatement that would be considered material to the financial statements, management's assessment of misstatement risk for the financial reporting element generally would increase correspondingly.

The first step in starting a scoping analysis is to determine a materiality level so you can better assess risk. Question 40 in the Public Company Accounting Oversight Board (PCAOB) Staff Questions and Answers (Q&A) states that accounts and disclosures that have only a remote likelihood of containing misstatements that could cause the financial statements to be materially misstated can be eliminated from further consideration as long as the proper qualitative and quantitative risk factors have been evaluated.

Quantitative Analysis

Quantitative considerations in an audit of financial statements are essentially the same as in an audit of internal controls. These considerations relate to whether individual or collective misstatements that would not be prevented or detected by internal controls would have a quantitatively material effect on the financial statements. The PCAOB confirmed this practice and simplified its advice on materiality in Auditing Standard No. 5 (AS No. 5). It states in Paragraph 20: "In planning the audit of internal control over financial reporting, the auditor should use the same materiality considerations he or she would use in planning the audit of the company's annual financial statements."

Using a top-down approach, materiality should be assessed first at the overall level, then broken down to the individual account level. Both levels of materiality should be used for planning, scoping, and risk assessment. Overall materiality is used for the entire project and relates to amounts in the annual, consolidated financial statements. Since deficiencies in individual accounts eventually will be aggregated, materiality at the individual account level should be less than overall materiality. Hence, you should establish an overall materiality level to guide the project and an individual materiality level (tolerable level) to apply to accounts, transactions, and particular locations.

Quantitative financial data for your scoping analysis can be derived from a variety of sources, including the company's most recent Forms 10-K or 10-Q filings, budgets, or forecasts. The goal is to choose the source that would best reflect the organization's operations by year-end. For example, it is not a good idea to use the second-quarter 10-Q financial data if the business is cyclical, with the bulk of transactions occurring in the fourth quarter. In this case, a better document to use for the quantitative scoping analysis may be the prior year's 10-K or a combination of the prior year's 10-K adjusted for data in the forecast. If the business operations are consistent throughout the year, the best decision may be to annualize the most recent 10-Q financial data.

Numerical Thresholds

Your scoping analysis can use numerical thresholds for its initial assessment during the year to determine which accounts, disclosures, and locations are in scope for Section 404 procedures. These thresholds can be a percentage of these consolidated income statement or balance sheet indicators:

- Revenues
- Pretax income

- Net income

- Operating expenses

- Total assets

- Total equity

For example, the overall materiality level could be calculated for a certain company as 5% of pretax income or 5% × $50 million = $2.5 million. However, calculating materiality is usually not so simple. The indicator and percentage you select should be tailored to the company's situation. If the company is operating at a loss, for example, you might not choose pretax income (loss) to determine your base for a materiality amount.

Practice Tip

Consider evaluating multiple indicators from *both* the income statement and the balance sheet to determine materiality thresholds for your quantitative scoping analysis. Doing this will help to ensure that you are accurately scoping all significant accounts and locations/business units regardless of the business structure.

For example, a licensing business unit with high revenues and minimal assets will likely be considered significant using the two-pronged approach but may incorrectly be descoped from a company's Section 404 procedures using only a balance sheet metric.

In addition to using consolidated revenues, pretax income, or other indicators in your quantitative analysis, the percentage you choose will vary depending on risk factors, such as the nature of your business, the company's history of financial errors, and the overall control environment. A profitable, low-risk manufacturer with a strong control environment may choose to use 5% of pretax income as one of its metrics, while a more risky start-up software company may choose 3%. As always, analyze, document, and confer (with your external auditor). While external auditors may not share their own materiality calculations with you, they will most likely tell you if they agree or disagree with your levels.

Keep in mind that when referring to a typical 5% threshold to determine materiality, SEC Staff Accounting Bulletin No. 99 (SAB No. 99), *Materiality*, reminds registrants and auditors that "exclusive reliance on this or any other percentage or numerical threshold has no basis in the accounting literature or the law." Although numerical thresholds can be a starting ground to evaluate whether an account is material, they should not be the only factor considered.

Overall Coverage of Financial Operations

Auditing Standard No. 2 (AS No. 2) required a *large portion* of coverage of financial operations at the financial statement level for internal control audits. While the "large portion" language has been excluded from AS No. 5 in favor of a more risk-based approach, auditors and management still should strive for significant coverage of financial operations. In the past, external auditors would look for their Section 404 procedures to cover 60 to 75% of the company's selected financial indicators (revenue, pretax income, assets, or equity). Instead of a hard quantitative assessment of coverage, it is a good idea to use the "financial coverage" percentage as a reasonableness check to ensure your program is comprehensive. Company procedures with far less coverage of the financial statements or financial indicators may not adequately assess the company's process and internal controls.

Practice Tip

Monitor business units with fluctuating revenues, assets, or net income regularly throughout the year. It may be more cost-effective to bring marginal business units into scope up front than to risk a costly addition to scope at the end of the year. Just because the business unit is in scope does not mean it requires extensive Section 404 procedures.

Qualitative Analysis

A risk-based approach has become the standard for efficient SOX programs because it focuses programs on the most significant issues at a company, taking into consideration both quantitative and qualitative aspects. Risk assessments help management and auditors consider the "softer qualities," or qualitative factors that affect a business instead of focusing only on rigid quantitative calculations. Qualitative factors generally will not exclude accounts, disclosures, or locations from being in scope for Section 404 procedures but may cause them to be included in scope even if they are not quantitatively material.

According to SAB No. 99, you cannot rely exclusively on quantitative thresholds when determining materiality. "A matter is 'material' if there is a substantial likelihood that a reasonable person would consider it important." Using the guidance in SAB No. 99, many external auditors believe that every line item on the balance sheet and all disclosures are material, regardless of the amounts, and indeed few financial statement line items at the consolidated level are found to be immaterial.

Although qualitative factors are discussed in early guidance on materiality, SAB No. 99 gives examples that may cause a quantitatively small misstatement to be considered material. A sample of qualitative considerations to use in your scoping analysis based on SAB No. 99's examples follows.

- Does the account or disclosure include estimates, and, if so, what is the degree of imprecision inherent in the estimate?
- Is the account or disclosure subject to changes from period to period, or is it highly complex?
- Has the location or segment been identified as playing a significant role in the organization's operations or profitability?
- Could the account or location affect the registrant's compliance with regulatory requirements?
- Could the account affect the registrant's compliance with loan covenants or other contractual requirements?
- What is the likelihood of significant contingent liabilities associated with the account or disclosure?
- Does the account have the effect of increasing management's compensation (e.g., by satisfying requirements for the award of bonuses or other forms of incentive compensation)?
- Are there safeguarding issues related to the account or location? Are goods recorded in the account subject to theft?
- Is the account, disclosure, or location an easy target for fraud?
- Have there been errors in the past in the account or disclosure?
- Has the external auditor given management comments regarding an account, disclosure, or location?
- Does the account or disclosure include any related party transactions?

Practice Tip

Ask your external auditors about their own scoping guidelines early in the year and for their view of your scoping and testing plan, including your materiality assumption. Scoping lays the groundwork for the entire project, so it is essential for the company and the auditors to be in agreement on these points.

For additional guidance on materiality, refer to these documents:

- SAS No. 47, *Audit Risk and Materiality in Conducting an Audit* as amended by SAS No. 82

- FASB Statement of Financial Accounting Concepts No. 2
- SEC SAB No. 99, *Materiality*

HOW TO USE A TOP-DOWN, RISK-BASED APPROACH TO REDUCE THE SCOPE OF YOUR PROGRAM

Using a top-down approach can prevent you from spending unnecessary time understanding and documenting processes that do not affect the likelihood that the company's financial statements could be materially misstated. In a top-down approach, you evaluate the entity-level processes, policies, and controls to determine the specific risks that may affect the organization at the top. The risks identified at the top level will point you in the direction of the significant accounts at the financial statement and disclosure level. These significant accounts and disclosures will be broken down further into more detailed accounts and locations. The risk of material misstatement can be traced down through this detail until the specific processes and transactions can be identified. Ultimately, key controls will have to be established for the relevant assertions that apply to these significant processes and transactions.

12 Entity-Level Matters to Consider

By using a top-down approach in the initial planning and scoping stages, you will evaluate the organization's control environment, operations, risk assessment, and recent history to determine where to focus your efforts for Section 404. This analysis is best performed with input from key personnel in different parts of the business, such as the controllers of each business unit, chief counsel and the chief financial, operations, and information technology officers. Using employees outside of the internal audit or finance function ensures a robust analysis from many perspectives.

A list of 12 entity-level matters to consider that may affect your decisions about the control environment, operations, and specific risks at your organization follows.

1. The general tone at the top, commitment to excellence, and ethical behavior displayed by executives and employees
2. Knowledge of the company's existing internal control structure over financial reporting
3. Risks specific to the industry in which the company operates, such as financial reporting practices, economic conditions, laws and regulations, and technological changes

4. Internal business practices, including the company's organizational structure, operating characteristics, capital structure, and distribution methods

5. Recent changes in the company, its operations, or its internal control over financial reporting

6. The company's prior-year process for assessing the effectiveness of internal control over financial reporting

7. Preliminary judgments about materiality, risk, and the effectiveness of internal control over financial reporting

8. Control deficiencies from a prior-year Section 404 assessment or previously communicated to the audit committee in a management letter from your external auditor

9. Relevant legal or regulatory matters

10. The type and extent of available evidence related to the effectiveness of the company's internal control over financial reporting

11. A preliminary judgment on the number of significant business locations or units, and the methods management uses to monitor such locations or business units

12. Knowledge about the company's information technology (IT) structure, security, and the effectiveness of the company's enterprise resource planning (ERP) system, including how well users know the system.

Practice Tip

In the early implementation of Section 404, companies often tried to reduce the number of key controls by evaluating transactions at the bottom level. Instead, eliminate excess and focus your program on specific risks at the top (entity-level) first. The efficiencies will trickle down from there.

Using Entity-Level Controls to Reduce Scope

When guidance on a risk-based approach was introduced by the SEC and PCAOB staffs in May 2005, there was much hope that strong entity-level controls would reduce the scope of Section 404 projects. In practice, the benefits of that guidance and a risk-based approach were not so obvious.

The SEC and PCAOB tried again to reinforce a risk-based approach in subsequent reports. The SEC's Guidance for Management promotes the approach but probably would have had little effect in practice except for the more specific risk-based instruction for auditors described in the PCAOB's AS No. 5.

The standard allows auditors to rely on entity-level controls if they have a direct connection to process level transactions. Paragraph 23 states:

> Some entity-level controls might be designed to operate at a level of precision that would adequately prevent or detect on a timely basis misstatements to one or more relevant assertions. If an entity-level control sufficiently addresses the assessed risk of misstatement, the auditor need not test additional controls relating to that risk.

Strong entity-level controls can be used on a more pervasive level to exclude "borderline" locations or accounts from the scope of a SOX program. Even if they are not used to directly reduce testing, strong entity-level controls could be used as a compensating control to lessen the severity of deficiencies at year-end. However, weak entity-level controls could lead to scope increases. Additional locations and accounts could be included in scope, and more testing with larger sample sizes would probably result to compensate for the weakness.

Determining Significant Accounts

In a top-down approach, significant accounts can be identified by considering financial statement line items or captions and evaluating both qualitative and quantitative risk factors. Usually not as obvious as (quantitatively) material accounts, other accounts may be significant on a qualitative basis based on the expectations of a reasonable user. For example, investors might be interested in a particular financial statement account even though it is not quantitatively large because it represents an important performance measure.

When evaluating inherent risk in determining significant accounts, your evaluation should not consider the effectiveness of internal control over financial reporting. In other words, assume the financial statements are simply compiled and reported without any controls in place. What accounts and disclosures would have the highest chance of error?

When identifying significant accounts, the PCAOB advises auditors to assess these risk factors:

- Size and composition of the account

- Susceptibility of misstatement due to errors or fraud

- Volume of activity, complexity, and homogeneity of the individual transactions processed through the account or reflected in the disclosure

- Nature of the account

- Accounting and reporting complexities associated with the account or disclosure

- Exposure to losses in the account

- Possibility of significant contingent liabilities arising from the activities reflected in the account or disclosure

- Existence of related party transactions in the account

- Changes from the prior period in account or disclosure characteristics

As part of identifying significant accounts and disclosures and their relevant assertions, try to determine the likely sources of potential error or misstatement. One way to do this is to ask yourself what could go wrong with this account or disclosure, and if it did go wrong, would it be material to the consolidated financial statements?

Account Components   The individual materiality level will help dictate which accounts and locations are quantitatively significant and should be applied to both summary line items on the financial statement and individual general ledger accounts. For example, a company may determine an individual materiality threshold of $500,000 to determine which accounts are quantitatively significant. As such, the total inventory amount in the balance sheet may be over $500,000, but the individual account, raw materials, may be considered not significant because its balance of $98,000 falls below the threshold. Components of a significant account may be subject to differing risks and, if not significant, can allow certain components of significant accounts to be left out of scope.

However, other qualitative aspects of accounts need to be considered, such as the amount of inherent risk, whether the account includes estimates, and if items in the account are subject to theft. Additionally, the account should be analyzed for the amount of activity that flows in and out during the period, not just the ending balance.

Account Activity   Account activity, or the transactions flowing through accounts, is an important consideration when scoping because ending balances do not always show the entire picture. In the inventory example just given, the raw materials account may have had millions of dollars of purchases going into the account during the year with millions of dollars of work in process (WIP) inventory coming out, even though it happened to have a low ending balance at year-end.

Accounts at Different Locations   Accounts and their components should be analyzed separately for different locations or business units to determine the differing degrees of significance. For example, prepaid

---

Practice Tip

Make sure your scoping analysis looks at the number of transactions as well as the amount of dollars flowing through individual general ledger accounts and locations. Low ending balances due to timing or netting could cause you to overlook significant issues.

---

assets may be significant at one location but low risk and immaterial at another. Therefore, prepaid assets could be in scope at the first location but not at the second. In the same light, prepaid assets may be significant in two different business units, but the component, prepaid advertising, may be significant (and in scope) only at one.

High-Risk Accounts   Most accounts that include estimates or a degree of subjectivity will be considered high risk and should be included in scope. An account may also be considered significant because of its exposure to unrecognized obligations, even if the balance is typically low. For example, loss reserves related to a self-insurance program or unrecorded contractual obligations at a construction contracting business may have been immaterial historically in amount yet might represent a high risk of material misstatement because of possible material unrecorded claims. Remember that you have to analyze the risk of overstatement for certain accounts (such as revenue) as well as the risk of understatement for others (such as loss reserves).

Relevant Assertions and Significant Classes of Transactions

If you have properly established the specific risks for your organization at the entity level, the financial statement account, and the general ledger account levels, you have most likely already reduced the scope and narrowed the focus of your Section 404 process. The next steps are to determine the relevant assertions for each significant account and tie them to the relevant classes of transactions. With a systematic approach, you can select distinct business processes to include and exclude from the project.

Relevant Financial Statement Assertions   *Relevant* assertions are financial statement assertions that have a reasonable possibility of containing a misstatement(s) that would cause a company's financial statements to be materially misstated. For example, valuation may not be relevant to the cash account unless there is a material currency translation; however, existence and completeness are always relevant for cash.

Mapping to Significant Transactions   Once you have determined the relevant assertions for each significant account, you can map them to

Exhibit 6.1   Mapping the Top-Down Approach Sequence to Direction in AS No. 5

Top-Down Approach Sequence	Auditing Standard No. 5 Direction
Using a top-down approach	Paragraph 21
Materiality	Paragraph 20 and AU Sec. 312
Identifying entity-level controls	Paragraphs 22–27
Identify significant accounts and disclosures and their relevant assertions	Paragraphs 28–33
Understanding likely sources of misstatement	Paragraphs 32–40
Identifying controls to test	Paragraphs 39–41

the significant classes of transactions within each business area. Significant classes of transactions are grouped together by type and are referred to as subprocesses in practice. For example, a retail company may have two significant classes of sales transactions: in-store sales and Internet sales.

Think about how significant transactions are initiated, authorized, recorded, processed, and ultimately reported. Understand the flow of transactions, and then identify the points in the process that could cause a financial misstatement due to error or fraud. This will lead to the ultimate goal of determining the key controls necessary to address the possibility of misstatement.

Top-Down Approach Summary from the PCAOB

Since the SEC's Guidance for Management does not address scoping except in broad, risk-based terms, much of your scoping guidance will have to come from the PCAOB's auditing standards. Exhibit 6.1 is a summary of the top-down approach sequence and the related AS No. 5 direction to guide you in your scoping analysis.

METHODS FOR DETERMINING SIGNIFICANT LOCATIONS

In your scoping analysis, you should consider all of the company's locations and business units. As part of management's evaluation of financial reporting risk, you will have to identify which specific locations or business units are subject to Section 404 procedures. This process raised many questions in early years, especially with retailers and other businesses with multiple, same-size locations.

SEC Guidance

The SEC Guidance for Management gives some general advice for multiple location considerations and encourages management to consider whether there are location-specific or pervasive risks that might impact the way controls operate. The SEC gives basic advice for three different scenarios:

1. **Risks are adequately addressed.** Management may determine that financial reporting risks are adequately addressed by controls that operate centrally, in which case the evaluation approach is similar to that of a business with a single location or business unit.

2. **Risk is low.** In situations where management determines that the risk is low that a material misstatement would occur at individual locations or business units, management may determine that evidence gathered through self-assessment routines or other ongoing monitoring activities, when combined with the evidence derived from a centralized control that monitors the results of operations at individual locations, may constitute sufficient evidence for their evaluation.

3. **Risk is high.** In other situations, management may determine that, because of the complexity or judgment in the operation of the controls at the individual location, the risk that controls will fail is high and more evidence is needed about the effective operation of the controls at the location.

The SEC also advises management to consider the different risks for each financial reporting element rather than making a single judgment for all controls at a location. This is consistent with the PCAOB's guidance on locations.

PCAOB Guidance

Refocusing the multilocation testing requirement on risk rather than coverage was one of the biggest changes that was made in AS No. 5. The requirement to test controls over a "large portion" of the company, which was blamed for excessive confusion and costs, has been omitted from the new auditing standard.

Guidance for auditors in AS No. 5 has been scaled down from the guidance originally given in AS No. 2, allowing auditors more flexibility in their approach to multiple location testing. The PCAOB's advice for auditors, which can be considered by management, is summarized in this way:

- The amount of audit attention devoted to a location should correlate to the degree of risk.

- The auditor should test controls over specific risks that present a reasonable possibility of material misstatement to the company's consolidated financial statements.

- Locations or business units that, individually or when aggregated with others, do not present a reasonable possibility of material misstatement to the company's consolidated financial statements can be eliminated from further consideration.

- For lower-risk locations, the auditor first might evaluate whether testing entity-level controls, including controls in place to provide assurance that appropriate controls exist throughout the organization, provides sufficient evidence.

- The auditor should take into account work performed by others on behalf of management, such as internal auditors, to possibly reduce the number of locations where the auditor would otherwise need to perform auditing procedures.

- The auditor should vary the nature, timing, and extent of testing of controls at locations or business units from year to year.

- The auditor should include and consider specific risks at entities that are acquired on or before the date of management's assessment and operations that are accounted for as discontinued operations on the date of management's assessment.

- In situations in which the SEC allows management to limit its assessment of internal control over financial reporting by excluding certain entities, the auditor may limit the internal control audit in the same manner.

Although the guidance from the SEC and PCAOB is more flexible for multiple location testing than it has been in the past, management still needs to come up with a systematic approach for deciding which locations or business units will be covered by its Section 404 procedures. In order for management to feel comfortable with its assessment of internal control, a reasonable amount of financial operations throughout the company will have to be covered. The "large portion" language has been omitted from recent guidance, but the concept is valid.

Practice Tip

Perform a risk assessment for each location or business unit (or group of locations if there are multiple locations) to determine what the specific risks are at each location. Remember to consider entity-level controls in your analysis. Create a systematic approach for the nature, timing, and extent of testing for each risk level. Be sure to show your plan to your auditor for approval.

For example, a high-tech company has five locations with different operations and different risks. The company performed a risk assessment for each location, taking into consideration the materiality of each location's balances and transactions as well as other factors, such as the complexity of the accounting, fraud considerations, and the history of audit adjustments. The company varied its testing approach based on each location's specific risks. The results are summarized in the next table.

Location	Specific Risks	Testing Procedures
1. Corporate	All significant accounts	Perform operational tests for all significant accounts. Test monitoring controls of locations 2 and 3. Test entity-level controls at the location.
2. Business unit	Revenue to cash cycle	Perform operational tests for all revenue to cash key controls at location. Test entity-level controls at the location.
3. Business unit	Intangible	Test key controls surrounding Intangible. Test entity-level controls at the location.
4. Sales office only	Insignificant	Randomly select to test only entity-level controls at the location.
5. Sales office only	Insignificant	No procedures.

Performing a risk assessment can be a bit daunting for multiple locations. AS No. 2 originally included a decision tree developed by the American Institute of Certified Public Accountants to assist companies in their scoping of multiple locations. AS No. 5 omitted the decision tree, presented here as Exhibit 6.2, but it still can be used to assist in the risk assessment process for multiple locations.

Practice Tip

Although not always feasible to implement in the first year of compliance, the most efficiency will be gained by standardizing controls over relevant accounts and transactions at all locations if the company has a large number of individually insignificant locations.

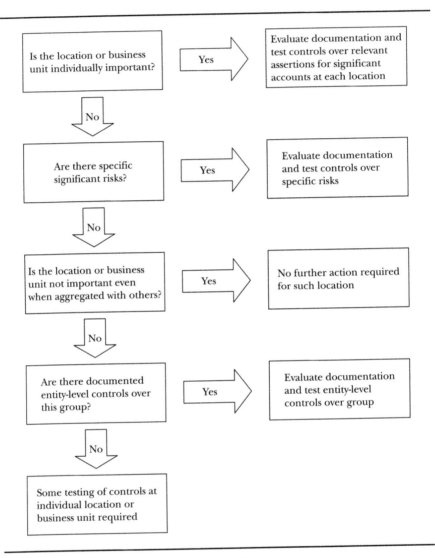

Exhibit 6.2 Multiple Location Testing Considerations

SPECIFIC AREAS INCLUDED AND EXCLUDED BY THE PCAOB

To assist in the scoping analysis, the PCAOB has issued guidance giving clarity to what should be included in Section 404 programs. The PCAOB stated that all information in the company's consolidated financial statements, including statements and footnotes, should be included in management's assessment of its internal controls. Yet there are other areas typically included with the financial statements and certain transactions that do not require assessment.

Supplementary Information

According to the SEC Staff, financial statement schedules required by Regulation S-X and supplementary disclosures required by the Financial Accounting Standards Board (FASB) "need not be encompassed in management's assessment of internal control over financial reporting until such time that the Commission has completed its evaluation of this area and issues new rules addressing such requirements."

Earnings Releases and MD&A

The PCAOB has determined that earnings releases, management's discussion and analysis (MD&A), or other financial information presented outside of the company's financial statements and disclosures are excluded from Section 404 procedures. See the PCAOB Staff Q&A, Q5, for additional guidance.

Newly Acquired Entities

The SEC will not object to the exclusion of purchased business combinations that were acquired within one year of the as-of date. (The one-year exclusion begins on the closing date of the combination.) The purchased business combination may not be omitted from more than one annual management report on internal control over financial reporting. Requirements for the acquired "business" are described in Article 11-01(d) of Regulation S-X.

If you choose to exclude a newly acquired business, you must disclose the exclusion along with the significance of the new business to the consolidated financial statements. Management should refer in its report on internal control over financial reporting to a disclosure in the body of the Form 10-K regarding the scope of the assessment. In addition, the company must disclose any material change to its internal control over financial reporting due to the acquisition.

Keep in mind that the controls around purchase accounting may be included in scope for qualitative reasons even if the controls of the acquired business are not.

Consolidated and Proportionately Consolidated Entities

The evaluation of the company's internal control over financial reporting usually includes controls over significant accounts and processes that exist at all consolidated or proportionately consolidated entities. If you have the right to audit, your auditor will most likely assume you have the right to assess controls under Section 404. Management should include entities in scope if it can assess controls, even if it cannot remediate those controls.

According to the SEC Staff in its *Management's Report on Internal Control over Financial Reporting and Certification of Disclosure in Exchange*

Act Periodic Reports Frequently Asked Questions (revised October 6, 2004), an exception can be made when management is not able to obtain the information necessary to make an assessment of an entity's internal controls because it does not have the ability (legally or in practice) to control the entity. Disclosure is required for entities excluded from scope because the company does not have the right to assess controls. These three criteria must be met to exclude a consolidated entity:

1. The entity was in existence prior to December 15, 2003.

2. The entity is consolidated by virtue of Interpretation No. 46 (i.e., would not have been consolidated in the absence of application of that guidance).

3. The registrant does not have the right or authority to assess the internal controls of the consolidated entity and also lacks the ability, in practice, to make that assessment.

Management's report on ICFR should provide disclosure in the body of its Form 10-K (or 10-KSB) regarding entities that are not included in the assessment. For example, the company could refer readers to a discussion of the scope of management's report on ICFR in a section of the annual report entitled "Scope of Management's Report on Internal Control over Financial Reporting."

The disclosure in Form 10-K is required in each filing and should include these points:

- The company has not evaluated the internal controls of the entity.

- The company's conclusion regarding the effectiveness of its internal control over financial reporting does not extend to the internal controls of the entity.

- Any key subtotals should be disclosed, such as total net assets, revenues, and net income that result from the consolidation of entities whose internal controls have not been assessed.

- A discussion that the financial statements include the accounts of certain entities consolidated pursuant to FIN (FASB Interpretation Number) 46 or accounted for via proportionate consolidation in accordance with EITF (Emerging Issues Task Force) 00-1, but management has been unable to assess the effectiveness of internal control at those entities. Further discussion could explain that the registrant does not have the ability to dictate or modify the controls of the entities and does not have the ability, in practice, to assess those controls.

Expect your auditor to evaluate and challenge the reasonableness of management's conclusion that it does *not* have the ability to obtain the necessary information as well as the appropriateness of any required disclosure related to the limitation.

If management is allowed to limit its assessment by excluding such entities, your external auditor is allowed to limit the audit in the same manner and report without reference to the limitation in scope. Although neither needs to report a limitation in scope, both need to disclose the exclusion. However, controls over the reporting of the company's portion of the entity's income or loss, the investment balance, adjustments to the income or loss, and investment balances and related disclosures should generally be included in scope.

Equity Method Investments

Internal controls at equity method investment companies are generally not in scope for your Section 404 project. However, controls for properly recording the company's equity investments according to generally accepted accounting principles (GAAP) will usually be included in your Section 404 procedures. Accordingly, you should consider, among other things, the controls over the selection of accounting methods for the investments, the recognition of equity method earnings and losses, and the investment account balance. The company might require that, at least annually, any equity method investees provide audited financial statements as a control over the recognition of equity method earnings and losses.

Although not required, nothing precludes you from evaluating the controls over financial reporting within an equity method investment. There may be circumstances where it is not only appropriate (e.g., the company is comprised solely of a few such investments) but also the most effective form of evaluation.

PCAOB AND SEC GUIDANCE ON OTHER COMMON SCOPING ISSUES

Countless unique situations may arise while performing your scoping analysis. As a general rule, you should analyze, document, and convey (to your external auditor) all unique scoping decisions. Refer to the listed guidance for several common situations that affect scoping:

- Implementation of a new accounting system: PCAOB Staff Q&A, Q6

- What is tested at significant locations?: PCAOB Staff Q&A, Q16

- When a company has a large number of individually insignificant locations: PCAOB Staff Q&A, Q18

- Excluding certain entities from the scope of Section 404 assessments: PCAOB Staff Q&A, Q19; SEC Staff's FAQs dated June 23, 2004, Q1 and Q 3

- External auditors' use of internal audit for their audit of internal controls: PCAOB Staff Q&A, Q36 and AS No. 5, paragraphs 16–19

- Auditor's assessment of risk and its effect on the amount of work: PCAOB Staff Q&A, Q40

- Qualitative factors and assessment of risk in identifying significant accounts: PCAOB Staff Q&A, Q41

TIPS FOR RESOURCE PLANNING AND DEVELOPING USEFUL TIMELINES

Once you have performed your initial scoping analysis to determine which areas are significant for your Section 404 program, you have a tool to create a preliminary schedule for the year. Section 404 projects require a large time commitment and generally take more time than expected, especially in the first year of compliance. Timelines for the entire program, from the beginning to analyzing deficiencies after year-end, should be developed annually. Not only do you have to manage your own schedule tightly, but you must coordinate your schedule with your external auditor because he or she has little time to complete the financial and internal control audits at year-end.

Practice Tip

At the end of the year, integrate your timeline with your external auditor's timeline. If timing is an issue, provide a control-by-control schedule (i.e., testing complete for Accounts Payable controls 1-10 by January 10) for the period after year-end, and be sure all deadlines are met.

Be realistic about your timeline and always include a buffer when possible. In general, documentation, testing, and remediation take longer than expected. There is no benefit to setting a schedule if deadlines are constantly pushed back.

Practice Tip

Avoid Section 404 procedures during the monthly and quarterly close periods. You will not be very productive, and employees may resent the distraction during their busy times.

Resource Needs

After your scoping analysis is complete, make a list of all business cycles that will be covered in your Section 404 project. Typically, each person on the Section 404 team can manage two to five cycles, depending on the size of the company and the number and complexity of significant subprocesses within each cycle. Try to match large cycles with small cycles. Take into account the size of your project, whether it is your first year of compliance, and whether team members will have other, non-Section 404 responsibilities. Finally, make a preliminary estimate of how many people you will need on your Section 404 team and staff up.

Practice Tip

Do not underestimate the IT cycle, which can be the most challenging. If your IT department is large or decentralized, consider assigning separate facilitators for infrastructure and applications.

SOX Training

Whether company employees or consultants are working on your Section 404 program, process owners should understand the meaning of a control, how it will be tested, why it is being tested, and the overall goal of the company's Section 404 program. If employees are performing the work, they must learn how to document and test the controls using proper descriptions and work papers. Although it seems surprising to most certified public accountants, professional skepticism and attention to detail are not innate.

Practice Tip

Hold regular training sessions to teach employees how to properly document a control, test it, obtain and describe adequate sample sizes, and write work papers with the details that are needed.

7

Advantageous Project Management Techniques

Key Topics:
- Areas to keep you focused for the second year and beyond
- Using a sound management approach to increase productivity
- Project management tips
- Staffing strategies
- Sustainable organizational charts for Section 404 teams
- Communicating effectively through emails, meetings, and advisories
- Identifying and addressing changes for Section 302 purposes

In year one of Sarbanes-Oxley (SOX) Section 404 compliance, the message for Section 404 teams was "just get it done." In the second year and beyond, the message has changed to "get it done right." Efficiencies in the planning, documentation, testing, remediation, and evaluation areas will come from strong management skills. Advice from auditors and industry leaders is to move SOX compliance to a process instead of a project mentality. This is true; SOX compliance needs to become a permanent part of process owners' day-to-day responsibilities and something that is expected as part of their job. It is not a one-time project. Most companies will have to manage SOX compliance as a year-round program that is headed by a compliance officer, SOX manager, or an existing finance employee and monitored by internal audit or management and the audit committee.

Process owners will have ideas on how to make documenting and testing their controls more efficient. Who better to suggest methods to streamline documentation and testing or even improve the performance of actual controls?

Practice Tip

Create an employee reward program for suggestions on improving controls
or efficiencies for documenting or testing controls. Process owners are often
the best source of knowledge for enhancing their own controls.

Although process owners can provide feedback and improvement
for controls in their area, the program team, internal audit, or compliance
manager generally will be the one(s) to create efficiencies for the program
as a whole. A person who can see the big picture is needed to advance the
planning, scoping, monitoring, evaluating, and testing processes. This
chapter presents concepts and actual plans for upgrading your Section 404
project (process) from just getting it done to getting it done right.

11 AREAS OF FOCUS FOR THE SECOND YEAR AND BEYOND

If you are an accelerated filer, the first-year fire drill is over and quality,
consistency, and efficiency is the focus for your program. Because there may
have been multiple people from different sources working on the project,
consistency may be an issue. Band-Aids may have been applied in the initial rush that can now be replaced by a more permanent solution. A list of
11 items that your SOX team can focus on for the future follows.

1. Is the documentation consistent? Are the formats, writing style, fonts,
   and quality the same for all processes?

2. Are the controls in place the best ones to mitigate the risk of financial statement misstatement? Are the controls being performed in the
   most efficient manner? Can some of them be automated?

3. Do you have the optimal number of key controls? Are there duplicates
   or complementary controls that can be made nonkey?

4. Are there too many processes in scope?

5. Are remediation plans sustainable? Did the remediation really mitigate the risk, or was it just a quick fix?

6. Do you have the best possible testing process? Does the testing schedule fit in to the company's operating plan?

7. Do employees need more or updated training?

8. Are you satisfied with the company's Section 404 software? Does it
   have the capabilities and reporting functions that you need? If you

are using spreadsheets, are they the best way to document controls, testing, and remediation?

9. Has your SOX team kept up to date on all the new guidance related to the Sarbanes-Oxley Act?

10. Are there ways to improve the return on investment (ROI) on your SOX investment? Can the documentation and testing be used for other purposes such training, quality assurance (QA), International Standards Organization (ISO), or other compliance?

11. How will changes in the business be addressed for SOX Sections 302 and 404 compliance?

Each one of these issues can be a source of waste in time, energy, and money for your company. Solving these problems could save thousands of dollars and give your company the best ROI for its Section 404 program.

HOW TO INCREASE PRODUCTIVITY WITH A SOUND MANAGEMENT APPROACH

Finishing the Section 404 work in time for management to attest on the effectiveness of its internal controls was an accomplishment itself in the initial year of compliance. The amount of time and resources Section 404 devoured shook most companies to the core. Even small companies that devoted one or two people to Section 404 work used a proportionally large amount of resources to ensure compliance. Documentation, testing, and remediation efforts often encroached on employees who had little capacity to absorb additional work.

For a good laugh (perhaps only those directly related with Section 404 compliance will laugh), refer to the Securities and Exchange Commission's (SEC's) Total Annual Burden estimate for the total annual incremental burden for annual and quarterly reports associated with the new internal control evaluation and disclosure requirements. It states that the SEC estimates the aggregate annual costs of implementing SOX Section 404(a) to be around $1.24 billion, or *$91,000 per company*.[1] (The estimate assumes a 75%/25% split between internal staff and external professionals and an hourly rate of $200 for internal staff and $300 for external staff.) Many companies will require substantial improvements and efficiencies to approach that estimate.

To reduce the amount of time and money spent on SOX compliance, project managers and their teams will have to change the way they view the program. It is important to remember the purpose of Section 404 compliance. Focus on management's opinion of its internal controls and the evaluation that will lead to the ultimate conclusion.

In the first year of compliance, many companies used a bottom-up approach and spent a great deal of resources on documenting controls.

Documentation is only a tool to understand the processes and controls within a company; it is not the goal for the year. Time and money should be spent accordingly.

The same goal-oriented concept can be applied to testing. Testing is time consuming and expensive, and it leads directly to management's ultimate opinion. However, it is still a mere tool to help management achieve its goal.

However, planning, remediation, and the final evaluation are essential pieces of your program and should receive a larger portion of your time and energy. Effective planning and remediation could also reduce the resources needed for documentation and testing.

Planning sets the stage for your Section 404 program for the entire year. A full project plan should be developed early in the year with planning updates performed throughout the year.

Remediation of ineffective controls is critical to the success of your project. Implementation of new or remediated controls is a lengthy process, and new controls must be effective for a considerable length of time to provide adequate sample sizes. A common mistake is to allow too little time to put new or remediated controls in place. In the past, this often led to implementation of poorly designed or temporary controls that had to be revamped the following year. Be sure new or remediated controls are well thought out and that you have involved the right people from the troubled area in the remediation process. Find out why the deficiency exists and what the deficiency could mean on a company-wide level. Obtain financial manager and process owner input on the best way to address their ineffective control(s). Process owners may need your guidance or suggestions to develop well-designed controls, but they usually can tell you what will and will not work in their area and why.

The last essential pieces of your project are the evaluation of deficiencies and forming management's opinion. Take the time to have the right people involved in the final evaluation, such as employees from internal audit, legal, financial reporting, and key operational areas. Brainstorm about compensating controls and the likelihood and magnitude of financial statement misstatements because of ineffective controls.

The goal of the project is for management to give an opinion on its internal controls. Documentation and testing are steps that are taken to come to that conclusion. Do not allow the same mentality that was used in the past dictate how you plan and budget your Section 404 program in the future. Spend less time and resources on documentation and testing and more on planning, remediation, and evaluation.

AIM FOR THE TARGET INSTEAD OF THE WAY TO GET THERE

The goal-oriented concept coincides with the idea of not being caught up in the process. Focus on the deliverables first and then on a way to get there.

Have you ever met people who work hard and put in long hours but cannot complete tasks on time? They always seem to be at their desk with their head down, work weekends and come in early, but deadlines elude them. These people are probably process oriented and focus on the road instead of the destination.

Practice Tip

Whether in a meeting or setting a deadline, first focus on the purpose of your task. What is going to be accomplished, and when? What are the deliverables? A discussion or thought process to describe the ways to get there can follow once the goals have been established.

By using a goal-oriented approach at a pricing meeting, for example, with directors from marketing, product management, and sales, the leader announces that the goal of the meeting is to agree on a new pricing structure and decide how it will be communicated to the rest of the company. During the meeting, deliverables are assigned to the director of product management to create a new price list based on the agreed-on structure and to the director of marketing to draft a memo for all employees explaining the new price list and its effective date. Both deliverables are due at the follow-up meeting scheduled in one week to review the results.

You can manage your Section 404 program using this method by focusing first on the objective for each phase of the project (such as planning, documentation, testing, etc.). Then you can focus on the final goal of management's assessment.

Specific Goals for Each Phase of the Project

- *What is the goal of planning?*

  o To properly include and exclude the appropriate locations, accounts, and disclosures from the scope of your program

  o To adequately plan for resources

  o To time the project to be complete 30 days after year-end

  o To reduce the number of key controls to the appropriate level

  o To save time and money

- *What is the goal of documentation?*

  o To describe in detail the key controls and processes surrounding significant accounts, disclosures, and locations

- *What is the goal of testing?*

  o To determine if the company's key internal controls are adequately designed and operating effectively

- *What is the goal of remediation?*

  o To implement new controls for gaps around key processes that will reduce the risk of misstatement in the consolidated financial statements

  o To correct and improve ineffective controls that could cause a misstatement of the consolidated financial statements

- *What is the goal of evaluation?*

  o To determine if management's internal controls are effective

Often managers get caught up in day-to-day duties and forget why they are documenting and testing controls. In other words, they cannot see the forest for the trees. It is easy to be caught up in the detail because the project is so big and involves so many details. Nonetheless, by concentrating on the purpose behind the process, energies and resources will be sent in the right direction.

Steps for Using a Goal-Oriented Management Approach

The goal-oriented philosophy can also be used to manage your team. Many people respond well to having a specific goal due on a specific day and having the freedom to choose how to accomplish the goal. This approach is especially effective when working with a group of professionals. However, this does not mean you communicate the goal, close your eyes, and hope for the best on the due date. A goal-oriented approach requires monitoring, follow-up, problem solving, and review of preliminary work as the project progresses. Setting mini- and intermediate goals along the way to the final goal is a good way to ensure your team stays on schedule.

The essential elements for a goal-oriented management approach are:

- Give adequate time to complete the goal.

- Clearly communicate the goal and the due date. Make sure everyone is aware of what is due when.

- Give clear instructions on all requirements needed to complete the goal.

- Think about consistency. A paper, presentation, or project with multiple participants is bound to look jumbled and inconsistent if attention is not given to coherence.

- Explain your expectations for quality.

- Set small goals along the way to the final goal.
- Monitor your team's progress. Small issues can become big problems if not addressed early.
- Compliment and reward your team when they accomplish a goal on time.

Case Study of a Goal-Oriented Management Approach

As an example of the elements of a goal-oriented management approach, assume you have three new locations that are in scope for your current-year Section 404 program. You are about to assign the responsibility for documentation of these new locations to three staff-level internal auditors who did some SOX testing in the prior year (so they have some audit and SOX experience but are still relatively new). The steps for a goal-oriented approach are summarized next.

- **Communicate goal and due date.** The goal is to have the narratives and control matrices complete by May 31.
- **Adequate time.** You assign one location to each of your three people, and explain that they have five weeks to create documentation for all significant processes at each location.
- **Clear instruction.** You give them a copy of the preliminary scoping analysis that has been performed for each location listing the significant processes and accounts based on quantitative factors. You instruct them to start with interviews and walk-throughs of the areas to gain an understanding of the business and its key processes, writing notes and descriptions to eventually be developed into narratives. Next, they are to meet with a senior finance, operations, and sales manager to discuss the specific risks that apply to their location. After identifying the risks, they can create a control matrix to include the risks for each significant area in the business and the related key control activities. After they have drafted the preliminary control matrix, they should check to make sure all relevant assertions are covered for each subprocess and then review the matrix with the process owners and managers of the specific areas. Once the control matrix is complete, they should revisit the draft narratives, inserting the key control activities into the text and refining the descriptions.
- **Expectations for quality.** You tell them your expectations of detailed control activities, listing the specifics of who, what, how often, and what evidence for each control. Narratives should include robust descriptions of key processes explaining complexities and controls. You review a sample narrative to verify the degree of detail needed.

- **Consistency.** You also expect each key control to be noted in the narrative in bold font and show them examples of the control matrix and narrative formats to use. You follow up by emailing them copies of the sample control matrix and narratives.

- **Monitor.** During the five weeks, you stop by to chat with each person at least twice a week to check on their progress, answer any questions, and address any problems.

- **Small Goals.** You tell them you will meet on April 30 to check on their status and review their initial narratives. On May 10 you will meet to review and advise them on the risks. By this meeting, they should have already met with the managers from finance, operations, and sales to gain their input on the risks. On May 20 you will meet with them to review their control matrix and key control activities. By this meeting they should have already analyzed the relevant assertions and reviewed the key controls with the process owners and managers. Finally, you will meet on May 31, when they will turn in their narratives and control matrix.

- **Compliment.** At the June internal audit department meeting, you publicly acknowledge their contribution to the project, noting individual attributes displayed by each person.

For some people, this style may seem overbearing with too much micromanaging. This is an active management technique, but over the five-week period, you are formally meeting with the staff five times and informally speaking with them twice a week. The weekly chats are important to get a feel for how your people are doing and to jump on any issues as they arise. Asking questions and discussing the tasks on a regular basis will allow your team to express their concerns and questions right away. The informal chats can help avoid surprises near the due date.

The scheduled meetings are an integral part of managing because it is beneficial to see the product as it is being developed. Also, it is not unusual for certain people to tell you all is well during the assignment, only to find they did not follow the instructions and have an inferior product that is not complete on the due date.

Keep in mind that not all people will need the same assistance. Some will be able and content to work on their own with minimal monitoring and produce great results. Others may struggle with quality and meeting deadlines. Good managers can read their people and determine who needs extra oversight and who does not.

Whatever your management style, focusing on the goal instead of the process in each phase of your Section 404 program will help you achieve your ultimate objective.

MORE PROJECT MANAGEMENT TIPS

The sections that follow include quick ideas to help manage any project successfully.

Avoid Analysis Paralysis

Gathering and analyzing information before making decisions is a good practice. But there comes a time for action when a decision has to be made and an action plan developed. Overanalyzing issues and putting off decisions will cause you to lose momentum. There is more time to analyze in the planning and documentation phases, but as the project nears completion, decisions have to be made more quickly. While snap decisions are not optimal, analysis paralysis will have you missing deadlines and scrambling at year-end.

Keep It Simple

There often is no need for complex controls and solutions. Simplify when possible.

Delegate

Any task that is repetitive can most likely be delegated. For example, it is not necessary for top-level managers to hold meetings. Hosting meetings is a repetitive task that can be delegated to a middle manager. The planning, scheduling, and preparing agendas for meetings can take several hours. Depending on the size of your department, the second, third, or fourth person in command can be responsible for holding meetings. This person would still be at a high enough level to know the issues that require discussion and could consult with you on the agenda to ensure all relevant topics are addressed. In addition, it might be a type of reward for up-and-coming managers to display their leadership skills in front of an entire department.

Match the Tasks to the Position

Consider adding lower and midlevel accounting staff to take over the more mundane tasks that your higher-level managers perform. For every task that a high-level manager performs, ask yourself, "Is this something a person making X dollars per hour should be doing?" Can another person making less per hour perform this task? If your managers are getting bogged down with administrative work, a department administrative assistant making $10 to $20 per hour may be more economical than hiring another manager.

Prepare Only Those Documents Required for the Engagement

Review your Section 404 documentation for redundancy and necessity. Because of the lack of guidance in years past, many companies prepared unnecessary supplemental information. For example, duplicate efforts commonly involve preparing flowcharts and narratives to document processes. Most auditors will accept flowcharts *or* narratives as long as they are detailed and complete. Be sure to stay focused on the explicit requirements, and do not prepare documents merely because they were prepared in the past.

Put Blackout Periods into Effect for Fourth-Quarter Material Changes

Fourth-quarter changes to computer systems or financial processes can be difficult to deal with from a SOX perspective. Narrative/flowcharts and control matrices will have to be updated and controls successfully tested, all within a three-month period. If remediation is involved, you could be stuck with a possible significant deficiency or material weakness late in the year. For these reasons, implementing new financial information technology (IT) systems or making material changes to control processes should be strictly monitored during the last three months of the year. Require a designated SOX team member to approve new systems or processes to be implemented near year-end.

Too Many Hands in the Pot

The more people who have to agree on a decision, the more difficult it is to come to a conclusion. It is important to make sure the "right" people, both politically and operationally, are involved in crucial decisions. However, when too many people are involved in the decision-making process, it can be a showstopper. This problem is seen often in small, growing companies; senior management is used to being involved in all types of decisions. As the company grows, those same senior managers are reluctant to give up their involvement in decision making. Try to keep decision making reserved for those directly affected. Decisions will be too drawn out if management outside the accountable area is routinely consulted. If other departments must be consulted before a decision is made, put a deadline on their input or invite them to the decision-making meeting. Once the decision is made, be sure to communicate it to all relevant employees.

Integrating Section 404 Compliance with Human Resource Policies

To be successful, SOX compliance should be embedded in employees' day-to-day responsibilities. Consider including SOX responsibilities in employee job descriptions or tying a portion of employee bonuses to SOX duties. Include a SOX memo as part of the human resource (HR) package new employees receive on their first day. The memo could give a short background on the act and explain the company's philosophy on compliance. By integrating SOX requirements with HR policies, compliance can become an expected part of all employees' jobs.

Use Some Executive Muscle

Getting people to do things they do not want to do can be difficult but if you are managing a Section 404 program, it is something that you will probably do frequently. Changing processes often means changing ingrained habits. Trying to motivate people to change their habits can be frustrating, especially if you are a consultant. Why should people listen to you? Most employees will not be confrontational, but they may fail to make a new control a priority, causing delays and setbacks. Many times you must find something to motivate people to change. Enlisting the help of an executive, such as the chief financial officer (CFO) or chief executive officer (CEO), usually does the trick. In many cases, you will not have to recruit the help of an executive. A process owner's manager may be able to motivate an employee to change a habit when you cannot.

Changing policies and controls can be political, but do not overuse your executive ally or she may become resistant. Try to implement new policies and controls with your own resources, saving executive muscle for the critical situations.

Train Process Owners on How to Speak to Auditors

Be sure to educate process owners on what to expect and how to communicate with your external auditors. You may find that people who do not deal with auditors regularly are often nervous about talking to them. Instruct them to be truthful, to the point, and not to deviate from the topic being discussed. They need to know that speaking to the auditors is not a time to vent, have other agendas, or speak of areas for which they do not have knowledge.

Repairing the Relationship with Your External Auditors

Year one brought controversy and confrontation that often tore apart solid business relationships between companies and their external auditors. Now that the drama is over, it is time to repair the damaged relationship; but putting months of disagreements behind you may be awkward. Do not underestimate the face-to-face factor. It is easier to build a rapport with people when they can see you and shake your hand. Email, voicemail, and telephone calls can be easily misconstrued and do not build as strong a relationship.

Finally, if you know you will continue to have disagreements with your auditors but want to maintain a solid relationship, consider splitting the tough negotiations and other auditor interactions tasks among different members of the team. One member of the team can disagree and negotiate the controversial issues while another maintains a strong rapport. This way, you can still take a hard stance on issues while not ostracizing your auditors.

STAFFING STRATEGIES

Most people in the auditing industry have heard the phrase that the Sarbanes-Oxley Act is more like the CPA (certified public accountant) employment act. Retaining or obtaining quality audit and accounting staff has been a challenge for most since SOX came into practice.

Employee Ownership and Staffing

The main staffing questions for a Section 404 program are how many people will you need to complete the project on time and which people will you use. In your program's initial years, the best results may have come from using a combination of consultants, internal auditors, and other employees. With the proper tone at the top, most employees will embrace your Section 404 work.

Section 404 programs typically are successful when a program team facilitates the work and business units take ownership for their own documentation, testing, and remediation of controls. You may find initial resistance from some employees to Section 404 work because it is not fun, exciting, or easy. Many employees may already be working at full capacity and may feel that the internal audit department or consultants are responsible for compliance work. However, the project is destined to fail if process owners do not take responsibility for their controls. Internal audit, the SOX team, or consultants can facilitate the Section 404 effort, but they do not have ownership of the processes being scrutinized.

Using Champions to Promote Employee Ownership

Regardless of the size of the company, consider assigning a champion to each significant cycle. The champion would be the person in charge of Sections 404 and 302 compliance in the area and would be the SOX team's contact.

Practice Tip

For each significant business process, assign champions who are responsible for all project coordination, deadlines, and deliverables. Champions should have authority in their departments and are most successful when they are at the director level or above. Involving high-level employees in your program sends the right message to the company. It tells process owners that Section 404 work is valued.

In a larger company, champions may not document and test controls but oversee the effort, ensuring it is given the priority it requires. In a smaller company, the champion may do it all, from documentation and testing to remediation and communicating with the program team.

Champions should know the time commitment required for each step of the program so they can adequately plan and meet their deadlines. Ample resources need to be deployed to ensure deadlines are met and testing and remediation efforts are successful.

Practice Tip

Consider adding administrative support to relieve employees of the considerable data entry and clerical tasks of the project. It is more cost effective to have an hourly employee complete these tasks instead of a well-paid manager, and it will improve morale.

Middle management is typically forgotten in the topic of program support. Executive commitment is important because it promotes the proper tone at the top that is needed to make your program a success. Process owners play an important role as well because they are the ones who perform the controls. However, middle management support is vital to meet deadlines, enforce new processes, and make sure controls are operating consistently. Without their support, process owners may not perform up to standard, causing the program to fail.

Getting the Most Out of Internal Resources

Many employees do not want to do SOX for a living or remain in the SOX program in year two (and beyond). Morale for internal auditors can be low because of the stringent nature of SOX compliance. The thrill of the first year compliance is over for accelerated filers.

Practice Tip

Resources are tight for quality accounting and audit staff; make sure the SOX team and internal auditors are adequately paid and have sufficient perks when it comes to vacations, time off, educational assistance, continuing education, and professional fees. Professionals who work long hours generally value time off and training.

When employees with SOX experience are ready to move away from internal audit or the SOX team, they can be rotated or placed within business units as assistant controllers, directors of finance, or other key accounting and finance positions. Their compliance experience will permeate the organization wherever they are placed.

A rotational program within the organization can be one answer to assist with scarce internal audit and SOX resources. It can also help employee morale, keep team members fresh, and provide excellent training for finance and accounting employees.

Practice Tip

Consider implementing an internal rotational program for finance and accounting employees where personnel work with internal audit or the SOX team for six months or more. Employees and the company will benefit from a well-rounded training program, and hard-to-staff compliance departments will have more resources readily available.

One area of caution for rotational programs: Although employees should have a dotted line back to their original department supervisor, they must report to a new supervisor while they are in a new department. Employees cannot be expected to keep their regular responsibilities or duties from earlier rotations while being rotated to a new area.

Be sure to recognize the SOX staff that remains in the program when they deserve it. Improvements to processes and maintaining compliance are usually not rewarded like initial implementation of processes, even if the initial process was substandard. Just as process owners should be rewarded for improvements to controls, the SOX team should be recognized for reduced costs, increased efficiency, and continued compliance.

Process Owners as Testers   In the first year of compliance, centralized teams often performed control tests because of the deadlines and because they often had audit experience. The trend for the future is to train process owners to think like auditors and give them ownership of control testing. Although teaching process owners concepts like professional skepticism and conservatism may require ongoing training, having employees perform control testing gives them a better understanding of the business and builds testing directly into routine job responsibilities. It also can be used as a way to build career paths or resource backup into different positions within the organization. Management may have to consider whether SOX staff will stay with the company if they have to do all the testing.

One high-tech company with over 8,000 employees and multiple business units has a SOX team made up of 4 employees and 3 consultants to facilitate the company's testing requirements. Over 80 employees are used to perform SOX testing, and 4 additional consultants are brought in for specialized areas, such as tax and IT or to plug any holes. Employees are exchanged between departments and business units to increase tester independence.

To Use or Not to Use Internal Audit for SOX Compliance   In the past, internal audit departments were commonly used to manage Section 404 projects. The internal audit function was put on hold while resources were shifted to SOX documentation and testing. It made sense at the time because these employees were usually qualified to head the project, drawing on their experience monitoring policies and procedures, performing risk assessments, and carrying out investigations. Internal auditors generally had the audit background and were independent.

While internal audit was busy with the demands of initial compliance, investigations ceased, monitoring diminished, and internal audit was no longer challenging policies and procedures. Having a separate team manage Section 404 (and 302) compliance allows the internal audit group to preserve its traditional role and enhances the monitoring component for the (Committee of Sponsoring Organizations, COSO) entity-wide controls. Although large companies may have the luxury of having an internal audit team and SOX program team, smaller companies may have only one or two people performing both functions.

Small-Company Staffing Ideas

Smaller public companies may be wondering if they really need a SOX person to head their Section 404 compliance, or if Section 404 compliance can be absorbed by someone else within the organization. While there are certainly some smaller companies that successfully complied with Section 404 by using the controller or other existing employee to head the project, it is not the best-case scenario for these reasons:

- The person to lead the Section 404 project should have an audit background to be able to understand concepts such as materiality, financial statement assertions, and financial reporting risks. He or she will also understand the documentation and work paper requirements for testing and may be able to anticipate many of your external auditor's decisions related to Section 404.

- Although the controller or other top financial manager may have the background and experience to manage the SOX program successfully, this person often has a full plate and does not have the time to devote to Section 404 compliance.

- SOX compliance is a specialized area that requires keeping up to date on new guidance and requires experience and planning to increase efficiencies. Existing employees may not be able to keep current on new standards, have the specialized knowledge, or manage compliance efforts efficiently.

If your company is not large enough to employ a full-time SOX person or does not have the expertise in-house, consider hiring a consultant who can help with your compliance and internal audit work as needed.

When and Where to Use Consultants

Because SOX compliance is a specialized area, it lends itself to the use of consultants. Consultants are best used when employees do not have the time or knowledge to keep up with the demands of Section 404. They can also be used to supplement internal audit or in-house SOX teams and can be hired and fired as needed, addressing the cyclical nature of Section 404 work. Because of the shortage of qualified staff, employees' distaste for Section 404 work, and the current job market for auditors, many companies will require some type of assistance with their program. A list of areas that lend themselves to the efficient use of consultants follows.

- If you do not have a qualified resource in-house, you may want to hire a consultant to lead the project. Consultants who do SOX compliance for a living should be up to date on new guidance and should have experienced several different scenarios for completing scoping, documentation, and testing. Be sure to manage the consultant well and make sure he or she is meeting deadlines and adhering to the company's standards and culture. For example, does the company have a passive relationship with the external auditors where you agree to most of their requests, or is it a more confrontational relationship often riddled with disagreement and debate? Be sure your consultant understands this philosophy and fits in.

- You can use consultants for quality assurance purposes. Most SOX consultants have worked with a variety of external auditors and have a good understanding of the expected standards for documentation of processes, testing, scoping, and management's final conclusion. Using consultants in a quality assurance capacity is the best of both worlds. Process owners still perform the bulk of the work, which saves costs and provides ownership, but consultants are used for their expertise to ensure that your program has the desired quality.

- Consultants can be used for Section 404 work in international locations for their language or interpretation skills. In addition, they can be sent to different sites without causing a hole in your internal audit or finance staff for weeks at a time.

- Areas that fall behind often need more resources that are not always available in-house. Consultants with Section 404 experience often can bring these areas up to speed or put them back on track.

- Consultants can be used for specialized areas such as tax, IT, or the COSO/entity-level controls, when in-house resources do not have the specialized knowledge required. Documentation, analysis, and remediation can require a thorough understanding of these areas to be effective.

- Training can be performed by consultants when in-house staff lacks the knowledge or experience. Consultants can provide training on new pronouncements or guidance and can be used to train the trainer.

- Consultants can be brought in to supplement your internal team during busy times. Many companies do not have the extra staff to devote to several weeks of testing two, three, or four times a year. Consultants can ease the burden during the busy periods and be released as the workload diminishes. They are the answer to the cyclical nature of an annual SOX project. As an added benefit, the level of independence increases when testing is performed by outside consultants.

- A fresh perspective from consultants who do not know your company operations as well as the employees creating the control activities can provide a reasonableness check on the number of key controls or a gap analysis.

There are many specialized areas where consultants can supplement your staff in your Section 404 program. Know exactly what you want them to do. Process owners still need to feel they own their controls but do not always have the time to dedicate to Section 404 work. With the deadline-intensive nature of SOX compliance, consultants often must be used to pick up the slack.

To Firm or Not to Firm

Because of the shortage of auditors since the inception of Section 404 compliance, consulting firms, external audit firms, and private companies have been fighting over scarce resources. Some firms have lowered their standards, especially in certain geographic locations, or have had to transfer staff from faraway cities because of the lack of qualified personnel in their areas. Consultant travel costs can be expensive. No one consulting firm will have all good people. Many times the important decision is not the firm that you chose but the person or people that will work on your program from that firm. Not all of them are stars.

Practice Tip

When hiring a consulting firm, ask to interview the actual consultants who will be working on your job. Use word of mouth to find quality consultants and consider using independents with a good reputation. Independents are often less expensive and good enough to make it on their own.

RESTRUCTURING THE ORGANIZATIONAL CHART FOR SUSTAINABILITY

Very few people would argue that executive management has to embrace Section 404 compliance in order to obtain positive fiscal results. Although CFOs and CEOs were often involved directly in the first year of compliance, many companies are moving toward a more suitable structure for the future. Whether large or small, companies will need a permanent SOX presence to lead their compliance.

Who headed (or will head) your SOX project in year one? Was it a controller or internal auditor? Is this the person who should head your Section 404 program in the future?

Now that the dust is settling, companies are finding a more permanent home and rightful owner for their SOX program. Many companies have a risk or compliance officer responsible for SOX compliance, while some have the program under internal audit. Company size and industry seem to dictate where SOX compliance is placed. Many small and medium-size companies do not have a risk or compliance officer unless they are in a highly regulated industry.

In any case, it is important to have a SOX leader, whether a manager, director, vice president, or officer, to guide the program throughout the year and a separate person or team to monitor the program, such as internal audit or the CFO. These positions can be new or rolled into existing positions at the company. It is important that the person leading your SOX program be the appropriate person; at a medium or large company, it is probably not the controller or chief counsel.

Large and Medium-Size Companies

When discussing Section 404 compliance with a medium or large company, you are really talking about a SOX team that is active and dedicated throughout the year. Some level of a permanent compliance team must continuously assess the company's scoping, business structure, and internal environment. This team would be responsible for keeping up to date on changes in the laws and new guidance, coordinating the internal Section 404 program within the company, and coordinating with the external auditors. Depending on the size, the team could have its own organizational chart or be a group of professionals with one leader. In the company's organizational structure, the team could be under the internal audit department's umbrella or operate separately.

For example, a larger company with approximately $5 billion in revenue and 8,000-plus employees had its corporate controller oversee the SOX project in year one. The SOX team was made up mostly of consultants with a few employees and a project manager to lead the team. An internal manager, who was an employee, helped facilitate and coordinate the

Exhibit 7.1   Year-One SOX Organizational Chart

project. Champions were assigned for each significant business process to monitor the progress and results. The organization chart for year one is shown in Exhibit 7.1.

The organizational chart was simplistic, but it worked. The SOX team ranged from 7 to 20 people and contained all levels of abilities. Because a consultant was heading the SOX team, an internal resource was involved to push the project along when needed and provide company-specific guidance. The controller oversaw the project, attended key meetings, and was the liaison for the CFO and other executives.

Although this structure worked in year one, it was not the optimal structure for this company. In year two, it hired a vice president of corporate audit who reports to the audit committee and oversees both the internal audit department and the SOX program. The structure provides the

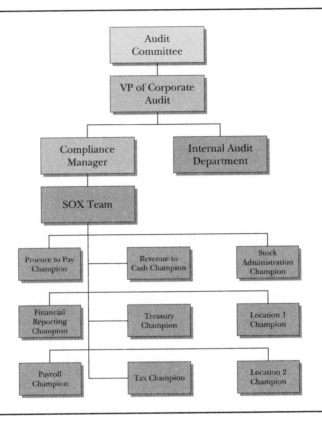

Exhibit 7.2   Year-Two SOX Organizational Chart

best of both worlds because the departments are compatible and could operate under the same umbrella, yet they are still separate and derive the benefit of independence. The company continues to have consultants on the job because their numbers can be reduced or increased as the program dictates. Their organizational chart beginning in year two is provided in Exhibit 7.2.

Small Companies

Smaller companies required to comply with Section 404 often do not have an internal audit department or compliance officer, but the same question applies: Is the right person heading your SOX program? In smaller companies, the appropriate person could be the controller or the sole internal auditor. Program oversight could appropriately come from the CFO or audit committee. Two possible organizational charts for small companies are shown in Exhibits 7.3 and 7.4.

Another option for this basic organizational structure is to have the SOX or compliance manager report to the controller or director of finance

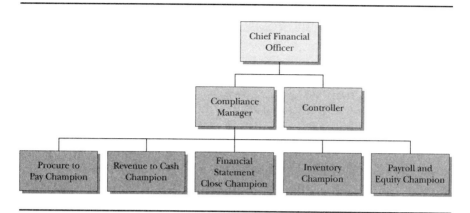

Exhibit 7.3   Small Company Potential Organizational Chart 1

instead of the CFO. If the SOX manager position is not a full-time job for your company, consider hiring a consultant who will work only when needed or assign additional special projects or other compliance responsibilities to the SOX manager position (see Exhibit 7.4).

In Exhibit 7.4, the director is responsible for the internal audit function and SOX compliance and reports directly to the audit committee, increasing independence. Your external auditors may consider the director truly independent only if he or she reports to the audit committee instead of management.

Smaller companies that lack an internal audit department or SOX group often have to be creative with their staffing. Do not be afraid to think outside the box.

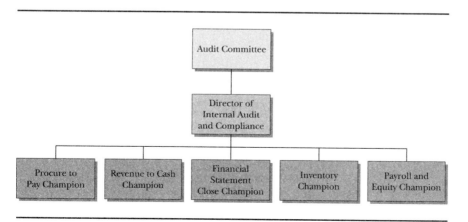

Exhibit 7.4   Small Company Potential Organizational Chart 2

HOW TO COMMUNICATE EFFECTIVELY THROUGH EMAILS, MEETINGS, AND ADVISORIES

Since your Section 404 project will touch many people and departments throughout the company, it is important to have regular communications with the team, employees who are involved, champions, executive management, external auditors, and the audit committee.

Four Successful Email Practices

Email is a wonderful tool to spread your message throughout the company. But unless your message is concise and the audience recognizes the sender's email address, there is a good chance the message will go unread. These four points will help readers pay more attention to your emails.

1. Keep you messages short and to the point. Most people only read the first few lines of an email message.

2. If you have to add more detail, use headings or bullet points to get your thoughts across

3. For important messages, have someone from executive management send the email. Most employees read a message from the president or CFO promptly.

4. When possible, follow-up an email message with a face-to-face meeting to make sure your message has been received clearly and to build a better rapport.

Holding Useful Meetings

Meetings should have clear agendas and follow a strict schedule, or they can become a huge waste of time. Be sure that only the necessary attendees are present, and cancel any meetings that are not essential. Do not let your meetings go off on tangents. If discussions become too detailed, encourage the individuals involved to meet independently and report the results back to the group at the next meeting.

Weekly Meetings   Weekly status meetings with your team are crucial to keep informed of challenges and problem areas that arise during the year. In addition, formal weekly meetings with the external auditor are helpful during busy project times when the auditor is on-site for an extended period. Although informal discussions should occur as needed, formal meetings help keep you in touch with your team's progress and any important findings. Both of these meetings should be limited to one hour.

Management Meetings   Monthly status meetings with other employees, management, and champions should be held regularly to discuss new requirements and challenges and to communicate how the program is progressing. These meetings show employees that they are not the only ones struggling with documentation and testing controls and are a good platform for your team to acknowledge those employees who are completing the work on time. You can also use these meetings as a training session for new published guidance. Try to put an element of fun in these meetings. Section 404 work can be tedious and dull, so think about providing lunch or dessert or having a drawing at your meetings. It is a small gesture, but it can raise morale for those employees doing extra work for your project.

Practice Tips

1. Consider having your CFO or other executive speak at some of your monthly compliance meetings to send the message that Section 404 work is vital.

2. If your company holds regular company-wide meetings, add SOX as a regular item on the agenda to keep the company informed of the program and promote the cause.

Audit Committee Communications   The audit committee is responsible for overseeing the company's internal controls over financial reporting and management's assessment of the effectiveness of these controls. The board is also responsible for assessing the risk of financial fraud by management and ensuring a program is in place to prevent, deter, and detect fraud. For years to come, your fraud program and Section 404 project are two of the most important areas the audit committee will monitor.

Status reports on your Section 404 program should be communicated regularly to the audit committee and documented in the meeting minutes. The status reports should include discussions on any control deficiencies or gaps that could ultimately result in a significant deficiency or material weakness. In addition to status reports, a meeting on the company's fraud program should be held with the audit committee at least once a year.

Getting the Message Out with Advisories

Published advisories can help guide and educate company employees on various issues in your Section 404 project that may be confusing to non-auditors. The purpose of the advisories is to clarify questions and give practical, easy-to-understand direction. Your advisories can be emailed to all employees involved in your project and should be posted on a company site for later reference. Possible topics for these advisories could include guidance on sample sizes, key versus nonkey controls, and deficiencies. Keep the advisories short and try to make the topics universal and timeless.

TACTICS FOR DEALING WITH BUSINESS CHANGES FOR SECTIONS 302 AND 404 COMPLIANCE

In the first year of compliance, many companies tried to eliminate any material changes to the business toward the end of the year for fear they would threaten their Section 404 compliance goals. Acquisitions were put off, enterprise resource planning (ERP) system implementations were delayed, and processes could not be altered for fear that documentation and testing would be found inadequate at year-end. The restriction on change often caused bad business decisions or stopped the implementation of improved systems and processes.

This delay of new transactions and processes is still in practice for some companies during their fourth quarter because of compliance concerns. But change can occur near year-end without a threat if it is properly managed. Your plan for managing change should have two components: identifying change and addressing change. Business process change is where the lines of Sections 302 and 404 cross. Material changes to internal controls have to be reported (identified) in Section 302 certifications on a quarterly basis and then evaluated (addressed) for the impact of the change on the company's internal controls for Section 404 purposes. Section 302 compliance is an issue in the near-term, but Section 404 will eventually become an issue at year-end.

Five Ways to Identify Change in Your Organization

How will the company identify change? You cannot identify change without the help of several key people in the organization. Training is essential so that these key people understand the reason why change must be identified and what types of changes should be called out as material. The best way to identify change in an organization depends on such factors as its size, structure, and communication style. Five methods that accelerated filers use today are listed next.

1. A combination of walk-through, observation, and inquiry testing as well as control testing is used each quarter to identify and document changes. For example, in the first quarter, the SOX team uses walk-throughs, observations, and inquiry to document changes for the Section 302 certification and to update flowcharts and narratives for Section 404 documentation. In the second and third quarters,

actual control testing is used for both Section 302 and 404 purposes. In the fourth quarter, update tests, control tests, and inquiry is used as needed for Section 302 and 404 purposes.

2. Finance and key operational managers are trained on the definition of a material change to internal controls and asked quarterly, via email from their site controller, a list of questions on their processes and controls to determine whether there have been any material changes. Site controllers discuss material changes to any of their processes with the CFO and SOX lead at their quarterly financial statement meeting.

3. The controller and president of each location are asked to sign a sub-certification statement, much like the Section 302 certification that is signed by the CFO and CEO for the SEC. Each subcertification statement states that all material changes to internal controls in their business unit are listed below, the financial information is accurate and complete, and all instances of fraud have been reported. After conducting interviews with key members of their business unit, the controller and president sign the subcertifications and forward them to the SOX team. All changes to internal controls noted in the statements, whether deemed material or not, are compiled in a list of quarterly changes to controls. The director of internal audit or compliance officer highlights all material changes in the list and discusses them with the CEO and CFO.

4. The CFO meets individually with each department head to discuss changes that have occurred in the department during the quarter. He or she asks the department heads to document process changes that could be considered material or that affect SOX compliance in an email to the SOX lead. The SOX lead compiles a report of changes and submits it to the CEO and CFO.

5. Testing of internal controls is performed quarterly throughout the year for each significant location. The SOX team monitors the results of testing and communicates changes to controls to the CFO quarterly.

For example, a company had a key control for stock warrant conversions during its first year of compliance although there were no occurrences during the year. Because any warrant conversion during the year would be considered in scope for Section 404, the company wanted to monitor the control for occurrences and test it when necessary. However, the company did not want to keep the control active because it would have to continually document "no sample" test results, keep the control updated, and include it in the company's internal control analysis. Instead, the company made the control nonkey and runs a report of all nonkey controls every quarter to monitor them for change as part of its Section 302 certification process.

Practice Tips

- Subcertifications are becoming a popular practice among companies complying with Section 302. Some companies require subcertification all the way down to the process owners. While this is a good practice, usually more than a passive subcertification process must be in place for CEO and CFO validation. Subcertifications should be accompanied by more proactive procedures such as interviews, walk-throughs, observation, and control testing of high-risk areas.

- Do not think that your auditors will accept only quarterly control testing as a valid method for Section 302 certifications. If it does not make sense for the company to formally test controls four times a year, plan less formal procedures, such as walk-throughs and interviews, during the quarters that you are not control testing.

- After you have performed your procedures to identify change, check to see if there have been any changes to significant positions at the manager level or above. Also check with the IT group to see if any new applications have been implemented. Both occurrences can be an indicator of changes to controls.

- Make your nonkey controls work for you. Instead of having outdated, meaningless nonkey controls documented in your application or database, document processes and controls that have to be monitored for change or materiality as nonkey controls. Every quarter when the company is doing its Section 302 assessment, you can run a report of the nonkey controls to remind you of processes and controls that should be specifically reviewed.

If there is a warrant transaction during any quarter, the company can switch the control back to key status and properly test it for compliance.

To streamline your Section 302 process, try to combine Section 302 and 404 procedures as much as possible. Do not think of your quarterly procedures in such a regimented fashion, such as testing one-quarter of your annual samples. Mix it up with a walk-through here, a control test there, and an interview in the end. Many companies are not performing quarterly control tests for their Section 302 certifications. There is more than one option. Put together a plan to identify and address change that works with your annual timeline and is acceptable to the CEO and CFO, then submit the plan to your auditor for comment.

Addressing Change: A Sample Change Plan Checklist

What is the plan for addressing changes to key processes that have been identified during the year? How will you determine if the change is in or out of scope? How will you address changes that occur late in the year? Do you have the resources to implement, document, and test new controls in the fourth quarter?

A proactive change plan can help your team deal with these questions. Be specific in your plan. A sample checklist for change plans follows.

❏ Perform a new scoping analysis and have the external auditors agree to your conclusion.

❏ Evaluate whether additional resources are needed to document, implement, and test new controls.

❏ Develop a timeline for testing and documenting new controls.

❏ Make sure the process owners involved in the new area understand what needs to be done for Section 404 purposes. Find out if a training update is needed.

❏ Schedule time with your external auditors for them to review and test the new processes. Their schedule will be tight at year-end too.

❏ Determine if the new process and controls will impact other processes and controls. If so, what changes will have to be made?

❏ Determine whether the new process requires any change in IT controls. Will any new applications be brought into scope?

❏ Evaluate whether a potential deficiency in the new process will cause a problem. If so, what are the largest risk areas? Could a deficiency in the new process be combined with a deficiency in a related area to create a significant or material deficiency?

Businesses cannot go on delaying important decisions because of impending attestation on internal controls. In a large or growing company, change is constant, unavoidable, and necessary. Dealing with change is one of the biggest challenges for sustainability of Section 404 programs. Having a plan for dealing with change is the best way to avoid a negative impact on your Section 404 compliance and to keep abreast of your Section 302 compliance.

NOTE

1. See Chapter 4 for first- and second-year SOX costs for smaller and large public companies, according to the CRA International *Sarbanes-Oxley Section 404 Cost and Implementation Issues: Spring 2006 Survey Update.*

8

Streamlining Documentation

Key Topics:
- Three ideas to improve your overall documentation process
- How to create and maintain meaningful control matrices
- Using relevant financial statement assertions for planning purposes
- Techniques for scrutinizing the optimal number of key controls
- How to reduce and improve controls with standardization
- Documentation at international locations
- Effective spreadsheet control programs
- Creating strong financial reporting controls
- Tools for assessing control design
- An alternative to gap remediation
- Three more ideas for improving documentation

The documentation phase was the most time-consuming and expensive step of compliance for many companies in their first year of Sarbanes-Oxley (SOX) Section 404 compliance. Companies became stuck in this phase, going around in circles with their external auditors because of the multiple iterations of identifying and designing key controls and deciding on appropriate documentation formats. This bottom-up approach, where key (control activity) controls were the focus before companies' specific risks were evaluated at the top level, came to be blamed for the excessive time and costs associated with first-year Section 404 compliance.

Although creating documentation from scratch is arduous, keeping documentation updated for changes and new processes can also be challenging. Documentation in the first year of compliance was excessive for many companies and will be difficult to maintain on an ongoing basis. The documentation phase objective now is to create or maintain accurate work papers and not waste extra resources doing so. If controls are not described correctly, they will fail testing. The goal is to document actual processes instead of the way process owners think processes should be performed.

Auditing Standard No. 2 (AS No. 2) clearly defined the purpose and requirements for maintaining control documentation, but the tone in AS No. 5 has changed for documentation requirements, especially for smaller companies. In Paragraph 51 of AS No. 5, the Public Company Accounting Oversight Board (PCAOB) advises auditors:

> Documentary evidence of the operation of some controls, such as management's philosophy and operating style, might not exist. A smaller, less complex company or unit might have less formal documentation regarding the operation of its controls. In those situations, testing controls through inquiry combined with other procedures, such as observation of activities, inspection of less formal documentation, or re-performance of certain controls, might provide sufficient evidence about whether the control is effective.

The Securities and Exchange Commission (SEC) in its Guidance for Management provides many options for documentation while still stressing its importance:

> As part of its evaluation of ICFR [Internal Control over Financial Reporting], management must maintain reasonable support for its assessment. Documentation of the design of the controls management has placed in operation to adequately address the financial reporting risks, including the entity-level and other pervasive elements necessary for effective ICFR, is an integral part of the reasonable support. The form and extent of the documentation will vary depending on the size, nature, and complexity of the company. It can take many forms (for example, paper documents, electronic, or other media). Also, the documentation can be presented in a number of ways (for example, policy manuals, process models, flowcharts, job descriptions, documents, internal memorandums, forms, etc.).

The guidance goes on to say that not all controls that exist within a process need to be documented, only those that address the company's key financial reporting risks.

Practice Tip

Weigh the options of reducing existing documentation and using less sufficient methods for documenting controls against having sufficient documentation on which your auditor can rely. Maintaining informal documentation may be enough for management to assess the effectiveness of internal controls, but it may provide little use for other business purposes. In addition, if auditors cannot rely on informal or insufficient documentation, the company may lose any audit fee savings it hoped for.

THREE IDEAS TO IMPROVE YOUR OVERALL DOCUMENTATION PROCESS

Preparing and maintaining accurate documentation is an art. The documenter needs to know whom to talk to and the right questions to ask while focusing on the controls, not the process itself. Although it is hard for one person to know everything needed to document an entire business process, you may be surprised at how little some employees understand regarding what comes before or after their individual tasks. Whether creating documentation or maintaining it, documenting processes is a collaborative effort, which makes it lengthy and subject to interpretation. You can improve your overall documentation process by remembering the goal of documenting your business processes, resolving the flowchart versus narrative debate, and using the secret to quality process documentation.

Remember the Goal of Documenting Business Processes

No matter how you decide to document the company's controls, the documentation process takes much time and effort to both create and maintain. It is easy to forget that the aim of recording a company's business processes for SOX purposes is to explain how employees are completing certain tasks and the controls that surround those tasks. The main goal of Section 404 documentation is to give others an understanding of certain key processes and the related controls so that management can properly test and evaluate them.

Practice Tip

It is important to remember that documentation is not the ultimate goal of a Section 404 project; it is only a step in the process used to help with testing and evaluating the company's internal control structure.

Flowcharts versus Narratives Debate

Should you use narratives or flowcharts to document your business process? Do you need both?

Each method has advantages and disadvantages. Narratives can be more user friendly and less intimidating. Most employees can write a few paragraphs describing what they do on a daily basis. However, narratives can be less useful if writers ramble on for pages without supplying the detail that is needed. Narratives also can be challenging for a growing or volatile company to maintain because of the constant changes.

Flowcharts tend to be more focused on the business process but can lack the necessary background information to give your controls context.

Some people may cringe at the thought of creating flowcharts or may not know the proper symbols or format to use. Flowcharting may take training but is easily transferable among business units or countries and can be easier to maintain than narratives.

In a survey of five accelerated filers that successfully completed their Section 404 assessments for 2004 (their first year of compliance), two out of five used narratives only and the other three used both.

Practice Tip

It is not necessary to prepare both narratives and flowcharts when documenting key processes. As long as your narratives *or* flowcharts are accurate, complete, and clearly note the key controls, there is no need for both.

Process documentation can be further simplified by eliminating the nonessential details around the processes but maintaining the specificity around the controls. In the end, either method can be used to accomplish the goal of robust process descriptions as long as information such as who performs what control when is included.

Secret to Quality Process Documentation

Whether you select narratives or flowcharts for your documentation, you must describe processes in such a way that a person who knows nothing about them can understand them from start to finish.

Although walk-throughs are not specifically required by management in any of the SEC or PCAOB internal control guidance, the secret to high-quality process documentation is to validate it with walk-throughs that encompass observation and examination techniques. Walk-throughs are a great tool to fully understand processes, make sure process documentation is complete, and confirm controls are working as described. Have a person from another department walk through the company's processes from start to finish using the narratives or flowcharts. Be sure they examine relevant reports or sign-offs for significant controls. If you are confident that the processes are accurately documented already, you can validate by inquiry. However, for areas with new or changed processes, nothing compares to walk-throughs with examinations to ensure accuracy.

Most teams will create or update their documentation at the beginning of the year. Do not forget to revisit your process documentation for updates after you have remediated controls.

In AS No. 2, external auditors were required to perform walk-throughs of your key business areas on their own. The requirements around walk-throughs have changed in AS No. 5. Auditors are still required to perform walk-throughs of key processes, particularly the period-end financial reporting process. However, in AS No. 5, auditors can reduce the amount of work associated with these walk-throughs by performing a walk-through for each significant process instead of each major class of transactions within each significant process and supervising the work of others for walk-through procedures if they provide direct assistance to the auditor. In addition, talk to your external auditors about using your process documentation in their work papers for their walk-throughs instead of creating their own.

For more information on the new requirements for auditor walk-throughs see AS No. 5, Paragraphs 34 to 38 and 49.

CLEARING THE CLUTTER: HOW TO CREATE AND MAINTAIN MEANINGFUL CONTROL MATRICES

Your control matrices are a conglomeration of vital information on the company's controls. They typically begin with the key business cycle or process and are further broken down into subprocesses, control objectives, related risks, and control activities in place to mitigate the risks. What other information is in, or should be in, your control matrix? Do your matrices contain information that you did not use previously?

At a minimum, this additional information should be included in your matrices:

- Priority

- Frequency

- Financial assertions covered by each control activity

- Whether the control is automated or manual

- Whether the control is preventive or detective

Priority

When first documenting key processes, most companies went overboard, referencing operational controls or controls over insignificant accounts. There are benefits to making a comprehensive listing of all the controls your company has in place. Later you can determine which are truly key or nonkey, but at least you will have a library of controls. In a pinch, a non-key control can be elevated to a key control to compensate for a deficiency found at the end of the year during testing.

Add a priority column to your control matrix, so you can sort your controls by key, mitigating, or nonkey designation as needed.

Frequency

Although the frequency by which a control is performed may be stated within the control activity, having frequency listed in a separate column can aid in project planning purposes at the beginning of the year or for planning a specific test phase (i.e., testing all quarterly controls at second quarter or testing after year-end). It also ensures that the information is included for each control activity.

Financial Assertions

Your external auditors will want to obtain sufficient competent evidence about the design and operating effectiveness of controls over all *relevant* financial assertions related to all significant accounts and disclosures in the financial statements. Your external auditors and SOX team will need to analyze the financial assertions that relate to each control activity to ensure your control matrices are complete. (See "Using Relevant Financial Assertions for Planning Purposes" for more information on financial assertions.)

Automated versus Manual Process

Your auditors will be looking for both automated and manual controls in each subprocess, so controls should be identified separately in your control matrices. Noting controls as automated or manual can also help you plan your testing.

Preventive versus Detective

A preventive control will stop an error or fraud from ever occurring. A system control that requires a journal entry to balance before it is posted prevents out-of-balance accounts. A detective control will monitor transactions for errors or fraud that have already occurred. A supervisor's review of a bank reconciliation is meant to detect mistakes made by the preparer.

There is much debate about which type of control is better. Although a preventive control may stop misstatements from ever occurring, no system is foolproof. If errors or fraud get past the control, there must be a detective control in place to circumvent a misstatement of the financial statements. However, without preventive controls, the likelihood of errors will be increased, causing a greater chance that an error or fraud will slip past the detective control. At least one of the Big Four firms believe that in the long run, it is better design to have sound preventive controls.

Still, the strongest system of internal control combines preventive and detective controls. Your external auditors will be looking for both types among your key controls for each cycle.

Additional Control Matrix Information You May Need

You also should consider including this information separately in your control matrices:

- Control type

- Fraud related

- Spreadsheet used

Control Type   The control type is commonly referred to as caviar (CAVR), which stands for completeness, accuracy, validity, and restricted access. Like the financial assertions, control types help your external auditor obtain evidence about the design of your controls. In many cases, CAVR will apply to information technology (IT) control activities that do not easily fit into the financial assertion categories. Unless you use this information for internal purposes or it is specifically requested by your external auditor, control type should not be included in your matrices.

Fraud Related   Certain controls are specifically in place to prevent or detect fraud, such as dual signatures required on checks over a certain threshold. These fraud controls should be separately noted so they can be analyzed and documented as part of the company's entity-wide fraud program.

Spreadsheet Required   Because of their manual nature, Excel-type spreadsheets are prone to numerous errors. This causes additional risks for processes that depend on these spreadsheets. Additional analysis on spreadsheets probably will need to be performed during your project. Marking the control activities that include spreadsheets will expedite the analysis.

There may be other information that your company requires for its particular project, but the aim is to eliminate unneeded information from your control matrices.

Practice Tip

Do not keep updating information in your control matrices that you are not using. Hide columns (in Excel) or make cells inactive for information that is not meaningful.

USING RELEVANT FINANCIAL ASSERTIONS FOR PLANNING PURPOSES

The financial assertions can guide you when developing a listing of risks for a new business cycle or location. Consider each relevant assertion and what the related risk would be while reviewing the key subprocesses in a business cycle. Keep in mind that not every assertion will apply to each subprocess, but it is a systematic approach to developing risks for your control matrix.

For example, in the fixed asset cycle, there are several subprocesses, including asset disposals and depreciation. In the fixed asset disposals subprocess, existence is a relevant assertions leading to the risk that assets may be incorrectly recorded in the system that no longer exist at the company. Valuation is relevant for the depreciation subprocess leading to the risk that fixed assets are not properly valued (at the net amount) in the financial statements.

Remember that you only need to document and test controls over *relevant* assertions related to *significant* accounts. Analyzing relevant assertions at the subprocess level will bring you to the same result as analyzing the assertions for each general ledger account deemed significant in your scoping exercise. Once you determine the relevant assertions for your significant accounts (or group of accounts), you will be able to tie the relevant assertions to specific transactions and control activities.

FINANCIAL ASSERTION HELP FOR NONAUDITORS

The financial assertions can be a tough concept for novice auditors or process owners to grasp. These questions may help beginners clarify the different assertions:

- How do you know all the transactions during the period are recorded? (Completeness)
- Is the asset/liability properly valued at the net amount? (Valuation)
- How do you know the asset/liability exists? (Existence)
- Does the company have the rights to certain assets? (Rights)
- Does a certain transaction cause the company to take on an obligation of some sort? (Obligation)
- How do you know the transactions are properly recorded or disclosed in the financial statements? (Presentation and Disclosure)

Although these questions may provide a guide, mapping your key controls to the financial assertions can be difficult and perhaps best performed by an experienced member of your team. Before you begin, ask your external auditors which assertions they use; occasionally cutoff and accuracy are added to the bunch.

TECHNIQUES FOR SCRUTINIZING THE NUMBER OF KEY CONTROLS

Even though you have identified the significant business processes and accounts through scoping, it is still easy to lose focus when documenting individual controls. To remain on track, the documenter should always consider whether the consolidated financial statements could be misstated if a particular control failed. Process owners often have difficulty seeing the big picture and differentiating controls that are important to their group from controls that are important to the company's consolidated financial statements.

Since companies tended to document and test more controls than necessary in year one, there is now a big push to reduce the number of controls to a suitable number. Finding the appropriate number of key controls has been a daunting task for many companies because there is no standard and no two companies will be the same. Factors such as the amount of gross revenue, whether operations are centralized or decentralized, the number of locations or entities to consolidate, the industry in which the company operates, and the degree of risk that management has assessed and the external auditors assign to your audit will all play a significant role in the number of key controls that the company will have.

As an example, one high-tech company brought in consultants to identify the key controls for their project. This company has centralized accounting functions, only five locations in scope, 85,000 employees, and $34.2 billion in revenue, and ended up with approximately 1,000 key controls. Another company with centralized operations, 7,600 employees, and revenue of $4.9 billion in the high-tech industry was able to reduce its key controls from 1,278 to 534.

Practice Tip

After updating controls for new and changed processes, review your control matrices annually to see if there are any controls you can change to nonkey without losing coverage of the relevant financial assertions in each subprocess. Reducing the number of key control activities will limit the amount of time and resources spent on testing and remediation later in the project.

Seven Principles for Finding the Right Number of Key Controls

The number of key controls clearly dictates the amount of time and resources your Section 404 program requires. Although there is no magic number of key controls for any type of company, it is safe to say that no company wants more key controls than it needs. Follow these seven basic principles before you start to analyze your key controls:

1. **Understanding.** You must truly understand the processes that you are scrutinizing. Except for the smallest companies, no one person can fully understand all the processes, so your analysis should include several different people.

2. **Risks and fraud.** Understand where the risks are and where fraud could occur in each area.

3. **Experience.** Be sure to use people with the proper experience and skills to evaluate the processes and determine which controls are key. Employees or consultants with an auditing background are usually well suited for this type of evaluation.

4. **Financial assertions.** Look at the relevant financial assertions for each subprocess and ensure that a key control addresses each one.

5. **Key controls.** Make sure the term "key control" is clearly defined for your SOX team and the process owners so everyone fully understands what your company considers a key control. Unfortunately, the term "key control" has not been clearly defined in SOX authoritative literature.

6. **Best controls.** Do not automatically replace controls that failed in a previous year with the compensating controls that saved you. Go for the best control that specifically mitigates the related risk.

7. **Manual controls.** Be careful with key manual controls that rely on one person to perform successfully. Develop compensating controls for risky areas.

Seven Ways to Analyze the Number of Key Controls

Once you have applied the seven principles, you can try the next seven techniques to analyze the number of key controls:

1. **Prioritize.** Ask process owners to prioritize the controls in their areas and have a SOX team person do the same to provide a second opinion. Analyze the controls at the bottom of the lists to determine (a) if they are really key controls, (b) if they are duplicate controls for other controls that may be farther up the list, and (c) if they are poorly designed controls that do not really address the related risks.

2. **Pick the controls that you cannot live without.** These key controls, of course, should remain key; but what about the other controls? Be sure not to pick only the detective controls. Doing this may be the easy way out, but detective controls are not always the most effective.

3. **Use an independent third party.** Use an outside consultant who has knowledge of the company's business but does not know the company's specific processes or politics to select the controls that seem to be nonkey. Doing this will provide a completely different perspective but the final analysis should be reviewed for accuracy.

4. **Use statistics.** Rate the risk involved in each process as high, medium, or low, and count the number of key controls for each area. For areas that seem out of proportion, delve down even deeper and rate the risk of each subprocess, and count the number of key controls in each area. Although numbers do not tell the entire story, there may be opportunities to reduce the number of controls for low-risk areas that have a relatively large number of key controls.

   For example, when rating each process and counting the number of key controls, a company determined that its low-risk accounts payable process had the second highest number of key controls. When they looked at the numbers at the subprocess level, they found that the invoice processing subprocess had six key controls and the cash disbursement subprocess only had two. The cash disbursement subprocess was considered a higher-risk area than invoice processing, so it seemed counterintuitive that there would be three times as many controls for invoice processing. The company analyzed the two areas and increased the number of controls in the cash disbursement area to three and reduced the number of controls in the invoice processing area to two (for a net change of -3 key controls)

5. **Set a reduction target.** Give each area a reduction target (i.e., 10%). Low-risk areas can have a higher target than high-risk areas.

6. **Observe the external audit testing.** Note the controls that the external auditors tested. If asked, your external auditors may not tell you which controls are key, but in their own testing they probably did not test any controls that they considered nonkey.

7. **Use comparisons.** Compare the number of key controls for similar business units or departments. Unless there are several different risks, an accounts payable department in one business unit should have a number of controls similar to another accounts payable department in a different location. There may be reasons why one location has more controls than another, but if the risks are alike, logic dictates that the number of key controls should be alike too.

In all these approaches, the idea is to prioritize a group of controls that have been identified as important and downgrade the controls at the bottom of the list. After you have completed your key control analysis, review the remaining key controls to make sure the relevant financial assertions are covered and there is a mix of both preventive and detective controls.

Do not delete from your documentation the controls that you determined are no longer key. Mark them as inactive and do not maintain or test them unless needed. You may have to update, test, and rely on these controls to lessen the severity of a deficiency or as a compensating control at year-end.

HOW TO REDUCE AND IMPROVE CONTROLS WITH STANDARDIZATION

One way to streamline your control documentation is to standardize certain key controls that are performed throughout the company at different business units or departments. Oftentimes similar controls occur at different locations during the company's period-end close. To ease documentation requirements, you can create a separate cycle to include standardized controls performed at the end of the period. If these transactions are performed by a centralized department, only one cycle would be necessary. However, if these transactions are performed by multiple business units or departments, each business would need its own period-end process.

Transactions to incorporate in the period-end process could include any controls that the company wishes to standardize that are performed by different locations. Examples include:

- Bank reconciliations
- Account reconciliations
- Lease accounting analysis
- Accruals
- Prepaid assets
- Journal entries
- Accounting memos
- Disclosure schedules

A partial period-end process control matrix is shown in Exhibit 8.1. See Appendix C for a full example of a period-end process control matrix.

Your external auditors may be able to reduce their procedures when processes and controls are standardized at different locations. If you have multiple locations that share the same process and controls, your external auditors may be able to perform the walk-through at only one location, condense testing, or rely more on management's testing, saving time and money on your audit invoice.

Exhibit 8.1 Sample Period-End Close Control Matrix

Cycle	Transaction	Control Objective	Risk	Control Activity
Period-end process	**Leases**	Leases are properly recorded as capital or operating based on terms of the agreement	Balance sheet may not accurately reflect all assets and liabilities	Accounting manager documents accounting treatment of leases in a memo based on terms of agreement and lease checklist. Lease memo and checklist are reviewed and signed by director of accounting. Copies are attached to the lease agreement and journal entry if applicable.
Period-end process	**Account Reconciliations**	General ledger balances are accurate and substantiated	Financial statements may be misstated due to an omission, clerical error, or incorrect entries	Staff accountants prepare reconciliations of all balance sheets and certain profit and loss accounts per the month-end accounts reconciliations schedule. Reconciliations are signed off by the preparer, approved by preparer's supervisors, attached to the related adjusting journal entries, and tied to the general ledger.
Period-end process	**Financial Disclosures Schedules**	All schedules prepared for disclosures are accurate and complete	Disclosures are misstated or incomplete	Senior accountants prepare and foot disclosure schedules quarterly. Preparers' supervisors review and tie numbers on disclosure schedules to supporting documentation to ensure accuracy. Review is evidenced by signoff on schedules.

Practice Tip

Ask your auditors about minimizing walk-throughs and testing for identical processes at separate locations. Although manual processes may have different performance standards, controls that are automated or mostly automated may provide savings.

PRACTICAL IDEAS FOR DOCUMENTATION AT INTERNATIONAL LOCATIONS

Documentation at international locations can be tricky if the employees' first language is not English and they are not familiar with U.S. generally accepted accounting principles (GAAP) or U.S. laws, such as the Sarbanes-Oxley Act. Cultural difference can add additional challenges. A few ideas on how to ease the burden of creating and maintaining documentation at international locations follow.

- Use flowcharts instead of narratives to document processes and controls. Flowcharts are universally accepted and generally will not require the grammar and language skills that full-length narratives need.

- Provide U.S. GAAP training to international accounting personnel so they will understand potential accounting issues and provide better information to the financial reporting group.

- Consider bringing significant accounting areas with strong GAAP concerns back to the United States.

- Supply training videos or hold seminars in the native language. Even though foreign employees may be required to document their processes and controls in English, they will have a better understanding of the requirements and will be able to think of the processes in the language that they understand if they are trained in their own language.

Local Business Unit Monitoring of International Locations

Just because an international location's business is material does not necessarily mean the related key controls have to be located at the foreign location. If there are no specific risks and the accounting is performed mainly at a corporate or U.S. office, you may be able to implement key monitoring controls in the United States instead of at the foreign location. The next seven factors will play a part in determining where the key controls can be located.

1. Is there any revenue recorded at the foreign location, or is it a sales or research and development (R&D) office?

2. Is there any inventory located at the foreign location?

3. What type of accounting personnel is at the foreign location? Does an independent third party perform the accounting?

4. Is an independent payroll service used for the international employees?

5. Is the international location's spending monitored closely with a budget?

6. Does the foreign location use the same enterprise resource planning (ERP) system as the corporate/local office?

7. Does internal audit perform regular investigations of the international location? What is the history of the results?

If you are able to answer no to the first two factors and yes to factors 3 to 7, you may have a strong argument for implementing key monitoring controls at a U.S. location without having key controls at the international location. Keep in mind that the international location is still in scope but controls to ensure its financial data is materially correct are located elsewhere.

Typical Monitoring Controls for International Locations

If the company is able to implement monitoring controls for its foreign locations, the corporate or U.S. office may require controls surrounding these processes:

- Review of bank reconciliations and payroll reports
- Balancing intercompany account(s)
- Currency translation
- Funding
- Expense reporting
- Procurement
- Spreadsheets

HOW TO CREATE AN EFFECTIVE SPREADSHEET CONTROL PROGRAM

Spreadsheets have received a great deal of attention as a result of Section 404 compliance programs. In general, calculations performed in spreadsheets are manually driven, so they include a high degree of inherent risk.

Often spreadsheets are developed by one individual at his or her desk but drive a substantial amount of investor decisions.

Several studies have documented the frequency of errors in spreadsheets. The consensus is that error rates in spreadsheets increase as the complexity and/or size of spreadsheets increases. According to a study by Raymond Panko at the University of Hawaii,[1] out of 88 spreadsheets that were audited, 94% contained errors. (These were actual, real-world spreadsheets used in business.) It has been suggested that the error percentage approaches 100% for spreadsheets with over 200 lines.

The financial close process often requires the use of several complex spreadsheets. It is crucial for the integrity of your data to have an adequate spreadsheet control program. If certain spreadsheets directly affect financial reporting, they should be included in your spreadsheet control program, even if they are not complex.

An earnings per share spreadsheet, for example, that uses simple addition, subtraction, and division formulas may not be considered complex. The spreadsheet still should contain hash totals and math checks to ensure accuracy and be fully included in your spreadsheet control program because its information is reported directly in the financial statements. It is a risky spreadsheet because it cannot be tied to a source document or a general ledger, so errors may go undetected.

Practice Tip

Wherever possible, replace spreadsheets that are used for complex calculations or account information with applications that can perform the same functions. Applications can automate calculations, provide better reporting capabilities, and store data, minimizing the risk of human error. Application testing requires fewer samples and is more reliable than spreadsheet testing.

For example, some companies still use spreadsheets for their fixed assets listings and, even worse, depreciation calculation. The fixed asset function will be more accurate, and functional and have more reporting capabilities if recorded in an application instead of a spreadsheet.

Fixed assets and the related depreciation recorded in a spreadsheet are obviously not optimal situations. Evaluate your company's financial spreadsheets to see how many calculations could be automated into an existing or new application. Does the company consolidate multiple entities or prepare the statement of stockholders' equity in a spreadsheet? What about the allowance for doubtful accounts or excess and obsolete reserve calculations? These may be functions your ERP system can perform if fully utilized or customized correctly.

Practice Tip

Do not just go through the motions with your spreadsheet tests. Use the tests for a thorough review of your financial reporting calculations. Although timing is usually tight at the end of each quarter, spreadsheet tests should occur before your calculations or work papers are handed over to your external auditors. Errors your auditors find in your spreadsheets can be an issue for both your financial and internal control audits.

Regardless of their accounting system, most companies will continue to use some spreadsheets in the financial reporting process. All spreadsheets used for financial reporting purposes should be tested for minimum controls regardless of their complexity. Minimum spreadsheet controls include controls over:

- User access

- Ensuring final versions can not be changed

- Backups

- Naming conventions or version controls

Highly complex spreadsheets should be checked for formulas and mathematical accuracy. Spreadsheets could be considered complex if they:

- Use macros

- Contain links to multiple worksheets

- Change frequently

- Use intricate formulas

Practice Tip

Assign spreadsheet testing to an employee(s) with strong spreadsheet skills who is not directly involved in the period-end close process. Provide training to the spreadsheet tester so he or she understands the purpose and methodology of the spreadsheet. Using an employee who is not directly involved in the close process will allow spreadsheets to be tested by an independent person who will have time to check the accuracy of financial reporting spreadsheets in a timely manner.

For more information on spreadsheet controls, refer to the PricewaterhouseCoopers white paper entitled "The Use of Spreadsheets: Considerations for Section 404 of the Sarbanes-Oxley Act" published in July 2004.

HOW TO CREATE STRONG FINANCIAL REPORTING CONTROLS

The period-end financial reporting process is always a significant process because of its importance to financial reporting and to the auditor's opinions on internal control over financial reporting and the financial statements. One of the Big Four accounting firms claims that 80% of its clients' financial statement close controls are manual. These mostly manual financial reporting controls are the most relevant controls to the financial statement risk of misstatement.

The typical period-end financial reporting process includes five procedures:

1. Procedures used to enter transaction totals into the general ledger

2. Procedures used to initiate, authorize, record, and process journal entries in the general ledger

3. Procedures used to record recurring and nonrecurring adjustments to the annual and quarterly financial statements

4. Procedures for preparing annual and quarterly financial statements and related disclosures

5. Procedures related to the selection and application of accounting policies (added in AS No. 5)

In many companies, the first two processes occur throughout the organization, but the last three are centralized to a specific group. Therefore, certain financial reporting controls, such as controls around journal entries and preparing supporting documentation for SEC schedules or disclosures, will have to be included at each significant location. As mentioned, these controls can be standardized for all locations or departments and included in a period-end process in each significant cycle. In addition to the standardized controls, a separate cycle for the controls performed by the financial reporting group will exist. Deficiencies in the financial reporting area are commonly significant or material.

Seven Steps for Evaluating Financial Reporting Controls

Compiling information from a variety of sources and people provides ample possibilities for mistakes. Add subjectivity, nonroutine transactions, and complex accounting principles, and you have a recipe for disaster (or misstatement). Smaller companies may not have to deal with a large number of people or locations, but they have their own challenges, such as segregation of duties or a limited number of qualified accounting personnel. In either case, errors can occur in a multitude of areas that have a direct impact on the financial statements.

Nevertheless, it is not the responsibility of the financial reporting group to catch all errors. To ensure accuracy, quality financial data must come from each business unit, location, and department. When it is time to create or reassess controls around the period-end financial reporting process, consider the next seven topics for both individual locations or departments and the centralized reporting group.

1. **Staff.** How qualified is the staff preparing the financial data? How qualified are supervisors and managers reviewing the data? Who is responsible for the selection and application of accounting policies? Is the accounting/financial reporting department adequately staffed?

2. **Inputs and outputs.** How do you know that the inputs used by business units/locations are reliable? How do you know the output is accurate?

3. **Automation.** How much reliance is placed on the ERP system? How much of the period-end process is automated? How much is manual? How many spreadsheets are used?

4. **Locations and entities.** How many other locations, business units, or entities are involved? How do you make sure their information is accurate, complete, and timely?

5. **Adjusting entries.** Are the consolidation and eliminating adjustments performed manually? Are spreadsheets used? What standard and nonstandard adjustments are made?

6. **Drafting.** What are your procedures for drafting the quarterly/annual financial statements? How are the disclosures drafted?

7. **Monitoring.** Who in management oversees the process? Who reviews the financial statements? How involved are the audit committee and/or board of directors?

In year one, a high number of material weaknesses were reported in the period-end financial reporting process. Weaknesses such as accounting policies and practices, inexperienced or inadequate staffing, and the financial close process have been at the top of the list as the most common issues cited in internal control weakness disclosures.

It will be difficult to persuade external auditors that a deficiency in the financial reporting cycle is not material because each key control has a direct impact on the financials. Errors found in prior-period statements and major audit adjustments can be an indicator of a material weakness in the financial reporting process. Internal controls over the financial reporting process have to be sound to minimize the chance of misstatement and for management to conclude that its internal controls are effective.

Addressing Year-End Controls before the End of the Year

Year-end financial reporting controls may occur in the subsequent year even though they apply to the year under audit. Thus, there is no time to remediate. New year-end controls cannot be put into place after the end of the year if they apply to the year under audit. These controls must be in place at the as-of date.

Practice Tip

Pay particular attention to the year-end financial reporting process before the end of the year. Annual reporting controls may be different from quarterly controls, and it is unlikely that you will be able to remediate these controls at year-end. Consider pretesting these controls before year-end to practice and correct controls if needed.

At quarter and year-end, two separate processes need attention: the actual close of the books and reporting to the SEC and stockholders. Companies often have controls in place for recording transactions, reconciling accounts, and making adjustments to close the books. However, controls over the reporting process are often lacking. Is the final review of the financial statements documented, or are there several drafts floating around with the controller or chief financial officer's (CFO's) initials? How does management know that all changes made it into the final version?

Practice Tip

Strong controls surrounding reporting, not just closing the books, can prevent typos, simple mathematical errors, and other cosmetic mistakes as well as material omissions and misstatements.

Other than the high-level controls of the controller, CFO, and audit committee review and approval of the financial statements, financial reporting controls should include controls that fine-tune the statements and look at the detail. Possible controls to enhance your company's financial reporting could include these procedures:

- Use version control with the financial statement drafts by marking the statements "draft + date" or "draft version 2" so executives know which version they are reviewing.

- Include a cover page with each successive draft that summarizes the changes made to each version. For example, Draft 2 made variance analysis changes and Draft 3 incorporated audit committee comments.

- Have a staff accountant foot all statements and tables in the entire document, including disclosures.

- Have an accounting manager tie all line items on each statement to the source documents, check all dates for the proper period, and ensure amounts are consistent between statements (i.e., net income is not $94,321 on one statement and $94,322 on another).

- A person who is not involved in drafting the financial statements can read through the entire document for typos and grammatical errors.

- Have an accounting manager match all prior-period statements and tables to the statements filed with the SEC in that prior period.

The last few days before a company's financial statements are filed can be a stressful time for the financial reporting group. They are usually working long hours and have a black cloud over their heads for fear an error will be found, whether material or cosmetic. Management and the financial reporting group will have more confidence if there are strong controls over the final review of the financial statements and time is made for various reviews of the final draft.

TOOLS FOR ASSESSING CONTROL DESIGN

The goal of a control design analysis is to determine whether your controls, if operating properly, can effectively prevent or detect errors or fraud in a timely manner that could result in material misstatements in the financial statements. Even though your controls passed the control design in a prior year, you should look at control design every year for new risks that have been identified and new controls that have been added. Additionally, remediated controls from a prior year may have been a quick fix and upon further analysis may prove to be poorly designed.

Good control design is achieved when your control activities specifically address the related risks. It is vital for your risks to match your control activities. Often good control activities that are already in place at a company are added to control matrices without regard for the risks.

Practice Tip

In your documentation process, control activities should evolve from control objectives and risks, but your analysis of control design should progress in the opposite direction. Begin at the control activity level and ask yourself if each activity fully and distinctly mitigates the risk. Then confirm that each risk would be a direct result of the control objective not being achieved.

Additional questions to consider when evaluating the design of your controls include:

- Are controls preventive or detective? Do your manual, subjective, or high-risk processes require both types?

- Will the control prevent or detect an error or fraud in a timely manner so that corrections can occur before the financial statements are issued?

- Is the person performing the control qualified to do so?

After your design evaluation, perform a final check to make sure your key controls provide adequate coverage of the relevant financial statement assertions for each cycle. If you find that not all the relevant assertions are covered by your existing key controls, you may have a gap that must be filled with a new key control.

As always, document your analysis of control design and obtain external auditor approval.

AN ALTERNATIVE TO GAP REMEDIATION

The term "gap" is commonly used in SOX programs to mean a hole in the process where a control is missing. You should maintain an ongoing log of all gaps that were not addressed in a prior year and new gaps that were discovered after the company's most recent risk assessment. Just because there is a gap in a significant process does not necessarily mean the company must add a control to address it. Management should use sound professional judgment to rate gaps as high, medium, or low risk. The company can devise a policy on the plan of action for each level. For example, the company may require that all high-risk gaps be repaired but leave medium and low-risk gaps to the discretion of the area's finance director or champion.

Document the status of all gaps on your log, and create a control activity for gaps the company has decided to address. If there is no action planned for certain gaps, it should be duly noted. At least once a year and every time a risk analysis is performed, complete a new gap evaluation. In theory, low-risk gaps that the company decides to leave alone will remain on the gap log year after year. Once the gap evaluation and documentation is complete, the log should be turned over to your external auditors for review. It is important that your auditors agree that the gaps you do not plan to remediate will not require action.

THREE MORE IDEAS FOR IMPROVING DOCUMENTATION

Thoughts on Automated versus Manual Controls

Often manual controls can be combined or replaced by automated controls. For example, a manual control in the accounts payable cycle for the three-way matching of the invoice to the purchase order to the receiving report is often an automated function that can be activated in your ERP system. Test one automated control instead of 30 payment voucher packages. Another example is an automated approval process. Many applications obtain email approvals in a predetermined order for such items as requisitions, purchase orders, or expense reports. Automated approvals will minimize exceptions in control testing due to missed signatures.

Practice Tip

Let your ERP system work for you. Include all automated controls that address relevant financial statement assertions as key controls in your control matrices. They are easy to test and usually will pass.

Well-designed automated controls that operate effectively provide more assurance than their manual control counterparts. Nevertheless, no matter how technically advanced companies are today, they still have many manual controls. Manual controls are subject to human error and inconsistency and often require some form of judgment. Automated controls do not have these risks. In addition, automated controls require only one or two samples for the year, making them easier to test.

Using Ranges of Detail to Reduce the Number of Updates

There is a fine balance between having too much detail in your control activities and not having enough. Your auditors will want all the relevant details included in your documentation so it can be precisely tested.

Writing test plans will be easier if you include such details as who performs the controls how often and specifically state the evidence.

Experienced SOX people may cringe at the thought of perpetually updating documentation because the details change. But how can you write a test plan for a control with no detail? For example, try writing a specific test plan for an inexperienced tester with this following control: Finance confirms access to bank Web sites is restricted to appropriate employees. Your test would have to be just as vague as the control, such as: Confirm that finance performed access checks for bank Web sites and access was restricted to appropriate employees. This test does not provide adequate direction and requires judgment. Who would the tester go to in finance? How would he or she confirm that bank access was checked? What if access was checked at the beginning of the year only, and who are appropriate employees?

By writing your controls using an acceptable range of details, you can add the specificity that you need and your auditors want, yet still avoid the burden of endless documentation updates. Using a range of details is especially helpful if the control is in transition or is performed by different people or if the company is growing rapidly and changing its controls. Consider using these phrases to implement ranges of details to describe your controls:

> **Or above.** Journal entries are reviewed and signed by the accounting manager *or above*.
>
> **One level up.** Account reconciliations are reviewed and signed by accounting personnel *one level up* from the preparer.
>
> **Preparer's supervisor.** Account reconciliations are reviewed and signed by the preparer's supervisor.
>
> **Or.** The calculation is reviewed by the accounting manager *or* controller. Approval is evidenced by email *or* signature.
>
> **At least.** The open purchase order report is reviewed *at least* monthly by the purchasing manager. (This phrase works well when the control happens sporadically. However, the "at least" frequency should be appropriate for the control. In the last example, it would not be appropriate to use "at least annually.")

In addition to using ranges of details to minimize updates to documentation, always use positions instead of names in your narratives, flowcharts, and control activities. People leave or transfer out of jobs far more frequently than titles change.

Use Section 404 Documentation for Other Compliance Programs and Risk Assessments

Increase the return on investment (ROI) of Section 404 work by using the documentation and testing of controls for other compliance programs when possible. New policies and updated process documentation can be turned into control documents for International Organization for Standardization (ISO) or other compliance programs. In addition, accurate process documentation can contribute to the company's risk assessments or enterprise risk management.

NOTE

1. Ray Panko, Shidler College of Business, University of Hawaii, http://panko.shidler.hawaii.edu/

9

Economical Testing Techniques

Key Topics:

- Practical steps for applying guidance on the nature, timing, and extent of testing

- Suggestions for testing significant manual nonroutine transactions

- Using update tests to ease the burden of testing at year-end

- Five ideas for the timing of control tests

- Types of control tests and when to use them

- Why the use of self-assessment tests should be minimized

- Maximizing your auditor's reliance on the work of others

- More inspiration on efficient testing

Companies have a variety of options available to them for testing and evaluating controls throughout the year. When planning Sarbanes-Oxley (SOX) Section 404 testing, companies should consider all the alternatives for the nature, timing, and extent of testing, seek internal guidance, propose a course of action, and then discuss the plan with their external auditors. In the end, tests of controls must help evaluate the design and operating effectiveness of the controls over financial reporting to ultimately support companies' assessments.

TESTING CONTROL DESIGN AND OPERATING EFFECTIVENESS

According to the Public Company Accounting Oversight Board (PCAOB), internal control over financial reporting is effectively designed when the controls in place would be expected to prevent or detect errors or fraud that could result in material misstatements in the financial statements.

Additionally, controls are properly designed when they accomplish the related objective and mitigate the related risk. Control design is easily addressed when creating a control matrix and should be evaluated at least annually or as business processes change. For more information on evaluating control design, refer to Chapter 8 on documentation.

In addition to control design, management must determine if controls operate effectively or are functioning as planned by people with appropriate authority and qualifications. Frequently controls are in place and operating at some level, but not according to formal policies and procedures. When this occurs, management should evaluate whether the controls in question are effective as they are operating in practice and whether formal policies should be updated. Unlike control design, operating effectiveness can be accurately evaluated only through actual tests, not by analyzing a control matrix. The recent Guidance for Management from the Securities and Exchange Commission (SEC) as well as Auditing Standard No. 5 (AS No. 5) give management (and auditors) many more options for the nature, timing, and extent of operating effectiveness testing.

PRACTICAL STEPS TO APPLYING GUIDANCE ON THE NATURE, TIMING, AND EXTENT OF TESTING

Starting with the guidance published in May 2005, the SEC and PCAOB have provided a better understanding of possibilities for companies on the nature, extent, and timing of control tests. More recent guidance from the SEC and PCAOB has reinforced the multiple testing possibilities. The expectation that controls should be tested at year-end with a high-assurance method and large sample sizes is no longer valid. The recent guidance promotes more flexibility in testing, emphasizes the risk associated with a control, and takes into account the specific characteristics of controls to dictate the appropriate type of testing. It also gives auditors more options for using the work of others, interim testing, and considering prior-year procedures.

Nature

With all the possibilities for control tests, it is important to match the nature of a test of a control to the nature of the control. The nature of testing refers to the method used to test a control, such as reperformance, examination, observation, walk-throughs, inquiry, or self-assessment. The nature of a control refers to the amount of inherent risk, subjectivity, complexity, and whether it is routine or nonroutine. The history of the control or process can come into play if there have been exceptions in prior testing, audit adjustments, or financial statement misstatements. The nature of the control should dictate the nature of the test used.

Reperformance supplies a high level of assurance and should be utilized for high-risk controls. Inquiry or self-assessment provides a low level of assurance and generally is used only in combination with other tests or for update tests. External auditors usually want to see a combination of the different type of tests, even in low-risk areas.

Practice Tip

Look at each cycle as a whole and use different methods of testing within each cycle. Both high- and low-risk areas can have some form of inquiry and reperformance.

Timing

Management's assessment of its internal controls is *as of* the end of the company's fiscal year, so controls must be in place and effective at that date. That does not mean that you have to test all your controls near the end of the year. The timing of your tests of controls can vary depending on the nature of the controls being tested and the frequency for which the controls operate. This means that you may be able to test low-risk, routine controls (nature) earlier in the year (timing) but should save nonroutine controls that require judgment, period-end financial reporting controls, or manual controls for the end of the year.

AS No. 5 emphasizes the use of interim testing in paragraph 55:

Roll-forward Procedures. When the auditor reports on the effectiveness of controls as of a specific date and obtains evidence about the operating effectiveness of controls at an interim date, he or she should determine what, if any, additional evidence concerning the operation of the controls for the remaining period is necessary.

However, it is a good idea to test high-risk controls with a high degree of subjectivity or judgment and controls over the recording of period-end adjustments closer to the as-of date rather than an interim date.

The SEC's Guidance for Management is not as clear, but it does state that different combinations of the nature, timing, and extent of evaluation procedures may provide sufficient evidence for management's assessment.

Extent

The extent of testing relates to the amount of testing (i.e., number of samples) needed to provide reasonable assurance that a control is effective. Most audit firms have published sample guidelines with ranges of sample sizes based on the frequency of the control. The extent of testing for low-risk controls does not have to provide the level of assurance needed for the higher-risk controls. So you could use the lower end of the sample size range for low-risk controls and the high end of the range for controls that are high risk, subjective or complex, or where you expect exceptions.

As a general rule:

- **Nature.** The more manual or subjective a control, the higher level of assurance will be needed.

- **Timing.** The higher the risk or closer related to financial reporting, the closer the control should be tested to the as-of date.

- **Extent.** The more significant, complex, or nonroutine a control, the more extensive testing you will have to perform using a higher assurance method with a larger sample size.

For example, a quarterly executive bonus accrual that is based on annual performance should be tested near year-end using some type of reperformance because it has several high-risk elements: It only happens four times a year, it is most likely a material amount, it could be complex, and it includes estimates. But a control to test that new vendors are not entered in the system until properly approved could be tested earlier in the year with a smaller sample size using examination of the approval evidence.

SUGGESTIONS FOR TESTING SIGNIFICANT MANUAL AND NONROUTINE TRANSACTIONS

Significant transactions that are nonroutine and are performed manually will always be high risk because of their nature and chance of error. If these transactions require the use of judgment, the risk and chance of error is even higher. Control testing for these areas is relatively new. Before Section 404 came into practice, auditors generally did not rely on control testing for these transactions in financial statement audits. They performed substantive tests to provide stronger assurance. Significant manual, nonroutine transactions requiring judgment typically can be found in these areas:

- Reserves and allowances, such as an excess and obsolete reserve, allowance for doubtful accounts, or legal reserve are usually manual and require judgment.

- Warranty accounting can be routine but still requires some subjectivity and estimates.

- Pension and Financial Accounting Standard (FAS) No. 123R calculations use estimates, are complex, and, as seen in recent news, can involve errors and fraud.

- Business acquisitions and mergers may require a valuation of the assets and liabilities purchased, can be highly subjective, and are usually nonroutine.

- Income tax calculations require the use of estimates and rely on changing laws. The calculations are usually manual and complex and in year one often were the source of material weaknesses.

Because of their high-risk nature, some sort of testing for manual, nonroutine controls will have to occur near the as-of date.

Practice Tip

Review your key controls for significant nonroutine transactions, controls with a high degree of subjectivity, and controls over the recording of period-end adjustments. Plan to test these controls (at least partially) in the fourth quarter using reperformance or a combination of methods to include reperformance.

Testing high-risk controls using reperformance will provide the most assurance but may require the tester to have specialized knowledge in certain areas such as tax, information technology (IT) or FAS No. 123R. The tester may need a general understanding of the process to reperform part of the control.

Practice Tip

Using reperformance and examination of the evidence when testing significant, manual, nonroutine controls that require judgment may be challenging for the average tester because of the complexity of the calculations. Consider using a tester from the same department where the calculation is performed to allow for more understanding of the controls and process surrounding the calculation. The level of independence will be low, but the test results may be better. Your external auditors probably will test these areas themselves, regardless of the quality of management's testing.

For example, many tax calculations, such as a research and development (R&D) credit, may require testers to have some basic tax knowledge. Just looking at an R&D calculation spreadsheet can be intimidating for junior testers, and they may not be able to tie numbers in the calculation to the tax return or source documents. Using a tax person not involved in the

R&D calculation to test will allow for more detailed testing and an accurate evaluation of whether the controls are effective.

USING UPDATE TESTS TO EASE THE BURDEN OF TESTING AT YEAR-END

Update testing or roll-forward procedures are being used more frequently to allow for full sample testing earlier in the year but still provide evidence of the continued operating effectiveness of key controls closer to the as-of date. Controls successfully tested at an interim date would require only minimal testing to "update" the results as of the end of the year. Management needs assurance that controls that were effective earlier in the year are still working at year-end, and most audit firms will expect to see some testing of transactions within 45 to 90 days from the end of the year. Key controls at all sites should be included in update testing, but update testing would not require travel to all locations with key controls, saving time and money.

Specific Guidance on Update Testing

Early guidance on update testing was originally described in AS No. 2, although it was not generally used in practice until highlighted in PCAOB Staff Question and Answer No. 51. Update testing and roll-forward procedures are encouraged again in AS No. 5, but surprisingly they are not specifically discussed in the SEC's Guidance for Management.

AS No. 5 explains that as certain factors decrease in significance, the evidence auditors obtain can be less persuasive and the necessary update procedures can be less extensive. The PCAOB recommends considering these factors to determine if update testing is needed and, if so, the types of procedures to use:

- **The specific controls tested prior to the as-of date and the results of those tests.** This factor considers the nature of the control and the risks associated with it. The lower the risk of the control, the less extensive the update procedures can be. If testing exceptions were found for a control during the interim test, the new or remediated control is considered to be of higher risk.

- **The sufficiency of the evidence of effectiveness obtained at an interim date.** The more persuasive the evidence obtained as of an interim date, the less extensive the update tests can be. If a combination of reperformance and examination of evidence of the control's operation was used to test controls at the interim date (highly persuasive), a less persuasive method could be used for update procedures, such as observation and or inspection of relevant documentation.

- **The length of the remaining period.** The update tests can be less extensive if the updating time period is closer to year-end. So for a calendar-year company, the update tests could be less extensive for controls initially tested in October than for controls initially tested in May.

- **The possibility that there have been any significant changes in internal control over financial reporting subsequent to the interim date.** If you can show that there has been no change to controls as of the interim date, your update procedures can be less extensive. For example, if there have been no changes to the design of the control, the business operations surrounding the control, the personnel performing the control, or other factors, the update tests can be less extensive.

Do not confuse update testing with the initial testing of remediated controls. Update testing is for controls that were successfully tested earlier in the year. Remediated control testing is also a second testing effort, but for controls that initially failed.

Update testing options could include using the same tests used in the beginning of the year with smaller sample sizes or using a different, less reliable testing method, such as inquiry, walk-throughs, or self-assessment. The "update testing" that was performed in year one tended to be overdone and was more of a full test phase rather than a mere update. To help combat this overdone approach to update testing, AS No. 5 now specifically says, in Paragraph 56, that "inquiry alone might be sufficient as a roll-forward procedure."

Although now superseded, AS No. 2 Appendix B contained specific examples of update tests in that are still good examples of techniques to use to plan testing during the year. PCAOB Staff Q&A, Question 51 summarizes the examples, as shown in Exhibit 9.1.

Exhibit 9.1   PCAOB Staff Q&A, Question 51 Summary

Examples of Extent of Testing Decisions	Timing of Interim Tests	Nature and Extent of Update Procedures
Daily programmed application controls and daily information technology-dependent control	Through September	Inquiry and observation
Monthly manual reconciliation	May and July	Inquiry and inspection
Daily manual, preventive control	Through September	Walk-through of one December transaction
Programmed preventive control and weekly IT-dependent manual detective control	Through July	Inquiry, observation, and inspection

To illustrate the third example in the exhibit, if a calendar-year company successfully tested 30 receiving transactions from June through September where the physical delivery date was compared to the receiving date recorded in the system, update testing could consist of a tester observing (walking-through) a receiving transaction in December to make sure the control was still effective and there was no change to the process. The observation would have to be documented along with a conclusion that the control was in place with no change and still effective.

These are not the only scenarios for acceptable update procedures. Another possible example is for a company headquartered in the United States with a significant location in Singapore. The company could perform a full-sample test phase in August for all key controls and use inquiry and some examination of key documents and reports to ensure the controls were still effective at year-end. The inquiry and examination could be performed remotely, saving an extra trip.

Or, if a calendar-year company tested 40 journal entries successfully in May using examination and reperformance testing, it could perform update testing in November using the same tests with a small sample size of eight (20% of the original sample size).

The closer the full-sample testing is performed to the fourth quarter, the more flexibility you will have with the update testing method. Test methods providing more assurance should be used for high-risk and early tested controls. In the examples just given, sample testing that occurred in May was matched with small-sample-size update tests (providing greater assurance) near year-end.

IT Update Testing

Similar to manual control update tests, IT or automated controls can be tested earlier in the year and, because of their nature, may require only minimal test procedures near year-end. Discuss with your external auditors the possibility of using inquiry only to confirm that there have been no changes to applications at year-end. Many auditors will agree that update testing of automated application and accounting process controls is not necessary if the initial tests were successful and ITGCs (IT general controls) were found to be effective in earlier testing. However, ITGCs will more than likely require update testing using one or more of the methods just listed.

Practice Tip

If ITGCs (especially change management controls) are found to be effective in earlier testing, automated application and automated accounting process controls that were successfully tested at an interim date may not require additional testing. However, update testing of the ITGCs should be performed. Confirm the approach with your external auditors.

If you find that your ITGCs are not effective at an early test date, try to remediate the controls and test again. If your ITGCs are still found ineffective, you will have to test both ITGCs and automated application and accounting process controls near year-end.

Practice Tip

Wait to test application controls until your ITGCs have been successfully tested. When ITGCs are effective, application controls can be tested once, earlier in the year.

When Using More Persuasive Methods for Update Tests Can Save Time

It may seem that using inquiry, self-assessment, or observation would be the most efficient way to perform update testing. The actual test may be less obtrusive and time consuming for process owners because there are no samples to select or prepare. But consider the entire test process. A new test plan has to be written, the tester and process owner are unfamiliar with the testing method, and documenting the results of inquiry, self-assessment, or observation can be more lengthy, subjective, and less precise. You may even have to change your test results template for these types of tests.

Practice Tip

Consider the entire testing process when planning which test methods to use for update testing. Think about writing the test plans, performing the tests, and documenting and analyzing the test results. Establish standard, update testing sample sizes based on your original sample size guidelines (i.e., 20% of the original sample size).

If you chose to use smaller sample sizes for the same control tests that were performed earlier in the year, your test plans would require only slight modifications and your test results would be objective and straightforward. Your testers would be familiar with the tests, and your analysis of the results would be simplified.

When Using a Less Persuasive Test Method Can Save Time

In theory, using update tests with an easier, less time-consuming and less persuasive method seems more efficient. Sometimes using a different testing method from what was used earlier in the year (such as inquiry) is the most efficient way to perform update testing. An accelerated filer in San Diego with strong entity-level controls is taking a more assertive approach to update testing and the timing of tests. The company considers controls that were successfully tested in the prior year, that do not involve estimates or period-end reporting, to be low-risk. These low-risk controls are tested in period 7 of the current year using full sample sizes. The controls that had no exceptions would not be tested again during the year unless the process changed. The only update tests performed at year-end for these controls consisted of emails (inquiry) to process owners confirming that there were no changes to the controls.

Before you try this on your own, there are four points to note regarding this example:

1. The company has strong entity-level controls with a culture of integrity and a solid commitment to competence.

2. The controls in question had no exceptions in the prior year or the current year and are considered low risk.

3. Full sample sizes were tested at the interim date.

4. The company's external auditors agreed to the testing approach.

The benefits of this approach are obvious. You could perform a large portion of your testing relatively early in the year and have only minimal additional procedures for those controls in the fourth quarter. Yet this scenario may not work for you unless you have a similar situation to the four points described.

If your company is not quite ready for this minimalist approach, five other methods follow that will integrate efficiency into the timing of your testing.

FIVE IDEAS FOR THE TIMING OF CONTROL TESTS

The best time to perform control tests differs at each company, but the goal should be to optimize the timing of testing to reduce the amount of disruption to your business. This section presents five different philosophies regarding the timing of tests, each having advantages and disadvantages. Find the one that will fit best into your company's culture and operations.

1. **Quarterly testing.** The company would test one-quarter of its annual sample sizes on a quarterly basis.
   Advantages
   - Supports the company's SOX Section 302 certification by promoting the timely recognition of changes to controls. You would

be evaluating the effectiveness of disclosure controls and procedures quarterly through control tests.

- Spotlights potential material weaknesses and other deficiencies early in the year, providing adequate time for remediation.

- Allows Section 404 testing to become a part of an employee's job instead of the entire job.

- Lets management (and your external auditors) know that controls are working throughout the year, not just at year-end.

Disadvantages
- Quarterly testing may seem like it never ends and makes employees feel as if they are always being audited.

- It is less cost-effective because you are setting up four test periods during the year.

Quarterly testing would work well at most companies, but especially at companies that have many manual controls or frequent control changes throughout the year.

2. **Three distinct test phases.** The company would plan to have three phases of testing during the year. The first phase can be completed during the second quarter and is a gauge to determine which controls are not working and need remediation. The first phase should be a medium-size testing effort with smaller-than-required sample sizes. This phase is mainly to gather information and can be used to reduce future sample sizes for controls that pass testing. The first phase is performed early in the year to give enough time to remediate those controls that failed testing.

The second test phase would be the most intensive, testing all remaining samples for controls that passed in phase I, and full samples for all remediated controls. Phase II can occur during the fourth quarter to show that controls are working effectively at year-end.

The final phase, to occur at or immediately after year-end, should be the smallest test phase, and would include only annual controls, new controls, or controls that previously failed testing.

Advantages
- You will have adequate warning of material issues.

- Testing at year-end is minimal.

- Timing is more flexible than performing tests every quarter.

Disadvantages
- Having the work spread throughout the year could be a disadvantage for some companies.

- Employees may still feel that they are constantly testing throughout the year.

This method would work best for a company that expects to have several controls requiring remediation or many new controls that have never been tested.

3. **One big test phase.** Most of your testing would be performed in one test phase near year-end using full sample sizes for all tests. Testing would begin before year-end and be finished after year-end to enable tests of annual controls.

Advantages
- The company would have to test only once during the year with minimal testing after year-end for annual tests.

- It is the least disruptive SOX testing method.

- Process owners would not feel that testing is an ongoing effort.

- This method lends itself to cost savings by allowing you to hire consultants for a short time when there is a specific need for many people during testing. You can keep your Section 404 team small during the rest of the year.

Disadvantages
- This can be a dangerous strategy because it leaves little or no time for remediation.

- Because of the need for many testers during a short period, staffing may be an issue.

- A large testing effort would occur during the accounting department's busiest time.

- Process owners may "forget" about their controls since testing occurs only once during the year.

This method would work best for a company that has had minimal change in its key processes and has tested its controls in the past with only minor issues. It would also work well at foreign locations for a company with many locations in scope. The plan would be for each location to perform all of its testing at once. If you are sending a team out to perform the testing, it would save on multiple trips and travel costs too. Yet if the annual testing at certain locations was performed early in the year, you may have to use update testing near year-end. (See 4.)

4. **One big test phase plus update testing.** The answer to the one-big-test-phase method could be to have one big test phase in the middle of the year and then perform update testing at year-end. You would have the benefit of minimal test periods and still allow time for remediation if needed. However, update testing (inquiry, observation, small sample sizes) may have to be performed near the end of the year to update your results.

   Advantages
   - The bulk of your effort would be performed once in the middle of the year, and you would still have time to remediate if needed.

   - Testing would not be spread throughout the year, improving employee morale.

   - Cost savings could be realized by utilizing consultants for a few months during testing and keeping the SOX team small during the remainder of the year.

   Disadvantages
   - One big test phase would require a lot of resources for a short time. If resources are scarce, staffing could be an issue.

   - Different test plans may have to be written for the update tests.

      Both of these disadvantages are easy to overcome. This method would work well for most companies, especially in the second year of compliance (and beyond).

5. **Cycle tests.** Testing would be performed on a continual basis throughout the year, moving from one process to another. You could also move from one business unit to another depending on the structure of the company. Schedules would be planned at the beginning of the year to allow testing of high-risk or changed processes earlier in the year, leaving time for remediation if needed. Testing could be performed by employees or a special corporate test team that was well trained, consistent, and efficient.

   Advantages
   - You could customize the timing of your tests based on risk.

   - There would be time for remediation of controls tested early in the year.

   - There would be no huge test period during which much of the company was not focused on its regular responsibilities of running the business.

Disadvantages

- This method would require an ongoing testing effort throughout the year.

- It could be hard to analyze the program as a whole because cycles would always be at different stages (i.e., testing, remediating, completed).

- A team of corporate testers may be hard to retain.

- Corporate testers can take ownership away from process owners.

   This method could work for any company if it fit into the culture and structure.

TYPES OF CONTROL TESTS AND WHEN TO USE THEM

Using different types of tests can make your project more efficient if you pick and choose the method to complement the type of control. A list of eight types of tests and when to use them follows.

1. **Inquiry.** According to AS No. 5, Paragraph 50, inquiry alone does not provide sufficient evidence to support a conclusion about the effectiveness of a control, but it can be used in conjunction with other tests or as an update test. The actual inquiry can be oral or written, but it should be documented if used as part of a control test.

Practice Tip

Email is an efficient way to document inquiry testing. Emails are time/date stamped, name the sender, and can easily be saved electronically or in hard copy.

---

2. **Observation.** Observation is largely used for automated or system controls where evidence does not exist. Observation is also used in walk-through procedures or certain update tests. Inventory activities such as shipping, receiving, physical counts, and fulfillment lend themselves to observation testing.

3. **Walk-throughs.** A form of observation, walk-throughs could be used as testing for routine, low-risk processes that have tested successfully in the past (i.e., accounts payable invoice processing). Walk-throughs

could be used in alternating years to test these types of areas. AS No. 5, Paragraph 49, specifically allows walk-throughs as a form of testing:

> Walkthroughs usually consist of a combination of inquiry of appropriate personnel, observation of the company's operations, inspection of relevant documentation, and re-performance of the control and might provide sufficient evidence of operating effectiveness, depending on the risk associated with the control being tested, the specific procedures performed as part of the walkthrough and the results of those procedures.

Practice Tip

Walk-throughs can be very time consuming and may not be an efficient form of testing for some processes. However, you can gain efficiencies by using walk-throughs together with observation or examination for both updating process documentation (narratives/flowcharts) and performing control tests.

---

4. **Examination.** Much of your control effectiveness testing will be obtained through examination of evidence of control operations. Examination alone works best for tests of approvals, such as examining a purchase order or wire transfer form for proper approval signatures. Examination is also a good method to use in conjunction with walk-through procedures for confusing areas or processes with new employees.

5. **Reperformance.** Each business process should have some reperformance included in its testing. It is best to use reperformance for tests where the quality of the control evidence does not persuade you that the control is effective, such as a cursory signoff on a complex R&D tax credit calculation. The signoff does not prove that the R&D tax credit calculation methodology has been thoroughly reviewed, the result has been checked for reasonableness, or the input data has been tied to source documents.

6. **Examination.** Examination used in conjunction with reperformance testing can create a strong test for a complex, high-risk control. In the example of the R&D credit, you could use examination of the supervisor's signature and a reasonableness calculation, along with reperformance of tying the inputs to the source documents (such as R&D labor dollars and R&D supplies) for a thorough test. Examination together with reperformance provides the highest assurance of any testing method.

Accounting and financial reporting controls work well when tested with a combination of examination and reperformance because these controls are scrutinized by both management and the external auditor. For example, account reconciliations can be tested by examining the documents for reviewers' signatures and reperforming parts of the reconciliations, such as footing the ending balance and tying it to the general ledger.

Practice Tip

Use reperformance, or a combination of testing methods to include reperformance, for controls that mitigate the company's most significant risks.

---

7. **Internal audit investigations.** Reports that are issued as a result of an internal audit investigation can be used for control tests of certain processes or as tests of entity-level controls. For example, internal audit may investigate the expense reporting process testing for proper approval and adequate documentation (receipts) of all expense reports in the month of October. Their testing methodology, results, and conclusions should be well documented and could be used by management to conclude that the controls around the expense reporting process are effective. Be sure to check with your auditors for their requirements for using internal audit investigations for control testing. Internal audit is typically staffed by qualified auditors, so their investigations could be used for any significant process of testing internal controls. Additional testing may be required in a process for areas not covered by their investigations.

8. **Self-assessment.** Self-assessment testing, where the process owner rates the effectiveness of controls performed, is subjective and provides little assurance that controls are working as they should. Because of the subjectivity and indefinite results of self-assessment, it can be difficult to come to a conclusion on the effectiveness of controls. External auditors generally will not rely on self-assessment testing, so it is not an optimal method to use for control testing in those areas where auditors may rely on the work of others. Self-assessment testing is best used as an initial evaluation of controls, as preliminary testing, or as update tests for low-risk controls.

Your testing program can vary the types of tests depending on the level of risk surrounding a certain process or, more specifically, a certain control. Well-thought-out test programs include a mix of all types of tests and match the appropriate test to the risk and control. The level of assurance is greatest with reperformance testing and is lowest with inquiry and self-assessment.

WHY YOU SHOULD MINIMIZE THE USE OF SELF-ASSESSMENT TESTS

There is a lot of information in the accounting community about self-assessment processes where process owners document their opinions on the effectiveness of their own controls. The idea is that the process owners would know, firsthand, if their controls were operating as planned. However, self-assessment of controls can be time consuming, impractical, and yield little benefit for these reasons:

- Process owners are not auditors. Without knowledge of the objectives and risks, they cannot determine if a control is operating effectively.

- Process owners may see only a piece of the control and mistakenly believe the entire control is working effectively.

- Process owners can be optimistic and rate their controls as effective when they are only working part of the time.

- A self-assessment process for an entire company usually involves a large number of people and is time consuming.

- Because the self-assessment process is not objective, it generally will not be relied on by external or internal auditors.

By definition, self-assessment testing is not, objective, and in many cases, the cost and time involved outweigh the benefits. Its limited uses in a Section 404 program may include using it for an initial evaluation of control effectiveness at the beginning of the year or for update testing for low-risk areas at year-end.

SEC and PCAOB Guidance on Self-Assessments

In the SEC's Guidance for Management, self-assessment is explained in this way:

> Self-assessment is a broad term that can refer to different types of procedures performed by individuals with varying degrees of objectivity. It includes assessments made by the personnel who operate the control as well as members of management who are not responsible for operating the control.

The SEC goes on to explain what is already accepted by the audit community: (1) the evidence provided by self-assessment depends on the personnel involved and the manner in which the activities are conducted, and (2) self-assessments performed by the same personnel responsible for the operation of the control would provide less evidence of effectiveness due to the low degree of objectivity.

The SEC does introduce a concept that was seldom used in practice in the early years of Section 404 compliance. If management determines that internal control risk is low for controls at individual locations or business units, evidence gathered through self-assessments, when combined with evidence from a centralized control that monitors the results of operations at individual locations, may constitute sufficient evidence for an evaluation.

Earlier guidance from the PCAOB is in agreement with statements from the SEC on self-assessment. The PCAOB "clarified" its stance on self-assessment tests in Staff Q&A Nos. 47 and 48. In Q&A No. 47, the PCAOB again lists examples of procedures that management could use to obtain sufficient evidence of the operating effectiveness of controls, including "testing by means of a self-assessment process, some of which might occur as part of management's ongoing monitoring activities." It goes on to cite an example of management's direct and ongoing monitoring of the operation of controls:

> a supervisor's review of a monthly account reconciliation prepared by one of their subordinates could be a monitoring control that also provides management with evidence supporting its assessment of internal control over financial reporting, if the results of the supervisor's review were evaluated and documented as part of management's assessment.

Thus the PCAOB's clarification on self-assessment tests is essentially examination performed by the process owner's supervisor. This method still lacks the objectivity and independence desired for a tester, and may involve managers and higher-level employees in testing, which could increase costs. Also, most external auditors will place little or no reliance on this type of self-assessment testing.

In Q&A No. 48, the PCAOB goes on to explain that "self-assessment has become a broad term that refers to different types of procedures performed by various parties." It states that auditors should not use self-assessments made by the same personnel who are responsible for performing the control.

More recently, in AS No. 5, the PCAOB describes self-assessment procedures as a means of ongoing monitoring at the entity level. This is in line with its previously published guidance as well as with the Guidance for Management published by the SEC.

As part of your ongoing Section 404 effort, your company will try to find more efficient ways to monitor its internal controls over financial reporting. Although traditional self-assessments may provide value in other areas, they usually are too impractical, unreliable, and subjective to be used for Section 404 testing. While external auditors can use judgment to

---

Practice Tips

---

1. Use examination, observation, or reperformance testing with small sample sizes for testing in the beginning of the year instead of self-assessment tests. Traditional testing will be a more accurate indicator of whether controls are working as planned, and the first test phase can be a practice run for testing efforts later in the year. In addition, samples successfully tested during this early phase can be used to minimize sample sizes or reduce testing in later test phases. If performed early in the year, testing will bring attention to problem areas, and you will have sufficient time to remediate deficiencies.

2. Use inquiry instead of self-assessment at year-end for update tests in low-risk areas. The difference is the tester; inquiry can be performed and documented by an independent person (as opposed to the process owner) and is more likely to be relied on by your external auditor.

---

determine the extent to which they will use these tests, most will be reluctant to rely on any of management's tests labeled as self-assessment.

MAXIMIZING YOUR AUDITORS' RELIANCE ON THE WORK OF OTHERS

In the past, auditors were reluctant to rely on the work of others in a Section 404 audit because of the requirement in AS No. 2 that auditors use their own work to provide the "principle evidence" for their opinion of a company's internal control. But AS No. 5 removes many of the barriers to using the work of others in internal control audits.

AS No. 5 gives more options for external auditors to rely on the work of others for walk-throughs, risk assessments, and testing of the company's internal control. Auditors use of the work of others falls into two categories: (1) using the work of others under the direct supervision of the auditor and (2) relying on the work of others in the ordinary course of business, such as in control testing. Either method provides a big opportunity for audit-fee cost savings.

Allowing company employees to work directly with your auditors could be a big incentive for accountants trying to obtain their CPA (certified public accountant) license. Keep in mind that you can use employees *or* consultants to work under the direct supervision of your auditors. If you do not want to hire an employee full time to work with your auditors at the quarter and year-end, you still could save by hiring a staff or senior-level consultant on an as-needed basis. (Most staff or senior consultants bill at lower rates than are charged by audit firms.) In any case, incorporating

---

Practice Tip

At your annual audit planning meeting with your auditors, devise a plan for the auditors to use company personnel during their audits. The cost savings in audit fees could be substantial and may even enable you to hire an additional employee or consultant to assist your auditors. For example, you could hire a staff or senior-level employee to assist the internal audit, SOX, or other compliance function during the year and to work directly with the auditors for their Forms 10-Q, 10-K, and SOX procedures. The cost savings for a medium-size company in which an employee performs staff work for the auditors can be estimated in this way:

Number of staff audit hours for the year	1500
Percentage replaced by company personnel	50%
Potential hours saved	750
Per-hour audit staff billing rate	$200
Potential savings	$150,000

---

your own people into the auditors' work could provide substantial savings and more than cover the cost of an additional employee or consultant.

Qualifications

In using the work of others, auditors will be looking for personnel who are sufficiently *competent* and *objective*. These terms are subjective, and auditors will be looking for a degree of competence and objectivity instead of making an absolute conclusion. Thus, the higher the degree of competence and objectivity, the more auditors will be able to rely on others' work.

Practice Tip

Try to find a balance between the degree of competence and objectivity that your personnel can provide and how much your auditors will be able to use their work. There is no need to go overboard. Hiring a staff-level person with a lower degree of competence and objectivity may work better for your department (and budget) than hiring a more senior-level employee or consultant.

AS No. 5 defines competence as "the attainment and maintenance of a level of understanding and knowledge that enables that person to perform ably the tasks assigned to them." Auditors typically will be looking for these attributes when evaluating competence:

- The educational level and professional experience
- The professional certification and continuing education
- Supervision and review of the person's activities
- Quality of the documentation of the work produced
- Periodic evaluation of the person's overall performance

Objectivity is defined by AS No. 5 as the ability to perform tasks impartially and with intellectual honesty. In evaluating objectivity, external auditors typically consider these attributes:

- Policies to address the individuals' objectivity about the areas being tested, and whether the policies are being followed
- Whether individuals are testing areas to which they are assigned, were recently assigned, or are scheduled to be assigned upon completion of their testing responsibilities
- The organizational status of the individual or person responsible for the individual, including whether they have direct access to the audit committee and report to a person of sufficient status
- Policies designed to assure that compensation arrangements for individuals performing the work do not adversely affect objectivity and whether the policies are being followed

Auditors may be able to use personnel whose core function involves permanently serving in a testing or compliance capacity, such as internal auditors, to a greater extent than those whose principal duties address other business objectives, because these people normally are expected to have greater competence and objectivity. Auditors are advised against using the work of individuals who have a low degree of objectivity, regardless of their level of competence, and individuals who have a low level of competence, regardless of their degree of objectivity.

Auditors' Use of the Work of Others in the Ordinary Course of Business

Auditors' use of the work of others in the ordinary course of business is commonly seen in SOX projects when auditors use some of management's testing instead of their own. This usually is seen in two different scenarios:

1. Auditors use all of management's testing for a certain (usually low-risk) control when they perform a review of the testing work papers and write-up.

2. Auditors review management's test results for a certain control in addition to performing some of their own, limited testing of the control.

How much they rely on management's testing will depend on several factors:

- Objectivity of the tester
- Quality and reliability of the tests
- Competence of the individual
- Methods used in the tests
- Degree of risk of the controls

Using Tester Objectivity to Increase Reliance

Greater reliance will be given to tests performed by internal auditors and consultants than to tests performed by employees from the same department as the controls being tested. This does not mean that employees cannot help with the testing effort. Employee testing should be carefully planned to encourage your external auditors to rely on management's testing to the full extent.

Practice Tip

As a rule, process owners should not test their own controls, and if possible, employees should not test controls performed in their own departments. Swapping testers from various business units provides increased objectivity.

For example, accounts payable employees from one business unit can test the accounts payable controls from another business unit. You will be able to maximize the benefit of testers who know the accounts payable processes at your company but still have an increased amount of objectivity.

Another idea is to have employees from business units that are not in scope for your Section 404 program perform some testing in other areas to spread SOX work throughout the company. The testing experience will help these employees in future years, should their business units come into scope.

In general, external auditors will rank internal auditors or consultants as highly independent, employees from a difference business unit or department as medium independent, and employees from the same department as low in independence.

Practice Tip

It may seem illogical, but tester objectivity is not as big of an issue in high-risk areas. While you should always strive for competent, independent tests of controls, your external auditors will probably test high-risk controls themselves, regardless of the tester used by management. Focus internal auditors and consultants on the medium- and low-risk areas to minimize external auditor testing of your controls.

Why Qualifications of Testers Should Not Affect Reliance

Many companies use employees or a combination of consultants and employees for SOX testing. Most of these employee testers are not auditors and may not have accounting or finance knowledge. It is important to tailor your approach to your testers in case they are not experienced or do not have an audit background. If employees are properly trained and monitored, and your test plans "are written for simpletons," there should be fewer issues with qualifications or competence.

Practice Tip

Actual testers do not always have to have the qualifications your external auditors would like in order for them to rely on management's testing. Although testers may be inexperienced, they should be well trained and have descriptive and thorough test plans. The people who write the test plans, monitor the testers, review the results, and analyze the effectiveness of controls should have the qualifications your auditors are seeking.

Moving testing away from internal audit and Section 404 teams will allow internal audit to focus on their other responsibilities and give more ownership to the employees who perform and monitor the controls. Having the process owners absorb the bulk of the testing may also result in the costs being absorbed, dissipated, and reduced overall.

Whether you have internal audit, consultants, or process owners perform the majority of internal control tests, document the testers, their level of independence, and the company's methodology on the level and independence of testers. Be sure to include internal audit's monitoring and review of your SOX testing, because internal auditors will (generally) have the qualifications required to ensure that your testing and documentation are adequate for management to conclude on the effectiveness of its internal controls.

Creating Quality Test Documentation to Increase Auditor Reliance

In addition to tester competence and objectivity, producing quality test work will contribute to the amount of reliance your external auditors will have on management's testing. In evaluating the quality of management's test work, auditors consider:

- The amount of detail and relevant information in your test plans
- The description, time frame, and adequacy of the samples selected
- The testing method and how the test is performed
- The quality of your test results and conclusions

Practice Tip

Make your testing documents easy to understand and concise for your auditors, giving them only the information they need to know. Keep the format simple and the descriptions of tests, conclusions, and exceptions detailed enough for your auditors to fully understand what occurred.

Writing Test Plans That Are Easy to Follow   Test plans will be the guide for testers, a road map for your external auditors, and should contain all the information testers will need to complete the tests. Test plans should be written so that people with no knowledge of the process can understand and perform the test required. Simplify testing by telling testers exactly what they need to know, whom they need to contact (both for the population report and testing), the name of the report that should be run, and where documents are kept. Make the testing documentation specific enough that outsiders could perform the tests based on the descriptions in the test plans. In other words, the test plan should be so descriptive and easy to follow that anyone could perform the test.

Practice Tip

If you are straightforward, simplify, and add particulars to your test plans, you can have lower-level employees perform testing. Your SOX team will need experienced auditors to write the tests and analyze the results, but your testers will not require audit skills if you are explicit in your instructions. Your testers can be less experienced and your costs can be reduced.

Include this information in your test plans:

- A number or reference to the control activity being tested
- The documents or specific report names needed and the person or position description that can provide the documents or reports
- The date range being tested
- The sample size to select for testing or a reference to the company's sample size guidelines
- A step-by-step description of the test to be performed
- The type of testing being performed (reperformance, examination, observation, inquiry, etc.)
- The name of the tester and date tested
- A work paper reference column for any evidence included with testing results

Testers should receive a copy of the related control matrix and process narrative or flowchart for each area they are testing. A short excerpt from a sample test plan at a small company is shown in Exhibit 9.2.

Exhibit 9.2   Sample Control Test Plan

Control Activity	Test Description	Type of Test	Tester and Date	Work Paper Reference
234	A. Obtain a list of all monthly account reconciliations from the Staff Acct. Randomly select 30 reconciliations prepared from Jan–May08. For the samples selected, ensure that (1) reconciliations' ending balances tie to the general ledger; (2) any reconciling items during the interim months are resolved by quarter end; (3) accounts are reconciled by Day 5 of the close and are reviewed by the Accounting Manager, as evidenced by signatures and dates; and (4) reconciliations have supporting documentation attached.	Reperformance, Examination	Mary Smith 6/10/X8	A.1 – A.5

Sample Sizes   The proper sample size is a crucial element in the testing process. Your external auditor may ask specifically how you selected your sample, what dates were covered, what was the population, and the number of items sampled from the population. Sample selection and sizes will play a large role in management's assessment of its internal controls and whether your external auditors will rely on some of management's testing. As an example, your external auditors may not want to rely on a sample of two for a weekly control that was newly implemented in the last month of the year.

Samples generally are selected randomly to provide the conclusion that the control methodology is being consistently applied throughout the population. In internal control testing, as opposed to substantive testing, selecting only a weighted sample or a sample of material amounts will not provide the assurance that the control is being performed consistently for all transactions.

For example, if you only test approvals for purchase orders over $100,000, you may find the process to be effective because all big-dollar purchase orders are high profile and heavily scrutinized. However, if you examined small-dollar purchase orders, you may find the control to be lax because these do not have a spotlight shined on them. By testing a random sample, you can determine if all purchase orders are consistently approved according to company policy.

The goals in selecting sample sizes for testing are to ensure that enough transactions are tested to have confidence that the remaining transactions are reflected in the sample results and to not waste time reviewing too many items.

You should always exercise professional judgment when determining the extent of testing (and your sample sizes) based on these criteria:

- Importance of the control for the business unit or department to prevent or detect misstatements

- Degree to which the control supports the effectiveness of other controls (i.e., general IT controls)

- Whether the control relies on performance by an individual or is automated (manual controls require more extensive testing)

- Frequency with which a control is performed

- Complexity of the control

- Whether there have been changes to the volume of transactions, the design of the control, or key personnel

Parameters for sample sizes should include ranges instead of exact amounts so that sample sizes can be increased or decreased based on the factors just discussed. For example, you may need to increase a sample size for a control that has recently been changed.

Practice Tip

Publish sample size guidelines for initial testing and separate guidelines for update testing. Post them on an accessible site so testers can refer to them easily. Be sure to obtain auditor approval for all of your sample guidelines.

Testers must know that once a sample has been selected, items in the sample cannot be replaced because they are missing or are known to contain errors. Missing or erroneous items should be marked as exceptions. Items already selected in a sample can be replaced only if they were inaccurately included in the population.

Using Standardized Sample Size Descriptions   Whether your testing is performed by employees, consultants, or internal auditors, it is difficult to ensure that all sample sizes are described adequately and consistently in your testing documentation. External auditors will require these descriptions to be robust so they can determine if the company has sufficiently tested its controls as of year-end.

Practice Tip

Use standardized sample size language for all test documentation. Standardized descriptions should always be detailed and complete, describing how a sample was selected, the dates covered, the annualized population, and the number of samples selected.

Examples of sample size descriptions follow.

- From the period of June 1 through July 31, 2008, there was a population of 200 account reconciliations prepared. The annualized population is estimated to be 1200. Because this control is considered medium risk, a sample of 40 was randomly selected based on the company's initial testing sample guidelines.

  Or

- The annualized population for account reconciliations is 1200. A remaining sample of 10 has been randomly selected for testing based on the update testing sample guidelines. The samples cover the period of October 1 through November 30, 2008. Ten (10) of 200 occurrences for that period are being tested.

In addition to a description of how the sample was selected, be sure to include in your work papers a list of each item tested.

Testing Results and Reliability   Just as in your test plans, testing results should be in a simple format with detailed descriptions. Do not make your auditors guess. For SOX purposes, control tests either pass or fail. Conclusions such as "needs improvement" or "satisfactory," which are sometimes used in internal audit investigations, are confusing for SOX testing. Whether the test passed or failed, explain explicitly how the test was performed and which specific samples failed (if any). Your failed tests should have just as much (if not more) description as the tests that passed. Make copies of all exceptions to help clarify the error and include them in your work papers.

The most important point for control testing is to be sure your conclusion is reliable. Whether to call a variance an exception or not sometimes requires judgment. Be conservative. Judge questionable results as you believe your auditors would, and be sure that the conclusion that a control is effective is valid. Sketchy test results can cause your auditors to question your testing. You will gain no benefit from your tests if your auditors concludes differently on a control's effectiveness.

Practice Tip

Be conservative in your analysis of control effectiveness and judge your results as your auditors would. Questionable test results and conclusions will reduce your auditors' reliance on management's testing.

Meaningful Exception Documentation   Thorough documentation of exceptions will provide support for your later evaluation of these exceptions as deficiencies. Although testers usually can explain the exception in detail, they may not be able to explain the underlying cause or impact the ineffective control will have on the financial statements. Process owners or department managers should review and clarify all possible exceptions to ensure that they are true errors and not due to a tester's misunderstanding.

Work Paper Methodology   Documentation of your testing efforts lays the groundwork for management's assessment on its internal control. Initially you may have decided to keep hard copies of your test documentation. However, just as with other business documents, keeping your documentation in electronic form eventually will save time and space. In either case,

---

Practice Tips

Here are some additional tips on how to address deficiencies.

- Have a standardized template to use for documenting confirmed exceptions. Have the tester fill out the exception description and the process owner and/or the process owner's manager fill out the cause of the exception. If qualified, have the process owner and/or process owner's manager describe the impact the failed control could have on the financial statements. This will help the process owner understand the error and take ownership for its remediation.

- Process owners and champions can estimate the impact a failed control could have on the consolidated financial statements, but have them rate the deficiency as high, medium, or low impact only without coming to conclusion on the severity of the deficiency. The decision to label an ineffective control as a deficiency, significant deficiency, or material weakness should be made by your Section 404 program leader and appropriate members of senior management.

- There is no need for external auditors to test controls that failed management's testing. Your auditors generally will not dispute management's conclusion that a control is ineffective. Be sure your auditors have your most recent test results during their own test period so they know which controls they can pass over.

---

the format of your test documents should be consistent. This was hard to achieve in prior years of compliance because companies usually had many different people performing their tests, and consistency was not a priority.

Practice Tip

Establish a methodology for your test work papers. Each control test documentation could start with a summary cover page listing the control, test procedure, tester, outcome, and so on, but it is not necessary to make copies of each report, invoice, or statement sampled. Perhaps you can decide always to include copies of two samples, the first page of any report that was tested, and a copy of each document with an exception.

Be sure to discuss your work paper methodology with your external auditors. There is a fine line between making too many copies and having your test documents readily available for your external auditors' evaluation.

For additional guidance for testing documentation, refer to PCAOB's Auditing Standard No. 3, Audit Documentation and Amendment to Interim Auditing Standards. Although written for external auditors, management can use similar documentation techniques.

Increasing Reliance with Persuasive Testing Methods

Management can use a multitude of methods to come to a conclusion on the effectiveness of its internal controls. However, the methods management uses for testing will directly affect the amount of reliance your auditors place on your testing. The less assurance provided by your testing, the less reliance by your auditors.

For example, management can use inquiry and observation testing as sources for their opinion on internal controls. However, because these methods offer little assurance that controls are operating effectively, your auditors will rely less on management's testing if these methods are used. Maximizing auditor reliance has to be weighed against spending more time and resources on persuasive testing methods. Nevertheless, the more the company moves away from a traditional audit approach, the more external auditors will want to do of their own testing.

Reliance and Control Risk

External auditors may use the work of others but will perform much of their own testing as well. What areas would you test if you were required to choose certain processes? Your auditors will most likely test controls surrounding the high-risk processes that are complex, subjective, have had errors in the past, or relate to period-end adjustments. The auditors' responsibility to report on a company's financial statements and internal control rests solely with the auditors and cannot be shared with the other individuals whose work the auditors use.

MORE INSPIRATION ON EFFICIENT TESTING

Some final thoughts on gaining efficiencies in your testing follow.

Supply Tester Training for Better Test Results

You can use lower-level employees for testing and still obtain reliable results if you train your testers and monitor their work. You will save dollars by using the lowest-level employees possible who can still maintain the necessary quality. Give them all the information they need to be successful and enjoy your cost savings.

Practice Tips

Two tips for tester training follow.

1. Plan to hold training sessions for all your testers before each test phase in your first year of compliance. Training sessions can be reduced in successive years but should occur at least annually or whenever there are new testers. Not all of your testers will have an audit background. Training sessions will educate them about sample sizes and expectations for work papers and ensure a consistent format of your test documentation. Prepare a tester reference guide with your guidelines on sample sizes, testing, exception templates, and other useful information.

2. Consider videotaping training sessions that demonstrate and document the company's testing approach so you will have a library of SOX training videos for new employees or employees who have new SOX responsibilities.

Reasonable Assurance

In some cases, an exception may be found during testing, but management can still conclude that the control is operating effectively. According to the PCAOB Staff FAQ No. 13, effective internal control over financial reporting is a process designed to provide *reasonable assurance* regarding the reliability of financial reporting. Because effective internal control over financial reporting cannot, and does not, provide absolute assurance of achieving financial reporting objectives, any individual control does not necessarily have to operate perfectly all the time to be considered effective.

The key concept in PCAOB's Staff FAQ No. 13 is reasonable assurance. In year one, some external auditors took a hard stance, striving for absolute assurance. The PCAOB and SEC addressed this problem in their May 2005 guidance: "Management is required to assess whether the company's internal control over financial reporting is effective in providing reasonable assurance regarding the reliability of financial reporting." Reasonable assurance over financial reporting includes the understanding that there is a remote likelihood that material misstatements will not be prevented or detected in a timely manner.

The SEC staff states that "reasonable assurance is a high level of assurance." This is a key point and most accounting firms will measure reasonable assurance statistically. In this case, reasonable assurance is usually associated with a 90 to 95% confidence level. In the first three years of compliance for accelerated filers, there were no big 7 firms (4 + 3) that went lower than a 90% confidence level for their "high level of assurance." If the number of exceptions is greater than the upper limit deviation rate, you have crossed over the reasonableness threshold. For more information on statistical and nonstatistical sampling, refer to various publications by the American Institute of Certified Public Accountants (AICPA), including the book *Audit Sampling—AICPA Audit Guide*. The guide notes 90 to 95% as the high assurance range.

To remain in the high assurance range, increase sample sizes to make up for errors if exceptions are found during testing. How much should you increase the sample size if exceptions are found? Sample sizes should be increased to the point that there is assurance that the control is operating effectively. This could mean doubling the original sample size.

If several exceptions are found, instruct your people to discontinue testing. It will be a waste of time to carry on. The tester should document the testing procedures, exceptions, and the decision to stop. Testing of the activity can resume once the errors are resolved or the control is remediated.

Help testers use judgment to determining when to increase the sample size or cease testing. Generally, if the minimum sample size is selected by the tester, it is assumed there will be no exceptions.

Integrating Control Testing and Substantive Testing

Not only are public companies trying to make their Section 404 projects less time consuming and expensive, audit firms are striving to improve efficiency as well. The PCAOB and SEC statements that came out in May 2005 both expect further integration of the two audits to increase audit quality and decrease audit costs. AS No. 5 devotes paragraphs B1 through B9 to integrating the financial statement and internal control audits. Your benefits from integration will depend on the history with your external auditors, the amount of substantive testing they have performed in the past, and their prior reliance on your internal controls.

If your external auditors test the internal controls in a certain area extensively, they may be able to reduce the substantive testing in that area. Efficiencies can also be gained by selecting one sample for both internal control and substantive testing. The more integration, the greater a reduction in audit fees.

Practice Tip

Ask your auditors early in the year for a specific plan to integrate the two audits. Strong internal and entity-level controls may reduce the nature and extent of your auditors' financial audit testing. In addition, the same samples selected for control testing can be used for substantive tests.

For example, your external auditors could request a sample of 50 vendor invoices with the related backup documentation and check copy. Fifty items may seem like a large sample, but they would have to request a larger sample to make sure each of three individual tests have enough samples. Fifty samples to cover three tests is better than 30 samples per test. The auditors could test the purchase orders that accompany the 50 invoices for proper approval (control test), test that the check signers are authorized (control test), and test the invoices for proper cutoff (substantive test).

Integrating the audits takes additional time up front for planning but will have the benefits of faster and less obtrusive testing in the long run.

Kill Two Birds with One Stone

In the test preparation stage, a large amount of time is spent requesting and obtaining samples. This often is time consuming for the tester and the process owner and can be the cause of testing delays. No one wants to pull a sample of 30 customer contracts when a large sale is hitting its deadline and ready to close.

Practice Tip

Similar to the external auditors' attempt to integrate the two audits, review your control tests to see if you can use the same sample for different tests. If so, specifically instruct your testers in each test plan to use the same sample for both controls.

Each company's operations and processes are different, so the examples that follow may not always apply. However, the company probably has similar controls in which you could combine tests. Possible scenarios where you could use the same sample for multiple tests are:

- When selecting a sample of stock option offer letters, you can test that the letters were properly authorized via signature, that the issuance dates in the letters are correctly recorded in the system, and that the sampled option grants were approved by the board of directors.

- You can test different receiving controls with the same sample of packing slips. The same sample can be tested for signoff by the person who physically verified the shipment and to match the date the shipment was delivered to the dock to the date received in the system.

- A sample for a three-way match control can be used to test several other controls depending on your company's operations. With one sample of 30 invoices you could test that the related purchase orders are properly authorized, the receiving cutoff date is accurately recorded in the system, the invoice cutoff date is accurately recorded in the system, or the check is signed according to company policy (i.e., if two signers are required over a certain threshold).

- One sample of customer contracts could be used to test for proper signature on the contract, evidence of review by legal, customer credit checks, and proper revenue recognition.

Centralize Testing

Consider using a corporate test team similar to a corporate cycle count team that roams from business unit to business unit testing controls. Because it may be hard to retain employees for SOX testing year-round, the corporate test team could be part of a training program for internal auditors, finance personnel, or employees wanting to earn audit hours for their CPA license.

Eliminate Duplication

There is no need to test complementary controls. Choose the one control that you cannot live without as a key control, and change the second control to a nonkey or mitigating control. Examine your documentation for controls that address the same risk and/or assertion(s). In most cases, there is no need for both controls to be key.

10

Methods for Remediation Madness

The remediation phase requires softer skills than the technical skills needed for the documentation, testing, and evaluating phases. Now it is time to brainstorm, negotiate, and ask questions to motivate process owners to improve their deficient controls. Different companies will require different levels of participation from their Sarbanes-Oxley (SOX) team for remediation. No matter the level of involvement, it is essential that the process owners take ownership for remediation.

If you performed an initial test phase or control analysis early in the year, you may have several months to remediate failed controls. However, if you are near year-end and must remediate controls, you will be racing against the clock to finish and retest.

Practice Tip

Start remediation efforts as early as possible because they often take longer than expected. Do not wait until the entire test phase is complete. Have process owners thinking about solutions, and start discussions on improvements as soon as you have all the information. In the first year of compliance, you probably will have to remediate more controls than you ever imagined.

DO ALL CONTROLS HAVE TO BE REMEDIATED?

The company may decide for business or operational reasons that it will not fix or put in place certain controls. Some controls are not practical to implement, and management should think about the costs of implementing these controls versus the benefits. Keep in mind that the business is operating with inefficient and/or ineffective processes that could be costing it money in the long run. In addition, weaknesses and gaps in financial reporting controls could cause the company to make large adjustments every quarter and generate surprises in financial reporting.

The decision to forgo remediation on certain controls should be limited to low-risk controls only. The benefits of remediating high-risk controls usually outweigh the costs when you consider that high-risk, ineffective controls could be labeled as material weaknesses at year-end.

Practice Tip

Give champions and process owners guidelines, but allow them to make the decisions on which controls to remediate. Making decisions regarding their own controls will give them a feeling of ownership and commitment. Of course, the Section 404 team, senior management, and the external auditors should be informed and agree to decisions to forgo remediation.

Although process owners and their champions should be involved in the decision to remediate controls, they may not know the best way to address the gap or deficiency. A person with audit experience may be needed to suggest possible control solutions. Sometimes employees can perfect a control that has been suggested but cannot come up with the control on their own.

Considerations for Controls That Will Not Be Remediated

Be careful about decisions not to remediate controls. Once initial decisions have been made, examine a list of controls that will not be remediated. Perform a preliminary evaluation of the controls individually *and in the aggregate* to make sure none of them could rise to the level of a significant deficiency or material weakness. (Refer to Chapter 11 to learn more about aggregating control weaknesses.) Although a control may not be important by itself, it could become essential if a similar control or a control in the same process failed testing or was not remediated.

According to Auditing Standard No. 2 (AS No. 2), a significant deficiency that remained uncorrected for a reasonable period of time (e.g., one year) could indicate a material weakness. This language was omitted from the listing of indicators of material weaknesses in AS No. 5. Even so, if the company decides not remediate a deficiency, there should be a clear reason and an annual evaluation of the impact on the financial statements. If possible, discuss the issue with your external auditors while there is still time to change the decision.

FOR-NOW APPROACH TO REMEDIATION

AS No. 5 promulgates the point-in-time concept where internal controls over financial reporting have to be effective as of the end of the year. Luckily, this enables companies to remediate controls during the year to allow management to conclude that its internal controls are effective at year-end.

In the first year(s) of Section 404 compliance, most companies found a surprising number of control weaknesses to remediate. Because companies had to demonstrate the remediated controls were operating effectively for a sufficient amount of time by year-end, a temporary approach was used to implement new controls or fix ineffective controls. These controls were put in place "for now" and were often manual, quick fixes that proved to be inefficient and ineffective in the long run.

Practice Tip

Be sure to reassess controls that were remediated in the prior year to make sure the new controls are the best permanent solutions to mitigate the associated risk. Interview process owners and others involved with the process to gain their insight on how to optimize the new control. Look for automated and preventive control solutions to make sure the control will stand the test of time and pass testing in future years.

For example, a manufacturer had a deficiency over purchase order authorizations in year one because change orders that increased the dollar value of the purchase were not rerouted through the approval process. The deficiency was found late in the year, so the company implemented a manual, detective control where the purchasing manager reviewed a monthly report of all change orders where the dollar amount changed from the original purchase order amount. He signed off on all change order increases up to $5,000, the director of purchasing signed off on change order increases up to $20,000, and the vice president of operations signed off on increases over $20,001.

While this control worked and large discrepancies were investigated, the approval occurred after the fact and was cumbersome. In year two, the company implemented an automated purchase order system where change orders that increase the amount of the purchase order were automatically rerouted through the approval process via email. Once this process was implemented, there were no lengthy reports to review or possible missed signatures or approvals after the order was placed.

Employees' sense of SOX compliance is heightened during the first year of compliance. When the excitement dies down, process owners may not pay as much attention to the manual controls causing exceptions to occur. Be proactive about evaluating and improving remediated controls from year one that are not the best solution to mitigate financial risks.

CREATING MEANINGFUL REMEDIATION PLANS

Outline a specific plan for remediation for each deficient control the company plans to remediate. Plans should include the steps that will be taken to implement or improve the control, deadlines for each step, and the person who is responsible for the remediated control. Be sure to monitor the plans closely to keep remediation efforts on track.

Practice Tip

Provide the tools needed to create remediation plans for deficient controls and work with the process owner and champion to design the plan. Require process owners to present their remediation plans to their department head, the chief compliance officer, or chief financial officer (CFO) to give them responsibility and ownership for the plan's success.

Thoroughly document deficiencies that the company has decided not to remediate. Include the decision not to remediate with a short explanation why along with a risk analysis showing why the ineffective control will not cause a material misstatement in the financial statements. Be sure to note any compensating or complementary controls in your documentation.

A sample remediation plan template can be as simple as the one described in Exhibit 10.1. Many existing SOX applications allow you to generate this type of template with the first five rows completed.

NINE PRACTICE TIPS FOR THE REMEDIATION PHASE

Short and Sweet

Keep remediation plans simple. The essential elements of the plans are (1) specific steps that will be taken to implement or fix the control, (2) a deadline for implementation, and (3) an owner. Focus remediation owners

Exhibit 10.1   Sample Remediation Plan

Accounts Payable Remediation Plan for CA# 466	
Control objective	All high-dollar checks are properly authorized.
Risk	High-value checks will be issued in error or without the proper authorization.
Control activity	#466 All checks over $50,000 require two authorized signatures per the signature authorization policy.
Deficiency	Four out of the 30 checks tested over $50,000 contained only one signature.
Steps for remediation	
Deadline for implementation	
Owner	

on improving controls, not lengthy documentation. If the control requires complex discussions and analysis, document your strategy, discussion, and analysis in a different document. Actual remediation plans should be short and sweet so they can be emailed as reminders or used as a reference guide by process owners.

Communication

It seems obvious, but often new processes are not communicated to everyone affected by them, causing confusion and frustration. New controls should be communicated to everyone involved, including all process owners, their direct supervisors, the head of the department if necessary, and anyone outside of the department who may be affected.

Timelines

If practical, establish a company-wide, specific window for remediation plans and communicate this period to everyone involved in the process. This way everyone will know the month of June, for example, is for remediating controls, and once July begins, all new processes should be in place. Try not to perform any testing during the remediation phase so all cycles can focus on repairing their controls.

Certain controls will not fit into the company-wide window for remediation because they are complex or involve too many people or locations. For all these controls, try to plan a final due date so the SOX team and management know that all controls have been remediated after that date.

Prioritize

Prioritize your remediation efforts, focusing first on high-risk and low-frequency controls. High-risk deficiencies may need to be disclosed to the audit committee and the public, and generally take more time to remediate and retest. In addition, quarterly and semiannual controls need to be repaired immediately. These controls may be hard to retest adequately because of their frequency.

Objectives and Risks

To ensure that remediated controls are properly designed, focus on control objectives and risks when formulating plans. Process owners will probably need your assistance in this area. It will be useless to implement new procedures if they do not address the financial reporting objectives and mitigate the related risks. After new (or remediated) controls have been established, have a different member of the SOX team review the control and related objective and risk to make sure the new control is designed properly.

Facilitate but Do Not Own

Although champions or members of the SOX team may have the responsibility to facilitate remediation plans, it is essential that process owners take ownership and are involved in developing the new controls. They have to believe that the controls can be implemented as written before they will perform them consistently.

Because process owners may not have an audit background or fully understand the financial risk, many will require assistance from the SOX team, champion, or finance manager in their area. Suggest possible remediated controls, but let the owners customize them to fit into their daily duties.

Monitor Plans

The Section 404 team should closely monitor the remediation effort to make sure controls are repaired or implemented on time. There is a sense of completion after each test phase, and process owners' priorities often revert back to their regular duties or month-end close. Be sure to communicate often and make sure remediation is a priority. Monitor deadlines closely with follow-up meetings, phone calls, and emails.

Involve the External Auditors (Sometimes)

For high-risk or controversial deficiencies, present your remediation ideas to your external auditors. While it is not necessary to involve the auditors in all remediation plans, the external partner or audit manager should be consulted for high-risk controls that have been spotlighted. Obtaining their comments early in the remediation phase will avoid surprises later in the year.

Add a Compensating Control When Needed

Although one of the biggest efforts for reducing compliance cost has been the reduction in the number of key controls, the company's goal is for successful compliance. Consider adding a complementary control for high-risk or newly remediated areas where there is a risk a significant deficiency or material weakness may result if controls are not performed perfectly. Even if the complementary control is not as strong as the primary control, it can minimize the effect of an exception and reduce the severity down a level (i.e., from a significant deficiency to just a deficiency).

SUFFICIENT PERIODS FOR REMEDIATED CONTROLS

After you have taken corrective action for your chosen deficiencies, you will need to determine whether the remediated controls are designed and operating effectively for a *sufficient period of time* prior to year-end. What is considered a sufficient period of time? Remediation must occur early enough in the year to ensure that there will be an adequate amount of transactions to examine during the next phase of testing.

Most accounting firms have their own suggestions for the length of time remediated controls should be in place before they can be retested. The necessary length of time a control must be operating depends on the control's frequency. The more often a control is performed, the shorter the time needed to gather sufficient evidence that it is operating effectively. As a general rule, remediated controls should be in place for the length of time illustrated in Exhibit 10.2.

Annual controls will not be able to be remediated and retested during the current year if they are deficient when tested or if the control was not in place and the transaction already occurred. There is more flexibility with semiannual controls. You may be able to avoid a deficiency if a semiannual control is tested successfully once during the year and management feels

Exhibit 10.2 Sample Time for Remediated Controls to Be in Place before Retesting

Frequency	Suggested Time Period of Operation Prior to Report Date
Quarterly	2 quarters*
Monthly	2 months
Weekly	5 weeks
Daily	20 days
Multiple times per day	25 times over a multiple-day period

*Can include the fourth quarter as one of the quarters

the control is effective. Check with your external auditors for guidelines on their *sufficient period of time*.

It is near year-end and you find a deficiency in your testing. You remediate the control, but it will not be in place long enough to meet the company's guidelines for a *sufficient period of time*. For example, you remediated a weekly control that will be in place only for three weeks before the end of the year.

Test the control for the amount of time that it was in place at year-end and note it as a deficiency (even if it passed) because it was not in place for a long enough period. You should be very clear and open about the lack of sufficient time. Analyze and document the deficiency at year-end along with the other ineffective controls. Although the control was not in place long enough to ensure that it was effective, the successful tests can be used to argue that the deficiency is not material or perhaps even significant (if you are lucky). Look for other compensating key controls or nonkey controls that can be tested to act as compensating controls if needed.

STEPS TO PREPARE FOR RETESTING

Changing established behaviors is painstaking and time consuming, but you must wait until new processes are applied consistently before you can progress past the remediation phase. Once controls are remediated and a sufficient period of time has passed, you get to start the testing phase all over again.

Update Documentation and Test Plans

Before testing of the remediated controls begins, update all affected narratives/process flows, control matrices, and test plans for the changes. If you will be testing controls that passed the first phase of testing along with the remediated controls, do not forget to update sample sizes in your test plans to reflect results from the first phase of testing.

Sample Size Planning Spreadsheets

Develop simple spreadsheets to track the number of samples needed for each testing period. The sample size planning spreadsheet is a tool to help you determine the number of samples the company should test for each individual control and how many samples need to be tested in remaining test periods before the end of the year. After your initial test period, the spreadsheet should be completed and updated after each test period during the year. The results of the spreadsheet can help you plan how much time and the number of people you will need for the remaining test period. An example of a sample size planning spreadsheet is shown in Exhibit 10.3.

Exhibit 10.3   *Sample Size Planning Spreadsheet*

Control Activity #	Frequency of Control	Number of Annual Samples Required	Exception in the Previous Testing Phase?	Number of Samples Successfully Tested This Year*	Remaining Samples to Test This Year
456	Daily	40	Yes	0	40
521	Daily	40	No	30	10

*Be sure to teach personnel that samples in this worksheet should be evaluated as a group. If there is one exception in a sample of 30, the entire group of 30 will not count toward the "number of samples successfully tested this year." As seen in the example, a daily control may require an annual sample of 40 items. In the first test period, if 2 of the 30 samples had exceptions, none of the 30 samples can be used toward the annual requirement. Therefore, 40 samples should be tested during the remaining test periods.

Practice Tip

Be sure the Section 404 team reviews each cycle's sample size planning spreadsheet, paying particular attention to the "Number of Annual Samples Required" and "Number of Samples Successfully Tested This Year" columns. These numbers are crucial for the successful testing of the company's controls and typically are confusing areas for nonauditors.

PROJECT MANAGEMENT TOOLS FOR REMEDIATION

Each period in your SOX program will bring unique challenges. Documentation and testing is time consuming and labor intensive. Scoping and evaluation take communication and analytical skills. Yet the remediation phase requires the strongest people skills. You may have to negotiate, persuade, facilitate, manage, and play politics all at the same time. It is not easy to persuade people to change their old ways and to sell a new way to do things. Some tools and ideas to help you through the remediation period follow.

Use Meetings to Your Advantage

Meetings will become your best tool during your remediation phase. It can be difficult to gather all the necessary people together to discuss new controls in their area. Reserve a specific time in advance to speak to the key players for each process that requires remediation. Then you can count on the relevant people being involved in remediation, and you will have their undivided attention for a short time. Meet in a conference room so that phone calls and emails will not cause interruptions.

Schedule short, regular meetings with process owners and their managers during the remediation phase for status updates on their new controls. Also schedule regular meetings for specific complex areas that require more attention from senior management. By scheduling regular weekly or monthly meetings, senior management will know that the inventory meeting is held every Tuesday morning, for example, and can attend when available.

Persistence Is the Key

At some point, new processes and controls may be stuck. Initial meetings went well, progress was being made, and suddenly the momentum is lost. Perhaps a person is delaying the forward movement, or a problem has been encountered. Whatever the case, persistent follow-up and request for action can loosen the knot. Call a meeting to find out what is slowing the process, send daily emails, and follow up with phone calls. No matter how frustrating the blockage, do not become flustered. Auditors are scary enough to most managers and process owners so remain friendly and professional.

Management Support Is Required

In order to remediate a control successfully, the process owner's direct supervisor and the area manager must support the new process. Managers must hold their process owners accountable, and senior management must send the right message from the top. If management does not care or enforce compliance, there is no reason for the owners to bother.

Beware of the Politics

Remediating controls may bring you into contact with people you have not worked with before. You will not have a rapport with these people, so it is harder to read them and harder to motivate them to do what you want them to do.

People may have their own agendas. Implementing new procedures can be very political. Is power being taken away from one department and given to another? Does a new person have the ability to influence decision making? Will resources be allocated away from one area and into a new area? Will a new manager be reviewing the work of an employee with more seniority? Be sensitive to the politics surrounding new processes. Real or perceived shifts in decision making and resources could produce stumbling blocks for your remediation efforts.

Evaluate the Way Controls Are Written

In some circumstances, a deficiency can be cleared if the control is rewritten. Rewriting controls is not always appropriate, however, and should not be done for the sole purpose of passing a control test. Yet if there is no reason why a control must be performed as it is written, and the way the control is performed in practice can mitigate the associated financial risk, it can be changed. For example, a control that states that all purchase orders (POs) are approved by the vice president of purchasing can be changed to POs over $50,000 are approved by the vice president of purchasing.

Control activities and process documentation often have to be reworked (especially in the first year of compliance) because process owners sometimes describe their controls as the way they are supposed to be, not the way they really are. In some cases, the way they are supposed to be has no purpose or is simply overkill.

If you decide to rewrite controls, do it the right way. Document any failed test results with the old control and note in the results and remediation plan that the control will be changed. Once the control matrix and narrative/process flow are updated for the new control, test it and document the results. Be very clear about what you have done, and point the new control out to your auditors. Keep in mind that if the new control is considered a material change to the company's internal control, it will have to be disclosed in the company's quarterly Section 302 certification.

Conclusion

The remediation phase of a SOX program can be a form of public relations if done right and can show the best return on your company's 404 investment. Process and control improvements created during the remediation phase can directly improve the bottom line. Be patient yet persuasive in your approach and allow more time than you think to ensure that the right controls are put in place.

11

Taking the Mystery Out of Evaluating Deficiencies

Key Topics:
- Deficiencies defined

- Analytical steps for evaluating deficiencies

- Are all exceptions considered deficiencies?

- Techniques for aggregating deficiencies

- Typical material weaknesses

- The unique nature of information technology general control deficiencies

- The market's reaction to process specific versus pervasive material weaknesses

- How to improve material weakness disclosures

- Auditing Standard No. 4 and reporting whether a previously reported material weakness still exists

- Successful communication of deficiencies to management and the audit committee

- Managements final assessment report

As you approach the completion of your remediation and control testing, controls that will be considered ineffective at year-end will become evident. Although there is some guidance to help analyze the severity of these deficiencies, the process is subjective and will require you to imagine what-if scenarios. It is important to remember that the significance of a deficiency in internal control over financial reporting depends on the potential for a misstatement, not whether a misstatement actually occurred, and that limits and thresholds to categorize deficiencies are not definitive.

External auditors are not required to search for deficiencies that are less severe than a material weakness. Auditors must, however, evaluate the severity of each control deficiency that comes to their attention. Experienced (internal and external) auditors will have an initial opinion or gut feeling for controls that are ineffective at year-end and whether they will be rated as material weaknesses, significant deficiencies, or just deficiencies. Even though the initial opinion can provide a preliminary evaluation, the final decision cannot be made until a full analysis using the concepts described in this chapter is performed.

DEFICIENCIES DEFINED

To help classify exceptions and gaps as deficiencies, the Public Company Accounting Oversight Board (PCAOB) has published definitions of the three different types of deficiencies. Although the terms have been used in auditing circles for some time, the definitions have changed.

Deficiency

According to Auditing Standard No. 5 (AS No. 5), a deficiency in internal control over financial reporting exists when the design or operation of a control does not allow management or employees, in the normal course of performing their assigned functions, to prevent or detect misstatements on a timely basis. The differences between design and operating deficiencies are explained in this way:

- A deficiency in *design* exists when a control necessary to meet the control objective is missing or an existing control is not properly designed so that, even if the control operates as designed, the control objective would not be met.

- A deficiency in *operation* exists when a properly designed control does not operate as designed or when the person performing the control does not possess the necessary authority or competence to perform the control effectively.

All breaches of controls that prevent or detect potential financial statement misstatements are deficiencies. However, each deficiency must be analyzed to see if it rises to the level of significant deficiency or material weakness. If the deficiency only has a remote chance of causing the financial statements to be misstated and/or the possible misstatement would be less than significant, the deficiency generally would not be elevated to a higher level.

Significant Deficiency

The definition of a significant deficiency has changed from AS No. 2 and changed again from the definition in the proposed standard that eventually became AS No. 5. After two prior definitions, a significant deficiency is finally described in AS No. 5 as a deficiency, or combination of deficiencies in internal control over financial reporting that is less severe than a material weakness, yet important enough to merit attention by those responsible for oversight of the company's financial reporting.

The definition is less precise than it was in its two former versions and lends itself to professional judgment with the phrase "important enough to merit attention by those responsible for oversight of the company's financial reporting."

Material Weakness

AS No. 5 changed the definition of a material weakness as well, mainly to rid it of the term "significant deficiency." Material weakness is defined in AS No. 5 as

a deficiency or combination of deficiencies, in internal control over financial reporting, such that there is a reasonable possibility that a material misstatement of the company's annual or interim financial statements will not be prevented or detected on a timely basis.

The key phrases in this definition are "reasonable possibility" and "material misstatement." Because they both require professional judgment, AS No. 5 refers to existing standards to explain their meanings.

Reasonable Possibility   AS No. 5 states there is a reasonable possibility of an event when the likelihood of the event is either "reasonably possible" or "probable." The PCAOB uses these terms as they are defined in Financial Accounting Standard (FAS) No. 5, *Accounting for Contingencies*. The statement defines these terms and the related term "remote" in this way:

a. *Probable*. The future event or events are likely to occur.

b. *Reasonably possible*. The chance of the future event or events occurring is more than remote but less than likely.

c. *Remote*. The chance of the future event or events occurring is slight.

So essentially, the new definition of a material weakness goes back to the original meaning in AS No. 2: If the chance of material misstatement is more than remote, you have a material weakness. One might say much ado about nothing.

Material Misstatement   Although both quantitative and qualitative factors need to be considered for the term "material," management is generally aware of the quantitative thresholds that are used for materiality. The qualitative factors are subject to professional judgment and are explained in more detail in SEC Staff Accounting Bulletin No. 99, *Materiality* (SAB No. 99).

Exhibit 11.1   Definitions of Deficiencies

	Likelihood		Magnitude
Control Deficiency	Remote	AND/OR	Less than significant
Significant Deficiency	Reasonably possible or probable	AND	Less than material but important enough to merit attention
Material Weakness	Reasonably possible or probable	AND	Material

Evaluating Deficiencies   Based on the definitions just described, management can evaluate a deficiency in internal control by considering the likelihood (reasonable possibility) that the company's internal controls will fail to prevent or detect a misstatement on a timely basis and the magnitude of the potential misstatement resulting from the deficiency or deficiencies. Exhibit 11.1 summarizes the definitions of the various deficiencies.

ANALYTICAL STEPS FOR EVALUATING DEFICIENCIES

The *likelihood* that an account or disclosure in the consolidated financial statements will be misstated and the *potential magnitude* of the misstatement are the essence for evaluating your deficiencies. However, other qualitative factors and compensating controls will also affect your conclusions. As a result, your evaluation will require significant professional judgment with input from various sources.

Practice Tip

Evaluating deficiencies is a lengthy process that includes many people and significant judgment. Instead of a full evaluation after each test period, have process owners and champions rank deficiencies as low, medium, or high risk after each interim testing period. Have the Section 404 team review the rankings to make sure all deficiencies are properly rated. Confirm your list of high-risk deficiencies with your external auditors to make sure you are both in agreement on the major issues. Possible significant deficiencies and material weaknesses should be labeled as high risk and fully evaluated, documented, and reported to senior management and the audit committee.

Developing an Appropriate Methodology for Evaluating Deficiencies

For the quantitative analysis of your deficiencies, a methodology with significant and material thresholds needs to be established as the first step. What is important to management and your stockholders? What amounts would they consider material or significant? Perhaps a one-cent change in earnings per share (EPS) is important for some investors. However, revenue may be the most important indicator for a start-up company that is moving toward the break-even point.

Each company will have its own unique indicators, and these indicators may change from year to year depending on what makes sense for the business in any given year. Neither the Securities and Exchange Commission's (SEC's) Guidance for Management or AS No. 5 gives strong guidance in this area except for the PCAOB's instruction that auditors' materiality considerations should be the same for internal control and financial statement audits. You may decide to use 1% of total assets or 2% of before-tax income as a significant threshold. The nine leading accounting firms in their white paper, *A Framework for Evaluating Control Exceptions and Deficiencies, Version 3* (referred to in this chapter as the *Framework*), suggest using 20% of the company's overall annual materiality as the threshold for more than inconsequential or "significant." The important part is to tailor your methodology to what is going on in the business. For example:

- What is the company's financial situation? Is it operating at a profit or a loss?

- What is happening in the industry?

- What are similar companies using?

- What indicators are important to management and investors?

- What would a "prudent official" use as a threshold for significant or material?

A biotech company, for example, that has been public for two years is operating at a net loss. Management is forecasting to break even in the first quarter of year four mainly by increasing its revenues. Total assets, loss per share, and loss before income tax are not as important to management or investors in the current year as revenues. As such, management had decided to use 0.5% of gross revenue as its significant threshold and 1% as its material threshold. These amounts are reasonable when compared to the auditor's annual overall materiality level.

Determining Reasonable Possibility

Evaluating whether there is a reasonable possibility (or likelihood) of a financial statement misstatement is a risk analysis that is largely qualitative.

Practice Tip

While it is management's decision to set the limits for significant deficiencies and material weaknesses, consider the amount of your external auditors' overall materiality as a reasonableness check. If your auditors' overall materiality for the year is $500,000, you may be off base if your threshold for a significant deficiency starts at $1.5 million.

Both the SEC and PCAOB list these factors as contributing to the likelihood that the financial statements will be misstated:

- The nature of the financial statement accounts, disclosures, and assertions involved; for example, suspense accounts and related party transactions involve greater risk.

- The susceptibility of the related assets or liability to loss or fraud; that is, greater susceptibility increases risk.

- The subjectivity, complexity, or extent of judgment required to determine the amount involved; greater subjectivity, complexity, or judgment, such as in an accounting estimate, increases risk.

- The interaction or relationship of the control with other controls; the interdependence or redundancy of the control.

- The interaction of the deficiencies; for example, when evaluating a combination of two or more deficiencies, whether the deficiencies could affect the same financial statement accounts and assertions.

- The possible future consequences of the deficiency.

Keep in mind that a reasonable possibility of misstatement might be different for the maximum possible misstatement than for lesser possible misstatement amounts. In other words, the probability of a small misstatement will be greater than the probability of a large misstatement. For example, a construction company has a deficiency in its bank reconciliation process because it did not reconcile some of its subsidiaries' bank accounts in a timely manner. Since the parent's bank reconciliation process is effective, and the parent consistently holds 90% of the total cash balance throughout the year, the likelihood that the entire cash account is misstated is low. However, a reasonable possibility that there is some type of error in the cash balance is much higher.

Compensating Controls

Compensating controls can be persuasive reasons why the possibility that an ineffective control would cause a misstatement is determined to be remote. The strongest compensating controls help to mitigate the same risk as the failed control, but there are exceptions, as in the next example.

A small manufacturer has a deficiency in its process to ensure that all shipped goods are invoiced in a timely manner. The potential magnitude of this deficiency could be material, since three or four large shipments that were not recorded in the proper period could cause revenues to be materially understated during that period. However, the company has a compensating control for monthly cycle counts that has a different objective but was successfully tested. Of their inventory, 100% is counted monthly, and all discrepancies are investigated and resolved before the general ledger is closed for the month. Since the shipped inventory (and related sale) was not yet recorded in the system, the inventory would be "missing" during the monthly cycle counts and investigated. The resolution of the "missing inventory" investigation would cause the company to record the shipments in the period in which they were shipped.

In this example, the failed control for shipped goods had a risk that revenues were not recorded in the proper period. The related assertion was for completeness and could also cover existence. The monthly cycle count risk was that inventory was not accurately recorded and addressed the existence and completeness assertions. Although the assertions were similar, the controls addressed separate risks for revenue and inventory. Luckily, the controls indirectly supported each other and could be used as compensating controls.

A few guidelines for documenting compensating controls in your evaluation of deficiencies follow.

- The strongest compensating control is a control that helps to mitigate the same risk and addresses the same financial assertion(s).

- A high-level variance analysis (such as actual amounts compared to budgeted amounts) is not the answer to all deficiencies. Unless the variance analysis is detailed and addresses specific transactions, it is usually too general to be used as a strong compensating control.

- Deficient controls cannot be used as compensating controls. Although you can refer to operational controls or other processes, financial controls that were successfully tested at year-end generally make the strongest argument.

- If an ineffective control does not have any compensating controls, it is hard to argue that the chance of financial statement misstatement is remote.

Compensating controls may, at a minimum, be able to reduce the magnitude of a deficiency. Compensating controls that follow the preceding criteria can reduce a possible significant deficiency or material weakness back to the level of deficiency.

Determining Magnitude

According to the SEC and PCAOB, many factors can be used to determine the magnitude of a potential misstatement of the financial statements, but the main factors are:

- The financial statement amounts or total of transactions exposed to the deficiency

- The volume of activity in the account balance or class of transactions exposed to the deficiency that has occurred in the current period or that is expected in future periods

When determining magnitude, it is generally understood that the maximum amount that an account can be overstated is the recorded amount. In contrast, the potential amount that an account can be understated does not have this limit.

Evaluate Reasonable Possibility or Magnitude First?

Although the SEC's Guidance for Management first refers to considering whether there is a *reasonable possibility* of misstatement and then to the *potential magnitude* when evaluating deficiencies, the *Framework* begins its evaluation process with an analysis of the magnitude of potential misstatements. Perhaps this is because many external auditors would like all deficiencies with the potential for a more than inconsequential misstatement to be documented through the entire analysis (of magnitude, then reasonable possibility). If reasonable possibility is analyzed first, a deficiency with the potential for a material misstatement may not be fully analyzed if the likelihood is remote. In contrast, by analyzing magnitude first, all deficiencies with a more than inconsequential amount of potential misstatement will be fully analyzed.

Unfortunately, this type of analysis leaves the door open for an unreasonable conclusion. *Potential magnitude* provides a wide spectrum of possibilities that is not easy to define realistically. If the chance of misstatement is *truly* unlikely, is potential magnitude even an issue?

In the shipped not invoiced example, the likelihood of misstatement is unlikely even though the amounts have the potential to be material. When analyzing whether there is a reasonable possibility of misstatement first, it is important to have a strong argument for the chance of misstatement being *remote* versus *reasonably possible or probable*. If the chance of misstatement is truly remote, discussing potential magnitude is a moot point.

Using the Prudent Official Test

In addition to magnitude and possibility, other qualitative aspects should be considered when evaluating the severity of deficiencies. The SEC's

---

Practice Tip

Whether you decide to analyze if there is a reasonable possibility of misstatement or the potential magnitude of misstatement first in your evaluation of deficiencies, document an example of the format you will be using and present it to your external auditors. A logical analysis that includes both the possibility of misstatement and magnitude is the goal.

Guidance for Management recommends that evaluators apply a reasonableness test when rating deficiencies. It advises management to

> determine the level of detail and degree of assurance that would satisfy prudent officials in the conduct of their own affairs that they have reasonable assurance that transactions are recorded as necessary to permit the preparation of financial statements in conformity with generally accepted accounting principles.

AS No. 5 uses the same language for the "prudent official test" but adds this comment in Paragraph 70:

> If the auditor determines that a deficiency, or combination of deficiencies, might prevent prudent officials in the conduct of their own affairs from concluding that they have reasonable assurance that transactions are recorded as necessary to permit the preparation of financial statements in conformity with generally accepted accounting principles, then the auditor should treat the deficiency, or combination of deficiencies, as an indicator of a material weakness.

Of course, this is a highly subjective interpretation that attempts to bring an overall sense of reasonableness to the analysis. However, it would be surprising for an auditor to override the magnitude and possibility arguments to rate a deficiency significant or material because of the prudent official test.

For more information, see the SEC Staff Accounting Bulletin Topic 1M2, *Immaterial Misstatements That Are Intentional* for further discussion about the level of detail and degree of assurance that would satisfy prudent officials in the conduct of their own affairs.

ARE ALL EXCEPTIONS CONSIDERED DEFICIENCIES?

For transactions that occur daily or several times a day, there may be some leeway for classifying an occasional exception found in testing as a deficiency. Sample sizes should be expanded to or past the maximum level if an exception is found or an exception is expected to be found during testing. It is often assumed that there will be no errors when minimum sample sizes are selected. The crucial issue is whether the exception represents transactions in the entire population or if it is just a chance occurrence.

AS No. 5 advises auditors to determine the effect of deviations on their assessment of the risk associated with the control, the evidence to be obtained, and the operating effectiveness of the control. In Paragraph 48 it further states:

> Because effective internal control over financial reporting cannot, and does not, provide absolute assurance of achieving the company's control objectives, any individual control does not necessarily have to operate without any deviation to be considered effective.

As an example, there may be a "several times a day control" stating all invoices are approved and signed by the accounts payable (AP) manager before processing. A maximum sample of 45 shows one invoice that is not signed. You may conclude that the one exception is not representative of the way the control operates in the entire population, there is sufficient evidence that the control is working, and invoices are routinely reviewed by the AP manager. The exception can be blamed on human error, and the conclusion can be made that the control is effective. Hence no deficiency would exist.

As another example, a company used a sample of 25 to test a daily bank deposit control where a second person compares the total on the bank deposit to the total receipts recorded in the system and signs off. One exception was found in the initial sample. The company expanded its sample and selected an additional 15 deposits, none of which had exceptions. The company concluded that the control was effective.

The idea that random exceptions may not be indicative of a deficiency is also supported by nine of the leading accounting firms. The *Framework*, created in 2004, takes a more conservative approach than AS No. 5 but still allows for exceptions in controls if control tests are extended. It explains that if the observed exceptions and resulting nonnegligible deviation rate are not believed to be representative of the population, the test may be extended and reevaluated.

To remain within acceptable standards for many auditors, the option to conduct additional testing is available for manual controls operating daily or more frequently when:

- Only one exception is observed in an initial sample of 20 to 40.

- The exception is not an indicator of systematic and recurring errors.

- The population is adequate to select additional samples.

Practice Tip

A person on the Section 404 team should evaluate daily or multiple times a day controls with one testing exception to determine if deficiencies actually exist. Determinations of no deficiency should be well documented with explanations of why the error(s) were so classified.

TECHNIQUES FOR AGGREGATING DEFICIENCIES

Both the SEC's Guidance for Management and AS No. 5 call for an evaluation of identified control deficiencies to determine whether the deficiencies, individually or in combination, are significant deficiencies or material weaknesses. Evaluating deficiencies in the aggregate is trickier than evaluating them individually because the process becomes more subjective when you evaluate controls in combination. Deciding which controls to combine, the effect of the combination, and its relevance is highly judgmental. Deficiencies should be evaluated in the aggregate when they affect the same items listed next:

- **Financial statement account or disclosure.** For example, if deficiencies for inventory controls are found in different locations, an aggregate analysis should be performed for all deficiencies related to inventory.

- **Entity-level controls.** All deficiencies for each individual Committee of Sponsoring Organizations (COSO) component should be reviewed in the aggregate in addition to all entity-level control deficiencies being reviewed together. For example, all deficiencies found for the risk assessment component should be analyzed in the aggregate before all deficiencies for the internal environment are evaluated together.

- **Business subprocesses.** For example, deficiencies that occurred in materials procurement, information technology (IT) procurement, and corporate procurement should be evaluated in the aggregate.

When evaluating whether there is a reasonable possibility that a combination of deficiencies could result in a misstatement, evaluate how the controls interact with each other. There are controls, such as IT general controls, on which other controls depend. Some controls function together as a group of controls, and other controls overlap achieving the same objective.

> **Practice Tip**
>
> When evaluating deficiencies in the aggregate, try using a worst-case-scenario approach. What would be the possibility and potential magnitude of a misstatement if all controls in the aggregated group failed at the same time? Be sure to take into account any qualitative factors.

Summary: Steps for Analyzing Deficiencies

Here is a summary of the seven steps to follow when analyzing deficiencies.

1. Determine the company's thresholds for significant deficiencies and material weaknesses based on company-specific indicators. Compare your amounts to your auditor's overall annual materiality for reasonableness.

2. Identify any *compensating controls* for the ineffective control.

3. Determine whether *the possibility* of misstatement of the company's financial statements due to the failure of the control is remote, reasonably possible, or probable.*

4. Calculate the *potential magnitude* of a misstatement that could occur because of the control's failure.*

5. Analyze whether a *prudent official* would have reasonable assurance that transactions are recorded according to generally accepted accounting principles (GAAP) if the control failed.

6. Conclude on the level of the individual deficiency.

7. *Aggregate* and analyze all deficiencies that could be logically grouped.

  *Note: Steps 3 and 4 can be reversed.

Sample Analysis for a Significant Deficiency

In analyzing their deficiencies using the seven steps, a company concluded it had a significant deficiency for this scenario.

The company uses a standard sales contract for most transactions and individual sales transactions range from $10,000 to $50,000 each. Sales personnel are allowed to modify sales contract terms with the proper approval. The company's accounting function reviews significant or unusual modifications to the sales contract terms but does not review changes to the standard shipping terms. Changes to the standard shipping terms could require a delay in the timing of revenue recognition. Management reviews gross margins on a monthly basis and investigates any significant or unusual relationships. In addition, management reviews the reasonableness of inventory levels at the end of each accounting period. The entity has experienced limited situations in which revenue has been inappropriately recorded in advance of shipment, but amounts have not been material. Although there are compensating controls, shipping errors have occurred in the past, so the likelihood of the deficiency is rated as reasonably possible. Based on limits set by senior management, the magnitude could be significant but less than material. The Sarbanes-Oxley team performed the prudent official test, and the deficiency did not aggregate with any others. The company concluded that the deficiency rose to the level of significant.

TYPICAL MATERIAL WEAKNESSES

When there are few or no compensating controls for a deficiency or group of deficiencies, and the potential misstatement could be material, the company is probably dealing with a material weakness. In addition to evaluating the possibility and magnitude of deficiencies, the SEC and PCAOB have identified these circumstances that indicate a material weakness in internal control over financial reporting may exist:

- Identification of fraud, whether or not material, on the part of senior management. According to the PCAOB, the term "senior management" includes the principal executive and financial officers signing the company's certifications as required under SOX Section 302 as well as any other members of senior management who play a significant role in the company's financial reporting process.

- Ineffective oversight of the company's external financial reporting and internal control over financial reporting (ICFR) by the company's audit committee.

- Restatement of previously issued financial statements to reflect the correction of a material misstatement. The correction of a material misstatement includes misstatements due to error or fraud; it does not include retrospective application of a change in accounting principle to comply with a new accounting principle or a voluntary change from one generally accepted accounting principle to another.

- Identification by the auditor of a material misstatement in financial statements in the current period in circumstances that indicate the misstatement would not have been discovered by the company's ICFR.

Deficiencies in these areas typically would be found by your external auditors. However, strong controls around financial reporting and audit committee oversight can help avoid surprises in these areas.

As an example of a material weakness analysis, a company followed the seven steps for evaluating deficiencies and concluded it had a material weakness for the next scenario.

The company has a standard sales contract, but sales personnel frequently modify the terms of the contract. The nature of the modifications can affect the timing and amount of revenue recognized. Individual sales transactions are frequently material to the entity, and the gross margin can vary significantly for each transaction. The company does not have procedures in place for the accounting function to regularly review modifications to sales contract terms. Although management reviews gross margins on a monthly basis, the significant differences in gross margins on individual transactions make it difficult for management to identify potential misstatements. Improper revenue recognition has occurred, and the amounts have been material. The likelihood of misstatement is reasonably possible or probable, and the potential magnitude is material. Since there are no strong compensating controls, the deficiency is classified as a material weakness.

UNIQUE NATURE OF IT GENERAL CONTROL DEFICIENCIES

Evaluating IT controls is unlike evaluating financial reporting controls because their impact on the financial statements is more indirect. Information technology general controls (ITGC) are policies and procedures that relate to many applications and support the effective functioning of application controls by helping to ensure the continued proper operation of information systems. These controls are pervasive throughout the organization. Because of their nature, it can be difficult to evaluate how a deficiency in ITGCs could affect the financial statements.

Evaluating ITGC Deficiencies

Evaluating ITGC deficiencies is similar to evaluating other control deficiencies. However, deficiencies in ITGC controls generally would not be the direct cause of a financial statement misstatement. The bigger risk is that ITGC deficiencies could cause or allow application controls to become ineffective resulting in a misstatement.

Compensating Controls   When evaluating ITGC deficiencies, compensating controls can be used to reduce the severity of a deficiency if they are successfully tested and address the same control objective (or risk) as failed controls.

Aggregating ITGC and Application Controls   ITGC deficiencies must be assessed in conjunction with their related application control deficiencies just as related financial control deficiencies must be assessed in the aggregate. A good understanding of how relevant applications impact the financial statements and the relationship of specific application controls to ITGCs is needed to assess deficiencies in this area accurately.

According to the *Framework*,

> if no deficiencies are identified at the application level, the ITGC deficiency could be classified as only a deficiency. If there is a control deficiency at the application level related to or caused by an ITGC deficiency, the ITGC deficiency is evaluated in combination with the deficiency in the underlying application control and generally is classified consistent with the application control deficiency.

Take the example of an ITGC deficiency found in change management where program changes are migrated into production without subsequent monitoring. This program change caused the application control of a three-way match in the accounts payable process to become ineffective. (The invoice is matched to the purchase order and receiving report.) You would first rate the application control deficiency, and that would dictate the deficiency level for the ITGC exception. If the application deficiency was labeled as a significant deficiency, your ITGC deficiency generally would be labeled as a significant deficiency as well.

Other Qualitative Factors and Prudent Officials   Similar to your financial control assessments, ITGC deficiencies must be evaluated for nonquantitative characteristics and pass the prudent official test. (Would a prudent official have reasonable assurance that the transactions are recorded as necessary to conform to GAAP?) Other qualitative factors to consider when evaluating ITGC deficiencies include:

- The nature and significance of the deficiency (i.e., does the deficiency relate to a single area in the program development process, or is the entire process deficient)?

- The pervasiveness of the deficiency to applications and data, including:

  - The extent to which controls related to significant accounts and underlying business processes are affected by the ITGC deficiency

  - The number of application controls that are related to the ITGC deficiency

  - The number of control deficiencies at the application level that are related to or caused by the ITGC deficiency

- The complexity of the company's systems environment and the likelihood that the deficiency could adversely affect application controls

- The relative proximity of the control to applications and data

- Whether an ITGC deficiency relates to applications or data for accounts or disclosures that are susceptible to loss or fraud

- The cause and frequency of known exceptions in the operating effectiveness of an ITGC; for example, the deficiency could be caused by (1) a control with an unacceptable deviation rate; (2) an observed exception that shows the ITGC is not operating effectively; or (3) a deliberate failure to apply a control

- A history of misstatements relating to applications affected by the ITGC deficiency, including misstatements in the current year

What Is Considered an ITGC Material Weakness?

Although it is unusual to have a material weakness in an ITGC deficiency, two situations in which an ITGC deficiency could rise to the level of material weakness are discussed next.

- An application control deficiency related to or caused by an ITGC deficiency is classified as a material weakness.

- The pervasiveness and significance of an ITGC deficiency leads to a conclusion that there is a material weakness in the company's control environment.

Keep in mind that when you are evaluating the consequence of an ITGC deficiency on effective application controls, you do not have to consider the likelihood that effective application controls could become ineffective in the future because of the deficient ITGC.

MARKET'S REACTION TO PROCESS SPECIFIC VERSUS PERVASIVE MATERIAL WEAKNESSES

If the company is unfortunate enough to have a material weakness in its internal control over financial reporting, there are several issues to consider for the future. Material weaknesses have to be communicated to the audit committee by both management and the external auditors. If the audit committee provides a strong oversight function, it will want to monitor any plans for remediation. Management and the audit committee may also wonder how the material weakness disclosure in their financial statements will affect the market.

Several articles and studies have been published on the market's reaction to a material weakness disclosure. Surprisingly, investors generally were not concerned with a company's disclosure of a material weakness. In the first years of compliance, there was often no correlation between a material weakness disclosure and a fluctuation in the company's stock price. In fact, in the earnings release where the first company to comply with Section 404 announced that management successfully completed its assessment of internal controls, analysts failed to mention or question anything about their compliance. The analysts' reaction, or lack thereof, seemed to be a preview for the market as a whole. However, there is hope on the horizon. Recent studies have started to show more correlation between a company's compliance record and its stock price.

In Moody's comment paper (April 2005), *Section 404 Reporting on Internal Control: Our Early Experience,* two distinct types of material weaknesses were identified. Moody's labeled as Category A process-specific weaknesses that relate to controls over specific account balances or transaction-level processes. Moody's tends to give companies reporting Category A material weaknesses the benefit of the doubt and does not take any related rating action based solely on the fact of the reported weakness. It assumes that management will take corrective action to address the issue in a timely manner. In the April 2005 paper, the most common type of Category A weaknesses related to income taxes, lease accounting, revenues and related receivables, and accrued liabilities.

Category B weaknesses are more pervasive and relate to entity-level controls, such as an ineffective control environment, weak overall financial reporting processes, or ineffective personnel. Moody's questions the ability of an external auditor to audit around Category B material weaknesses effectively. In Category B cases, Moody's would typically evaluate a company by its rating committee to determine whether a rating action (or change in rating) is needed. In April 2005, the most common type of Category B weakness related to ineffective or insufficient accounting personnel in company-wide functions and the inability to complete financial reporting on a timely basis (delinquent filers). More recent studies still show personnel and financial reporting issues among the top weaknesses.

As of April 2005, Moody's had taken rating action, in part because of control problems, in only 12 of 93 companies. In general, it found rating actions for companies with material weaknesses were not needed because:

- Control problems appeared to be specific, localized, and correctable within a short period (Category A).

- The rating already reflected Moody's impression of control weakness.

- Management's plan for remediating the control problem appeared to be credible.

Despite the lackluster effect of material weakness disclosures, Moody's average rating for the group with control problems was Ba3, which was three notches below the average for all U.S. companies rated by Moody's (Baa3).

HOW TO IMPROVE MATERIAL WEAKNESS DISCLOSURES

Once all the testing and evaluation is complete and you have determined you have a material weakness, management still needs to carefully draft a disclosure describing the weakness for investors and the public. Companies should be thorough and descriptive when disclosing their control weaknesses and planned remediation to the public for both Sections 404 and 302 purposes. Moody's suggests two areas of improvement for the disclosure of material weaknesses:

1. Companies with control problems could be more specific about the nature of the control problem they report. Vague generalizations raise more questions than they address. More detail would help creditors understand the relative severity of control problems and would reduce uncertainty about a company's financial reporting.

2. Companies could be more specific about their plans to remediate control weaknesses and the timing for doing so. Some companies disclose little about their remediation plans. Creditors want to be sure that management is taking its control problems seriously and that timely correction is under way.

The SEC's Guidance for Management suggests including this information in a disclosure of a material weakness:

- Nature of any material weakness

- Impact on financial reporting and its internal control over financial reporting

- Management's current plans, if any, or actions already undertaken, for remediating the material weakness

It goes on to add that companies should provide disclosures that allow investors to understand the root cause of the weakness and to assess the potential impact.

> This disclosure will be more useful to investors if management differentiates the potential impact and importance to the financial statements of the identified material weaknesses, including distinguishing those material weaknesses that may have a pervasive impact on ICFR from those material weaknesses that do not.

To address these considerations, companies can answer these questions when writing material weakness disclosures:

Nature of the Control Problem
- What is the problem?

- When did it occur?

- Who found the problem (management or the auditors)?

- Where does it occur (which business unit, or is it company-wide)?

- Why did it happen?

- How does it affect the financial statements?

Plans to Remediate
- What is being done to fix the problem?

- When will remediation begin, and when is completion expected?

- Who will be fixing the problem?

Creditors and investors may expect companies to provide updates in their quarterly filings on their progress toward remediation of control weaknesses. As a result, the PCAOB issued AS No. 4 to allow auditors to report on successful remediation on an interim basis. The SEC made the standard effective as of February 6, 2006.

AS NO. 4 AND REPORTING WHETHER A PREVIOUSLY REPORTED MATERIAL WEAKNESS STILL EXISTS

If management chooses, it can attest to and engage its external auditors to report at an interim date whether a previously reported material weakness continues to exist. According to AS No. 4:

> The external auditor must obtain an understanding of and evaluate management's evidence supporting its assertion that the specified controls related to the material weakness are designed and operated effectively, that these controls achieve the company's stated control objective(s) consistent with the control criteria, and that the identified material weakness no longer exists. If the auditor determines that management has not supported its assertion with sufficient evidence, the auditor cannot complete the engagement....

Although management may wish to clear only one material weakness, the engagement may require additional work beyond the documentation and testing of one control. All controls that are necessary to achieve the stated control objective(s) should be specifically identified and evaluated. The specified controls will include controls that have been modified or newly implemented as a result of management attempting to remediate its material weakness. They also may include existing controls that previously were deemed effective during management's most recent annual assessment of internal control over financial reporting.

As expected, this type of engagement can be cumbersome, time consuming, and expensive. Additionally, companies can report on their remediation progress in a Form 8-K or 10-Q without obtaining a report from their auditors but still sending the message to the market that the company is improving its controls. Since the market's reaction to many material weaknesses has been mild and companies can report on their remediation progress using other venues, reporting on whether a previously reported material weakness continues to exist will most likely be an infrequent event.

SUCCESSFUL COMMUNICATION OF DEFICIENCIES TO MANAGEMENT AND THE AUDIT COMMITTEE

Throughout the year, after each testing period, it is a good idea to perform at least a preliminary analysis of the deficiencies found and report the results to the audit committee, senior management, process owners, and process owners' supervisors. It is hoped that you will find that process owners become very concerned about the exceptions in their areas and want to minimize and remediate them. It is important to report the results of your testing after each testing phase to help in the remediation effort.

Practice Tip

If your test phases last more than a month, give management and process owners a progress report of test results midway through your testing. They will be able to start remediation efforts earlier and will be kept up to date on the status of controls in their areas.

Plan to give the audit committee status updates during every meeting so they can properly monitor management's assessment of internal control. Communications between management and the audit committee for the company's Section 404 program could include these topics:

- A project timeline for the year and where you are on that timeline

- Year-to-date results of control testing including the number of deficiencies found

- Status of remediation efforts

- Any issues or significant controls that have failed testing so far including financial, fraud, IT, and entity-wide controls

- Any disagreements with the external auditors

- At year-end, your analysis and conclusion for all outstanding deficiencies

Your external auditors are required to report all significant deficiencies and material weaknesses to the audit committee in writing. Although deficiencies that are found during the year may not be officially labeled as significant deficiencies or material weaknesses until the end of the year, your external auditors will most likely communicate any red flags to your audit committee whenever they meet.

Practice Tip

Prepare a formal memo for each controversial deficiency at year-end explaining why the control breech is not a significant deficiency or material weakness. Be sure to include your quantitative analysis, a discussion of compensating controls, and any other qualitative factors that impacted the final conclusion. To address the specific issues required, these memos generally have to be written by a person on the Section 404 team. The Section 404 team, senior management, area champion, and process owner should all agree on the severity of the deficiency before it is presented to the audit committee and external auditor.

SUGGESTIONS FOR MANAGEMENT'S FINAL ASSESSMENT REPORT

Once all testing is complete for the year, management must analyze all controls that remain ineffective at year-end and come to a conclusion as to whether the company's internal control over financial reporting is effective. Controls that are deficient for both operational and design reasons must be analyzed and documented. Your external auditors will want to know how management came to its conclusion.

There is no standard or industry-accepted format to use to document management's conclusion, but your documentation should contain:

- A summary of the final results of testing as of year-end. It is a good idea to give the number of total key control activities and the number of failed controls for reference. Deficiencies can be categorized and detailed further in various ways depending on what is important to

Exhibit 11.2   Deficiencies by Type of Exception

Type	Accounting	Treasury	HR	Tax	Finance	IT	Procurement	M&A	Total
Control ineffective		2	2		1	5			**10**
Control gap	2						2		**4**
Evidence	1					1	1		**3**
General computer controls						2			**2**
Developer access to production						8			**8**
Short sample size	1	2		7		1		1	**12**
Totals	**4**	**4**	**2**	**7**	**1**	**17**	**3**	**1**	**39**

Exhibit 11.3   Deficiencies by Operational or Design Effectiveness

Type	Operational Effectiveness	Design Effectiveness	Total
Control ineffective	8	2	10
Control gap		4	4
Evidence	2	1	3
General computer controls	2		2
Developer access to production		8	8
Short sample size	12		12
Totals	**24**	**15***	**39**

management and the audit committee. Exhibits 11.2 and 11.3 are examples of deficiency details that can be included in management's final report.

- Management's methodology for determining which deficiencies raise to the level of significant or material.

- An evaluation of each ineffective individual control at year-end, with a discussion of the compensating controls, likelihood, magnitude, and conclusion on the level of the deficiency as a material weakness, significant deficiency, or deficiency. Exhibit 11.4 is an example of a payroll control deficiency evaluation and conclusion.

Exhibit 11.4   Sample Deficiency Evaluation Form

Year-end Evaluation of Ineffective Controls	Payroll Cycle
Fiscal Period Ending December 31, 200X	**Control#PR01-C01**

Control Activity Name:
Approval of officer bonus awards

Reason for This Exception:
This is an annual control that occurs at the beginning of the year. It was not in effect during fiscal 200X.

Exception Categorized as a:
Deficiency

Risk:
Officer bonus awards may be paid without proper approval from the compensation committee.

Conclusion Rationale:

Compensating Controls:
The financial planning department reviews the bonus awards paid versus the amounts accrued throughout the year according to the company's approved budget. Any material variances are researched and resolved by the financial planning manager (see control# FP02-C05)

Possibility and Magnitude:
The possibility that a financial misstatement would not be prevented or detected in the event this control is not operating effectively is judged to be remote because of the compensating control. The potential magnitude of the exception is determined to be inconsequential because the total annual bonus accrual amounts to $9.5M, which is below the significant threshold of 1% of annual EBT. Since the annual bonus accrual has never exceeded $10M, it is unlikely that a misstatement over this amount would occur in the company's financial statements. This control occurs on an annual basis only.

Summary Conclusion:
Because the likelihood of misstatement is remote and the potential magnitude is less than significant, we conclude that the exception is a deficiency.

Control Activity Description:
The executive compensation committee reviews the proposed bonus awards for each officer annually. Evidence of approval is documented by the chairman of the compensation committee's signature on the summary bonus schedule. The approved schedule is attached to the committee meeting minutes, and copies are forwarded to accounting for the accrual and payroll for payment.

- An evaluation of each aggregated group of controls at year-end with a discussion of the compensating controls, likelihood, magnitude, and level of the deficiency.

- Any memos or documentation of positions that management has taken on any controversial issues or controls at year-end.

- Management's final conclusion on its internal control over financial reporting.

- Many companies forget the last step in the 404 assessment process. After all the documenting, testing, and analysis of internal controls are complete, it is important to document your final evaluation for communication to senior management, the audit committee, and your external auditors.

12

Common Areas of Concern and How to Address Them

Key Topics:

- Control options for the use of service organizations

- What to do with mergers and acquisitions activities

- A unique solution for managing the tax process

- How to minimize developer access to production issues

- What to do when your ERP system is not compatible with your access controls

- Tips for changing ERP systems and staying SOX compliant

- Practical ideas for document retention requirements

- Thoughts on changing accounting firms

As companies work their way through Sarbanes-Oxley (SOX) Section 404 compliance, certain issues seem to present the same challenges. The use of service organizations was tricky in the initial years of compliance, as was the tax process, acquisitions, developer access to production, and changing or upgrading enterprise resource planning (ERP) systems. Some organizations may have delayed certain decisions to acquire new companies or upgrade systems if it was scheduled near year-end. This of course is not good for business and was an unwanted result of Section 404 requirements. Over the last year or more, certain controls and practices have made it easier for companies to allow these events to occur as needed without compromising their compliance.

CONTROL OPTIONS FOR THE USE OF SERVICE ORGANIZATIONS

Medium-size and large public companies probably outsource multiple services. Some will affect financial reporting and others will not. Typical outsourced services that affect financial reporting include:

- Payroll

- Investment management

- Benefits such as 401k or stock option administration

- Contract manufacturing

- Asset storage

- Other outsourced services

For Section 404 purposes, your company will have to assess the design and operating effectiveness of internal controls at those service organizations that have a significant impact on the company's financial reporting. Steps to evaluate internal controls at service organizations as well as options that you have for evaluating them are presented next.

Steps to Evaluate Service Organizations' Internal Controls

Four steps to take to create a program to evaluate the internal controls of your company's service organizations are listed next.

1. **Create an inventory of all service organizations that the company uses.** Payroll and benefits service providers are visible for your Section 404 program, but how do you know when a new provider has been added? Remember to include foreign service providers, and update the list at least annually.

2. **Determine which service organizations are significant to the company's financial reporting process.** Once you have a full list of providers, document which providers will be in scope for Section 404 purposes. Remember to include service organizations that affect the company's information systems.

3. **Evaluate the internal controls that are in place at the significant service organizations.** If the provider has a Type II Statement on Auditing Standard No. 70, *Service Organizations*, (SAS No. 70) report with a year-end that is close to the company's year-end, you have the tools you will need to assess the providers' internal controls.

4. **Establish any alternative procedures needed to rely on internal controls of significant service organizations.** If the service provider does

not provide a Type II SAS No. 70 report or if the SAS No. 70 report is dated more than six months from the company's year-end, you will have to establish alternative procedures to assess the provider's internal controls.

Creating an Inventory of Service Organizations Gathering information on all the service organizations your company uses may be a difficult task. You can focus your search on the purchasing and legal departments in addition to checking with each significant business cycle.

Be careful not to confuse a "specialist" with a service organization. Specialists can be used for valuations, complex calculations, or interpretations of legal or technical terms. For example, the company may use a specialist to value its minerals or an actuary to calculate pension benefits. Because specialists' work may impact the financial statements, the company should make sure its specialists are qualified and reliable and that controls are in place to address accuracy and completeness. However, these specialists are not part of an outsourced process and should not be included in your listing of service organizations.

Which Activities Are Considered Part of the Company's Internal Controls?

SAS No. 70 states that activities are considered part of a company's internal control if they affect any of these areas:

- The classes of transactions that are significant to the company's financial statements

- The procedures, both automated and manual, by which the company's transactions are initiated, recorded, processed, and reported from their occurrence to their inclusion in the financial statements

- The related accounting records, whether electronic or manual, supporting information, and specific accounts in the company's financial statements involved in initiating, recording, processing, and reporting the company's transactions

- How the company's information system captures other events and conditions that are significant to the financial statements

- The financial reporting process used to prepare the company's financial statements, including significant accounting estimates and disclosures

Using the criteria outlined in SAS No. 70, you should document which organizations are significant to your internal controls over financial reporting (ICFR). Service organizations used to record transactions in each of your key business cycles should be labeled significant if the control covering a financial assertion is occurring at the service organization. In other words, ask yourself if the process being outsourced covers a relevant financial assertion and a material volume of transactions. If so, the service organization should be noted as significant.

Options for Relying on Service Organizations' Internal Controls

Once you have determined which service organizations are significant to your ICFR, you have these options for reliance on the service organizations' controls:

- Obtain and evaluate Type II SAS No. 70 reports.

- Obtain an auditor's report on agreed-upon procedures that describes tests of relevant controls.

- Perform your own tests of their controls.

- Do not rely on their controls, and test the company's controls surrounding the outsourced processes.

Evaluating Type II SAS No. 70 Reports   The easiest way to evaluate your service organization's internal controls is usually through a SAS No. 70 report. However, not all service organizations' such reports, and not all such reports are adequate. In addition, other factors such as the period covered by the report, the scope, the opinion, and user controls should be considered.

Type I and Type II Reports   There are two different types of SAS No. 70 reports, Type I and Type II. Both are audit reports from independent, external auditors with an opinion on the service organization's internal controls.

- In a Type I report, the auditors only give their opinion on the design of the organization's internal controls.

- In a Type II report, the auditors issue an opinion on the design and operating effectiveness of the organization's internal controls.

Since the Securities and Exchange Commission (SEC) requires the company to assess the design and operating effectiveness of its ICFR, a Type I report alone will not fulfill the entire requirement.

Scope   The report must cover tests of controls at the service organization that are relevant to the company's key processes and the related financial assertions. For example, if the company is relying on a payroll service for the valuation assertion, you should be sure the report covers controls surrounding translation from foreign currencies to dollars.

In addition, the report should cover general information technology (IT) controls, including controls surrounding relevant software applications used in the outsourced processes.

Period   The report will state the period of time covered by the tests of control at the service organization. These dates need to be compared to the company's year-end to determine if additional procedures are necessary.

What happens if the most recent report you can obtain from your service organization is for control testing as of December 31, 2006, but your company's year-end is September 30, 2007? Although Auditing Standard No. 5 (AS No. 5), Paragraph B24, discusses your options for when a significant period of time has elapsed between the period covered by the tests of controls in the service auditor's report and the date of management's assessment, it does not define a "significant period of time." Some external auditors believe a difference of six months between the dates in the SAS No. 70 report and the company's year-end would give the company limited benefits. Even with minimal time differences, you may be required to obtain an update letter from the service organization documenting any changes in its internal controls since the date of its SAS No. 70 report or perform additional procedures. As the period between the two dates becomes farther apart, the need for additional tests increases. For additional guidance, refer to the Public Company Accounting Oversight Board (PCAOB) Staff Question and Answer (Staff Q&A) No. 25.

Practice Tip

If there is any difference in the dates on the SAS No. 70 report and the company's year-end, you should consider documenting a few questions regarding changes to controls. Consider additional testing or documentation if there had been any changes in:

- Controls communicated to management from the service organization

- The people the company interacts with at the service organization

- Reports or data received by the service organization

- Errors in processing at the service organization

- Contracts or service-level agreements

Past errors, recent changes to the organization's controls, or an out-of-date Type II SAS No. 70 report may cause you to not rely on your service organization's SAS No. 70 report and determine that additional evidence about the effectiveness of their controls is required.

Client Controls   Many service organizations will refer to client controls that the service organization assumes are in place at their clients' companies. They may note that certain client controls are necessary for them to achieve the control objectives mentioned in their report. Typical user controls include ensuring that information sent to the service organization is accurate and complete, communicated in a timely manner, and updated as needed.

In addition, the auditors' reports included in the report may have a disclaimer for client controls when referring to the effective design and operation of service organizations' controls. Such language might read as shown next:

> The relative effectiveness and significance of specific controls at ABC, Inc. and their effect on assessments of control risk at client organizations are dependent on their interaction with the controls and other factors present at individual client organizations.

Practice Tip

Be sure to review the client controls section of your service organization's SAS No. 70 report, if applicable, to ensure that your organization has controls in place so it can submit accurate, complete, and timely data to your service organization. Missing client controls may indicate a gap in your company's internal control structure.

Opinion   To be fully relied on, the SAS No. 70 report should have an unqualified opinion. If a qualified opinion exists or there were any testing exceptions, you will have to determine the impact these exceptions may have on the company's ICFR. You may have to perform additional procedures to gain comfort that the service organization's controls are designed and operating effectively.

According to the SEC Office of the Chief Accountant's Frequently Asked Question (FAQ) No. 14, you would be able to rely on a SAS No. 70 report that is issued by your external auditor as long as you did not engage your external auditors to perform the SAS No. 70 audit at the service organization.

Practice Tip

A practical way to document your company's review of service organizations' SAS No. 70 reports is to have the process owners complete a short checklist to make sure the dates, type of report, opinion, and user controls have been reviewed. Users will have to be trained to complete the checklist accurately, and it can be saved electronically.

Exhibit 12.1   Service Organization Internal Control Checklist

---

Service organization name:

Date of SAS 70 report:

Is an update letter needed from the service organization?

If so, are there changes to the service organization's controls?

Type II or Type I report?

What is the auditor's opinion in the report?

Does it address the relevant service or function?

Are the applicable user controls in place?

Is this control effective?

Completed by:

Date:

Exhibit 12.1 is an example of a service organization internal control checklist.

Tests of the Company's Controls Surrounding the Outsourced Process   If you cannot rely on the service organization's controls at all, you may be able to test "user controls" (your company's controls). Typically, doing this is not as effective as testing controls at the service organization, and you will need to assess whether testing user controls will provide sufficient evidence that controls are operating effectively. You may need to add additional processes and controls to ensure that all assertions are addressed at the company instead of relying on the service provider. The company can test data from service organizations by reconciling information processed by the service organizations against information from an independent source or by independently recalculating certain transactions. Present your method to your external auditors if you plan to test user controls in lieu of testing controls at service organizations to make sure they agree with your methodology.

International Service Organizations   Obtaining Type II SAS No. 70 reports from international service providers can be a challenge. The running joke says if you ask foreign service providers if they have a SAS No. 70 report and their response is "What's that?" you may have a problem. Most providers that supply services to U.S. public companies know what these reports are by now, but they may not feel the need to go through the lengthy and expensive process of obtaining one. If your foreign service providers do have some type of report on their internal controls, you may be able to use it if it is audited and the tests of controls follow the same criteria outlined in SAS No. 70. However, if there is no report on internal controls or if the report is not adequate, you will have to rely on another option to determine if the organization's internal controls are effective.

For additional guidance on service organizations, see AS No. 5, Paragraphs B17 through B27, and AU Sec 324, *Service Organizations*.

WHAT TO DO WITH MERGERS AND ACQUISITIONS ACTIVITIES

Putting merger and acquisition (M&A) controls in place is not as difficult as initially thought and can provide real benefits to a company outside of mere SOX compliance. M&As are often challenging because each transaction is unique, and during a transition, the company may have to rely on people at the acquired company who are not loyal to the acquirer. Documenting mergers and acquisitions for Section 404 purposes is a two-pronged process. Besides implementing controls at newly acquired/merged entities that are determined material, controls may need to be put in place for the M&A process itself.

Internal Controls Surrounding the M&A Process

The first step in the M&A control process is to determine if M&A activities are in scope for Section 404 purposes. Look at the total dollars spent in the previous year, or the total amount budgeted for M&A activities in the current year, and determine if the amounts are over your materiality threshold. Do not confuse the overall M&A process with individual transactions. Remember to think about qualitative factors as well, such as errors in previous purchase transactions or purchases of complex intangibles such as intellectual property. M&A transactions may be considered high risk because of the uniqueness of each transaction. You may have to include them in scope even if the amounts do not surpass your materiality threshold.

Practice Tip

If the company is involved in frequent M&A activities, consider documenting your process, whether it is in scope or not. A last-minute acquisition at the end of the year may push your M&A activities over your materiality threshold for both internal control and financial audits. In addition, sound controls will help ensure transactions are correctly recorded.

Exhibit 12.2   Sample Mergers and Acquisitions Control Matrix

Subprocess	Risk	Control Activity
Due diligence	Transaction is completed without identifying key risks and potential liabilities	Financial due diligence is performed internally for transactions under $10 million and externally for transactions > $10 million. The due diligence report is approved and signed by the Vice President of Finance or above.
Approval	Company legally commits to transaction without proper approval from board of directors	Approval for the potential merger or acquisition by the board of directors, and any resulting shareholder vote is documented in the board minutes.
Accounting for M&A transactions	Tangible and intangible assets are inaccurately valued, causing a misstatement in the financial statements	Acquired intangible assets over $10 million are valued by an approved, independent third party. The valuation report is reviewed and signed by the Vice President of Finance or above.
Accounting for M&A transactions	Asset values and/or expenses are not accurately recorded	The Business Combinations Accounting Guide is completed for all transactions over $10 million and approved by the controller or above. A memo documenting the accounting treatment and relevant journal entries is prepared for all transactions under $10 million and approved by the controller or above.

For small and large companies alike, financial reporting risks in the M&A process center around the approval for the transaction, due diligence, and accurately valuing and recording the transaction. A sample control matrix for the M&A process is shown in Exhibit 12.2.

Internal Controls at New Entities

Hearing about a new entity that the company plans to acquire near year-end is enough to give most SOX practitioners a few sleepless nights. In addition to transitioning the newly acquired company into the existing organization, internal controls may have to be evaluated, documented, and tested in a short amount of time, whether the new company is already SOX compliant or not. However, the company has the option to include or exclude the new company from its assessment of internal control for one year from the date of acquisition.

Practice Tip

If the company decides to include a newly acquired company in management's current assessment, do not forget to evaluate entity-level controls as they relate to the new location. If a new acquisition is considered material, the company will have to make sure entity-level controls apply to the new location too.

Excluding Newly Acquired Entities from Management's Assessment

According to the SEC Office of the Chief Accountant's FAQ (revised October 6, 2004) No. 3, management's report on internal control over financial reporting typically includes controls at all consolidated entities. However, the SEC acknowledges that it might not always be possible to conduct an assessment of an acquired business's ICFR when the transaction occurs near management's assessment date. An exclusion of the entity for one annual management report on internal control is allowed if management discloses it in its assessment on Form 10-K. According to the SEC:

> In such instances, we would not object to management referring in the report to a discussion in the registrant's Form 10-K or 10-KSB regarding the scope of the assessment and to such disclosure noting that management excluded the acquired business from management's report on internal control over financial reporting.

In its disclosure, management is required to

- Identify the acquired business excluded.

- Indicate the significance of the acquired business to the company's consolidated financial statements.

The SEC granted this one-year window to ease the burden of compliance for public companies with newly acquired entities near year-end. It allows for business to carry on with the workings of industry.

According to the SEC's FAQ No. 9:

As an alternative to ongoing disclosure for such changes in internal control over financial reporting, a registrant may choose to disclose all such changes to internal control over financial reporting in the annual report in which its assessment that encompasses the acquired business is included.

A UNIQUE SOLUTION FOR MANAGING THE TAX PROCESS

For most companies, the tax process typically contains the most manual transactions and calculations. The tax process is even more risky because tax calculations are often complicated, contain estimates, and cannot be tied to source documents. Manual review typically is the only way to ensure these tax calculations are accurate and complete. Results of the calculations can have a direct impact on the financial statements. To make things even more difficult, tax departments often use multiple, complex spreadsheets that are large and change frequently. It is not surprising that there have been so many material weaknesses in the tax area. It would be hard to find a bigger financial reporting risk area than manual, complex processes that contain estimates, use spreadsheets, and directly affect the financials.

Manual Review

When it comes down to it, manual review by a qualified person may be necessary to ensure tax assumptions and calculations are valid. To date, no application can replace a tax manager's experience, tax law knowledge, and sense of reasonableness. The best way to deal with the manual review process for Section 404 purposes is to control it.

Consider adding some of these items to manual reviews if they are not already part of the review process:

- Tie totals or key figures to source documents when possible. Total research and development (R&D) payroll dollars can be tied to payroll reports, and prior-year amounts can be tied to prior-year tax returns.

- Perform a separate calculation as a reasonableness check. Try to use different data or different sources for the information, and see if the calculations are similar in amount.

- Have a second reviewer do a top-level review for reasonableness. The second review may not catch specific errors, but the second reviewer should be familiar enough with the transaction to know when it is off base.

- Have a tax person perform rotating spreadsheet tests on all tax spread-sheets with more than 150 lines. Statistics show that these spreadsheets will contain one or more errors, and a tax person will better under-stand the concepts used.

- Perform a variance analysis comparing current-year results with those from the prior year. Make sure that material differences from year to year can be explained.

- Confirm that the reviewer checked the calculation for recent tax law changes, and require signoff.

- Have a staff person foot schedules to ensure mathematical accuracy.

The tax process contains a high amount of inherent risk and may always rely to some extent on manual reviews. The goal for controlling the tax process is to implement controls to help ensure that the reviews are designed to catch material errors. A checklist approach can aid in a thorough review process.

What to Do When the Tax Process Is Outsourced

Companies that engage outside parties to prepare their income tax provi-sion and related assets, liabilities, or disclosures can face similar problems as companies that prepare their calculations and disclosures in-house. Outsourced provisions and disclosures can easily contain errors because the provider may not fully understand the business or may not have accu-rate or complete data. Just as with other service providers, you need to make sure the company has adequate client controls. Consider using a checklist control encompassing some or all of the review points listed ear-lier to help ensure your outsourced tax calculations and disclosures are materially correct.

HOW TO MINIMIZE IT DEVELOPER ACCESS
TO PRODUCTION ISSUES

IT developer access to production is a clear segregation of duties issue but for some companies, a necessary evil. Smaller and midsize companies often do not have the manpower to segregate these duties. Larger companies with complex systems may require an occasional developer to have access to production for data updates or just in case of an emergency. Companies may believe that the negative impact to business processes caused by increased debugging and resolution time that would occur without developer access to production outweighs the risk of fraudulent activity.

Any size company can use the following techniques to limit the risks of developer access to production. The goal is to explain explicitly who has access to what to show that the risk is limited.

- Define the word "developer." Developers can make changes to code. Do not confuse these people with other personnel who support the business system for functional users or make configuration changes to existing applications.

- Limit developer access where possible. Reduce the number of IT people who have access to production to the absolute minimum. In some cases, employees are granted access when they do not actually need it.

- Document only those true developers who have access to live data that could affect the financial statements. Although it is a good segregation-of-duties practice to limit and document all developer access to production, it is relevant for SOX purposes only in the financial reporting arena.

- Describe exactly what kind of access each developer has. Developers may have access only to the financial reporting application but not the application where the general ledger is recorded. Or developers may have access to a small portion of an application, such as the accounts payable (AP) module, because it frequently crashes. Be sure to be explicit when describing access or others may think they have more access than they actually do.

- Implement detective controls for any high-risk areas. Several public companies have sidestepped this issue by implementing a monthly monitoring control where a nondeveloper reviews a report that notes each time a developer accessed live financial data.

With these practices listed, management should be able to explain to the auditors the actual risk(s) for any developer segregation-of-duties issues and gain comfort that the risks are adequately monitored and controlled.

WHAT TO DO WHEN YOUR ERP SYSTEM IS
NOT COMPATIBLE WITH YOUR ACCESS CONTROLS

Many enterprise resource planning applications have recently updated their software to help companies comply with Section 404 access and security issues. Despite the updates, many popular applications, both small and large, still pose a challenge for implementing straightforward system access controls. Often the problem lies in generating a useful report to monitor system access rather than controlling and granting access.

For example, a small company with 125 employees and revenues of $70 million uses a popular ERP system and has an in-house programmer who can write code and custom reports for the application. The system allows the administrator to grant individual access privileges or assign security based on user groups, such as AP clerks or AP Managers. Each option allows the administrator to assign rights to specific windows or functions within the application.

Although the implementation of access rights for this software is unproblematic, no meaningful report shows the access granted to any individual or group. The company asks its programmer to develop such a report, but because the software assigns rights to specific windows/functions, the report is over 1,000 pages long.

The lack of succinct, descriptive access reports is still a common problem among ERP systems. Auditors want to ensure that there are no segregation-of-duties issues or users with inappropriate rights, but they can do so only if they have meaningful reports.

Practice Tip

Approach system access controls with the same risk tactic that you apply to other controls. What are the biggest access risks for each user or user group? Create your own document describing high-risk or controversial rights for each user group, then create a list of users in each group. User lists probably will have to be reviewed and approved quarterly to ensure they are current. However, the document describing rights assigned to specific groups may have to be updated only annually or on an as-needed basis.

Exhibit 12.3 presents a sample access document for several different user group–based rights that were granted for each drop-down menu in a popular ERP system. Blatant segregation of duties issues are called out, and screen prints are used to show detail where noted.

Exhibit 12.3   ERP Access Rights List

Group	Rights Granted Except Where Noted

AP Clerks

Inquiry and Reports—all
File—no maintenance, restore or backup functions
Tools

- Routines—Batch recovery
- Customize
- Macro
- Resource description

Transactions

- Purchasing
    - No vendor setup, maintenance, or changes
    - No purchase order creation or changes
    - AP windows only—see attached for screen prints

- Financial
    - No posting journal entries
    - No bank reconciliations

- No payroll, inventory, or sales transactions

Consultants

Inquiry and Reports—all
File—no maintenance, restore, backup functions
Tools—none
Transactions—none

Developer

Inquiry and Reports—all
File—no maintenance, restore, backup functions
Tools—none
Transactions—none

This document mirrors the risk-based approach in that it only documents areas of concern. Is there really a big risk if the AP clerks can access inventory reports? The bigger risk in this example is whether AP clerks can set up vendors or create purchase orders. Because access rarely changes at the user group level and there were no exceptions in the prior year, the company updates this document only annually.

In addition to the annual update and approval of the document, directors from each department review a list of employees in each user group quarterly to make sure it is current. In Exhibit 12.3, the user list is:

Group	Users
AP Clerks	Gordon Gustafson
	Amber Macko
Consultants	Betsy Straus
	Steve Auston
	Krystal Mattik
Developer	Mike Rodriguez
	Mark Koweski

Although this solution is a somewhat manual process, it can provide adequate control over access when an ERP system does not leave you with many options. It is hoped that, in the future, ERP systems will evolve to help companies conform to application access controls more efficiently.

TIPS FOR CHANGING ERP SYSTEMS AND STAYING SOX COMPLIANT

Changing and/or updating ERP systems was one of the activities that was avoided in the first years of Section 404 compliance because companies could not deal with such a large change to controls and still complete their attestation on time. Of course, delaying changes and updates cannot go on forever. Companies have and will continue to update and change their accounting systems. If your IT controls are properly designed, the company should have change management controls in place. Nonetheless, changing ERP systems directly affects accounting, financial reporting, and automated application controls that typically are left to the finance side of SOX programs. A few tips to help make sure the system change does not become an issue for Section 404 purposes follow.

- **Leave a large cushion when planning a system change live date.** Because of their pervasive nature and multidepartment involvement, system upgrades or changes commonly miss the deadline for their live date. Planning for the new ERP system to go live in August may not allow for adequate time to document, test, and remediate new controls for a calendar year-end company.

- **Set blackout dates.** With deadlines for quarterly filings shrinking and recurring month-end closes, there really is no good time for a public company to make a system change. However, there are definitely bad times to make a change. In the initial planning stages, find out when are the good times and the bad times to go live with a system change. Perhaps the best time is the week after a Form 10-Q filing. The bad time is probably during the year-end or quarterly close process. Since the live date may be a moving target, set blackout dates for when the implementation cannot occur.

- **Run the old system and the new system in parallel.** Since the actual date the company goes live depends on so many factors, have the new system fully operational and waiting for the best time. Running the new system in parallel with the old for a short time can allow for debugging and will give you more flexibility with the live date.

- **Train all users.** Be sure that all users receive adequate training on the new ERP system while it is still in the test environment. If the company plans to send only supervisors and managers to formal training, hold in-depth training sessions in-house for the staff before the new system goes live.

- **Evaluate both manual and automated application controls.** Determine how controls will change with the new accounting system before it is implemented. New systems may dictate new manual processes as roles and responsibilities change. Plan for new controls and evaluate existing controls for possible changes before the new system is put in place.

- **Do not start documenting the new controls too early.** Just like a new process that is put in place, new controls often sound good in theory but are found impractical when it comes time to execute. Once the new system is in place, let any new processes and controls "settle," allowing process owners time to find the best approach.

PRACTICAL IDEAS FOR DOCUMENT RETENTION REQUIREMENTS

SOX Sections 802 and 1102 describe criminal penalties for altering documents or tampering with records for official proceedings. These two sections have imposed requirements on auditors and their issuers for the retention and destruction of financial records. More specifically, these sections include these provisions:

- Individuals who knowingly alter, destroy, mutilate, conceal or make false entries in any record, document or tangible object with the intent to impede, obstruct or influence any matter involving federal agencies may be fined, imprisoned up to 20 years, or both. (See Section 1519.)

- External auditors must maintain audit work papers for a period of seven years. Fines, imprisonment up to 10 years, or both can be imposed for the violation of this provision. (See Section 1520.)

- SOX expands the obstruction of justice statute that prohibits tampering with witnesses. Whoever attempts to corruptly alter, destroy, mutilate, or conceal records for an official proceeding with the intent to impair the object's integrity or availability may be fined, imprisoned up to 20 years, or both. (See Section 1102.)

Because SOX empowers the PCAOB to subpoena documents that form the basis of an audit opinion, external auditors and their public-company clients are now required to retain work papers that support the audit opinion and management's conclusion on its assessment of internal controls. What this means for SOX purposes is that control matrices, testing documents, and any other work papers, both paper and electronic, to support management's decision must be saved for seven years. This includes any relevant correspondence, email, or other financial data.

Developing a Records Management Policy

Protect the company by developing a records management policy for both paper and electronic records. The goal of the policy is to ensure that documents are available when needed and to save time, space, and money. Possible points to document in your records management policy are:

- Describe how and when certain documents can be destroyed.

- Name a records custodian or department that is responsible for communicating, administering, and maintaining the policy.

- Include the storage format and location of all saved data.

- Ensure all changes after the archiving date are logged to indicate the modification and date.

- Train employees about the policy and show them how it will impact their daily tasks and transactions. For example, employees should know how often they are allowed to delete routine email and what kind of emails they should retain.

- Be sure the policy addresses "deleted" electronic data that may not be completely deleted. Temporary files or other data footprints can inadvertently be saved.

- Do not forget to include any online document repositories in the policy.

- Document a response plan for records retention should the company receive notice of a lawsuit or investigation.

- Create a log to document which records were destroyed and when.

Practice Tip

Consider allowing employees to save certain documents on a secured server only instead of on their personal desktops. Saving key documents on a server will ensure that the documents are backed up and properly controlled.

Many companies used paper files to document their assessments during the first years of compliance. Because of the document requirements imposed by SOX and the nature and volume of Section 404 documents, the trend will most likely be toward electronic documentation.

THOUGHTS ON CHANGING ACCOUNTING FIRMS

The days of the Big 8 accounting firms are no longer. The reduction to four major firms and the onslaught of Section 404 work has caused some firms to become short staffed, raise their fees, and, in some cases, reduce their services for certain clients or let other clients go. As a result, the "second-tier" firms are now more prominent and have been growing in size and skill level. Additionally, the trickle-down effect has sent more business to third-tier firms, which are gaining more public-company clients.

If your company is considering the possibility of switching to a smaller firm, you may find there are more pros than cons for doing so. Consider these thoughts on changing accounting firms.

- Second- and third-level firms hold more prestige now than they have in the past and are more accepted by the investment community and audit committees.

- Smaller firms have markedly lower fees. Many companies have seen a large increase in audit fees over the last few years both because of rate increases and additional audit requirements.

- For medium-size and smaller public companies, you may receive better service, time, and attention from a second- or third-tier firm. Sometimes it is better to be a big fish in a little pond.

- If you do not want to change audit firms, consider switching to a smaller firm for consulting and tax engagements. There are talented people at smaller firms who will almost always charge lower fees. Consulting personnel at the large firms often are recruited from smaller firms, especially since the recent shortage of CPAs and internal auditors.

In conclusion, if you feel your auditors' fees do not fit your budget, if your auditors have a hard time fitting into your schedule, or if you feel you come second to your auditors' bigger clients, it may be time to consider switching to a different firm.

Appendix A

Simplified Sample
Entity-Level Control Matrices

Control Environment

Subcomponents	Possible Controls	Performed by	Oversight by	Examples of Evidence
Integrity and ethical values	Code of conduct is approved by the board and communicated to all employees. Code is updated annually.	HR	Audit committee	Code of conduct document approved by the board of directors; copies of employee signoff forms confirming acceptance; emails or memos of code to employees; presentations to employees that include slides on ethics or code
Commitment to competence	Accounting, tax, and IT personnel perform tasks according to training manuals, desktop procedures, or policies. They receive ongoing training to keep skills current.	HR	Internal audit	Finance, IT, tax training manuals, desktop procedures, or company policies; samples of continuing education or credential certificates for key employees

(Continued)

Subcomponents	Possible Controls	Performed by	Oversight by	Examples of Evidence
Management's philosophy and operating style	Audit committee is independent of management; CFO attends board and executive meetings; turnover in senior executive positions is monitored; audit committee has at least one financial expert; effectiveness of audit committee is assessed and monitored by board of directors.	Senior management	Board of directors	Board of directors, audit committee minutes; financial expert biography for audit committee; assessment of audit committee; statement of independence of board/audit committee
Organizational structure	Organizational charts are maintained depicting titles and reporting structure.	Senior management	Board of directors	Current organization chart
Assignment of authority	Assignment of responsibility follows organizational charts; management has documented levels of authority in areas such as capital expenditures, cash management, purchases, and credit approvals.	Senior management	Board of directors	Signature authorization policy; purchase authority levels
Human resource policies and procedures	Company has an HR manual that covers procedures for training, promoting, and compensating employees; formal job descriptions exist; company has a well-established performance evaluation process with all employees evaluated at least annually; employee retention and promotion criteria are linked to the performance evaluation process.	HR and department heads	Board of directors	Copy of HR manual; samples of employee signatures showing they received a copy of HR manual; listing of job descriptions; performance evaluation policy and examples; evidence that bonuses and promotions are based on performance

Board of directors and committees	Audit committee charter is in place; board approved a 3-year strategic plan; board has several active committees.	Audit committee and board of directors	Board of directors	Audit committee charter; strategic plan approved by board of directors; listing of board committees and minutes; relevant board minutes; audit committee assessments
Information technology	IT strategic plan aligns with company's business plan; IT management understands its roles and responsibilities as it relates to internal controls.	IT management	Board of directors	IT strategic plan or IT section of company strategic plan; emails from IT management on access, security, or other internal control topics

Information and Communication

Subcomponents	Possible Controls	Performed by	Oversight by	Examples of Evidence
Financial reporting policies	Financial reporting policies and procedures exist and are communicated to relevant employees/management.	Department heads/regional managers	Board of directors	Emails or presentations to financial reporting staff; Edgar procedures; reporting procedures
Accounting and internal control policies	Accounting policies exist and are communicated to relevant employees/management.	Internal audit	Board of directors	Emails or presentations to accounting staff of policies
Lines of communication	Financial results are communicated at least quarterly to senior management, board of directors, and audit committee; relevant information on ethics and policies is communicated to employees and management.	Senior management	Board of directors	Presentations to board of directors or committees
Distribution of information	Company has a policy for the distribution of critical information to the public.	Senior management	Board of directors	Procedures or policy for reporting info to public; emails; board of directors meeting minutes

(Continued)

Subcomponents	Possible Controls	Performed by	Oversight by	Examples of Evidence
Section 16	Company has a policy for Section 16/insider purchases of company stock. Policy has been communicated to employees and management.	Senior management	Board of directors	Procedures or policy for reporting information to public; emails; board of directors meeting minutes
IT	Data integrity, information classification, and security ownership and responsibilities have been defined and communicated to management and employees.	IT management	Board of directors	Procedures or policy for reporting info to public; emails; board of directors meeting minutes

Risk Assessment

Subcomponents	Possible Controls	Performed by	Oversight by	Examples of Evidence
Company-wide objectives	Board of directors and/or strategy committee oversees the risk assessment process and takes action to address the significant risks identified.	Senior management	Board of directors	Board minutes
Business risk Identification	Management creates and follows a 3-year strategic plan.	Senior management	Board of directors	Strategic plan
Inherent risk identification	Management performs annual risk assessment and presents to board of directors.	Internal audit or senior management	Board of directors	Annual Business Unit planning/ strategy meetings; risk assessment; board presentation of risk assessment
Information and communication	Management's budget, forecast, and strategic plans are communicated to board of directors and employees.	Senior management	Board of directors	Board of directors presentations and emails or memos to employees of budgets and forecasts

Managing change	Management communicates changes that may have a significant effect on the entity to board of directors or audit committee.	Senior management	Board of directors	Board of directors minutes, company presentations, emails, memos
Managing change	Accounting department has a process in place to identify and address changes in GAAP, the operating and regulatory environment, and related party transactions.	Controller or chief financial officer	Chief financial officer or audit committee	Legal and accounting practices; meeting agendas and presentations; continuing education for accountants
Information technology	Information and systems risks are part of the company's annual risk assessment.	Internal audit or senior management	Board of directors	IT risk or strategy meeting agenda/minutes/ presentation

Monitoring

Subcomponents	Possible Controls	Performed by	Oversight by	Examples of Evidence
Separate evaluations	Self-assessment reviews.	Business unit managers	Board of directors	Self-assessment questionnaires and documentation
Reporting deficiencies	Internal audits or investigations performed to evaluate compliance and deficiencies. Results reported to the audit committee.	Internal audit	Board of directors or audit committee	Internal audit reports or presentations
Ongoing monitoring	Board of directors monitors company's performance, risk, and operations.	Senior management	Board of directors	Presentations or minutes to board of directors or committees
Ongoing monitoring	Audit committee monitors financial results and reviews financial statements before filing with SEC.	Controller or chief financial officer	Audit committee	Presentations or minutes for audit committee meetings

(Continued)

Subcomponents	Possible Controls	Performed by	Oversight by	Examples of Evidence
Information technology	IT management monitors adherence to IT policies, procedures, and standards.	IT management	Board of directors	Monitoring reports (backups/help desk); monthly/ quarterly IT meeting minutes/ presentations/ agendas

Anti-Fraud

COSO Component	Subcomponents	Possible Controls	Performed by:	Oversight by:	Examples of Evidence
Control environment	Code of conduct	Code of conduct is approved by the board and distributed to new employees. Code is updated annually.	Human resources	Audit committee	Board of directors minutes
Control environment	Whistleblower program	Whistleblower program is in place and is monitored by audit committee.	Audit committee	Board of directors	Hotline information, reports on hotline complaints, procedures for resolving complaints, logs of reporting incidents
Control environment	Hiring and promotion	Background and references are checked for new hires. Job descriptions and qualifications are prepared and followed for each open position.	Human resources	Board of directors	Hiring and promotion policies; reference and background check forms or examples
Monitoring	Monitoring	Audit committee effectively oversees the company's anti-fraud program and meets at least once a year to discuss the anti-fraud program and fraud risks.	Board of directors	Board of directors	Relevant audit committee or board of directors meeting minutes or emails

Risk assessment	Fraud scenarios	Fraud risk assessment including fraud scenarios is prepared by management and presented to the audit committee or board of directors at least annually.	Internal audit	Board of directors	Fraud risk assessment to include listing of scenarios, analysis, and controls in place to mitigate risks
Information and communication	Information and communication	Code of conduct and ethical tone at the top is communicated to management and employees.	Senior management	Audit committee	Emails, presentations, intranet addresses where code of conduct, HR policies, and other fraud-related matters have been communicated to management or employees
Control activities	Control activities	Specific fraud-related control activities are identified.	Internal audit	Audit committee	Listing of control activities that mitigate fraud risks

Appendix B

COSO's Internal Controls Checklist for Entity-Level Controls

Strong internal controls do not ensure success; bad decisions, poor managers, competition, collusion, and override of controls still can cause unreliable financial reports. However, strong controls put up roadblocks for fraud, bad decisions, and human error, and help to minimize pitfalls and surprises. An effective control system enables management to discover and manage significant risks and monitor the integrity of financial and operating information. It also ensures that the audit committee is a proactive agent for corporate self-regulation. The Committee of Sponsoring Organizations (COSO) of the Treadway Commission developed the questions listed here to help senior executives and directors of enterprises of all types and sizes gain a better understanding of their organization's control systems.[1]

Ethical Environment
- Do board members and senior executives set a day-in, day-out example of high integrity and ethical behavior?

- Is there a written code of conduct for employees, and is it reinforced by training, top-down communications, and requirements for periodic written statements of compliance from key employees?

- Are performance and incentive compensation targets reasonable and realistic, or do they create undue pressure on achievement of short-term results?

- Is it clear that fraudulent financial reporting at any level and in any form will not be tolerated?

- Are ethics woven into criteria that are used to evaluate individual and business unit performance?

- Does management react appropriately when receiving bad news from subordinates and business units?

- Does a process exist to resolve close ethical calls?

- Are business risks identified and candidly discussed with the board of directors?

Risk Identification and Management
- Is relevant and reliable internal and external information timely identified, compiled, and communicated to those who are positioned to act?

- Are risks identified, analyzed, and actions taken to mitigate them?

- Are controls in place to assure that management decisions are properly carried out?

Internal Controls Effectiveness
- Do senior and line management executives demonstrate that they accept control responsibility, not just delegate that responsibility to financial and audit staff?

- Does management routinely monitor controls in process of running the organization's operations?

- Does management clearly assign responsibilities for training and monitoring of internal controls?

- Are periodic, systematic evaluations of control systems conducted and documented?

- Are such evaluations conducted by personnel with appropriate responsibilities, business experience, and knowledge of the organization's affairs?

- Are appropriate criteria established to evaluate controls?

- Are control deficiencies reported to higher levels of management and corrected on a timely basis?

- Are appropriate controls built-in as new systems are designed and brought on stream?

Audit Committee Effectiveness
- Has the board recently reviewed adequacy of the audit committee's written charter?

- Are audit committee members functioning and, in fact, independent of management?

- Do audit committee members possess an appropriate mix of operating and financial control expertise?

- Does the audit committee understand and monitor the broad organizational control environment?

- Does the audit committee oversee appropriateness, relevance, and reliability of operational and financial reporting to the board, as well as to investors and other external users?

- Does the audit committee oversee existence of and compliance with ethical standards?

- Does the audit committee or full board have a meaningful but challenging relationship with independent auditors, internal auditors, senior financial control executives, and key corporate and business unit operating executives?

Internal Auditing Function Effectiveness
- Does internal auditing have the support of top management, the audit committee, and the board of directors as a whole?

- Has the written scope of internal auditing responsibilities been reviewed by the audit committee for adequacy?

- Is the organizational relationship between internal auditing and senior executives appropriate?

- Does internal auditing have and use open lines of communication and private access to all senior officers and the audit committee?

- Are audit reports covering the right subjects distributed to the right people and acted upon in a timely manner?

- Do key audit executives possess an appropriate level of expertise?

NOTE

1. To purchase *Internal Control—Integrated Framework* or *Internal Control over Financial Reporting—Guidance for Smaller Public Companies*, visit www.cpa2biz.com/index.jsp.

Appendix C

Standardized Period-End
Process Control Matrix

Cycle	Transaction	Control Objective	Risk	Control Activity
Period-end process	Leases	Leases are properly recorded as capital or operating based on terms of the agreement.	Balance sheet may not accurately reflect all assets and liabilities.	Staff accountant documents accounting treatment of leases based on terms of agreement and lease checklist. Lease evaluation is reviewed and signed by accounting manager and a copy is attached to the lease agreement and journal entry if applicable.
Period-end process	Accruals	Outstanding liabilities for goods/services received but not yet billed at period-end are properly accrued.	Liabilities will be understated.	Accounts payable supervisor emails all staff accountants the monthly "open receiving" report to ensure all items received but not matched to an invoice have been properly accrued. Based on email responses, accounts payable supervisor makes journal entry or documents the reason for no journal entry. Accounts payable manager reviews report for completeness and accuracy and signs off.

(Continued)

Cycle	Transaction	Control Objective	Risk	Control Activity
Period-end process	Impairments	All assets are properly valued in the financial statements.	Assets are overstated.	Finance manager sends quarterly email to all finance directors inquiring of any equipment or intangible impairments. If applicable, finance manager prepares impairment analysis, which is reviewed and signed by senior director of finance. Analysis is used for basis of adjustment to ledger and is attached to journal entry.
Period-end process	Journal entries	General ledger balances are accurate.	Financial statements may be misstated due to an omission, clerical error, or incorrect entries.	Staff accountant prepares journal entries on a monthly basis and attaches supporting documentation to journal entry form. All journal entries are reviewed for accuracy and signed by preparer's supervisor.
Period-end process	Accounting memos	Unusual or high-risk transactions are properly recorded according to generally accepted accounting principles.	Transactions will not be recorded properly, causing a material misstatement in the financials.	Accounting memo or justification why a memo is not necessary accompanies all agreements. Financial analyst sends a copy of all agreements with a value in excess of $1 million to accounting manager to document the proper accounting treatment. Financial analyst prepares journal entry to record transaction based on accounting memo guidance (if applicable). Preparers' supervisors review and sign memo and journal entry.
Period-end process	Account reconciliations	General ledger balances are accurate and substantiated.	Financial statements may be misstated due to an omission, clerical error, or incorrect entries.	Staff accountants prepare reconciliations of all balance sheet and certain profit and loss accounts per the month-end accounts reconciliation listing. Reconciliations are signed off by preparers, approved by preparers' supervisors, attached to the related journal entries, and tied to the general ledger.

Period-end process	Variance analysis	Identify variances, trends, or unusual changes and their causes by comparing actual results to budgets/prior periods.	Material errors or omissions will not be realized before financials are filed.	Finance group meets with vice president of finance quarterly to review actual versus budget and current versus prior variance reports. All unexpected variances are discussed and resolved during the day 2 review meeting. Final variance analysis with explanations for variances over $100,000 is signed by the vice president of finance and retained in the monthly close binders.
Period-end process	Financial disclosures	All schedules prepared for disclosures are accurate and complete.	Disclosures are misstated or incomplete.	Senior accountants prepare and foot disclosure schedules quarterly. Preparers' supervisors review and tie numbers on disclosure schedules to supporting documentation to ensure accuracy. Review is evidenced by signoff on schedules, and signed schedules are submitted to corporate accounting.

Appendix D

PCAOB Staff Question-and-Answer Index

Although many of the Public Company Accounting Oversight Board (PCAOB) Staff answers refer to Auditing Standard No. 2, most topics and concepts are still valid.

12. Compensating controls

13. Testing exceptions

14. Compensating controls to mitigate significant deficiencies or material weaknesses

15. Evaluation of material weaknesses

16. Significant accounts at significant locations

17. Multilocation coverage of a company's financial position

18. Sampling for multilocation coverage

19. Excluding an entity from scope

20. Auditor testing when using the work of others

21. Auditor testing when using the work of others

22. Auditor testing when using the work of others

23. Auditor testing of fraud controls

24. In scope outsourced activities

25. SAS 70 report more than six months from year-end

26. SAS 70 report from a nonregistered accounting firm

27. Compliance with laws and regulations

28. Scope limitation when SAS 70 reports are not available

29. Walk-throughs at service organizations

30. Using the report of another auditor in integrated financial and internal control audits

31. Federal Deposit Insurance Corporation (FDIC) and Section 404 requirements for insured depository institutions

32. Scope and timing of auditor's procedures when evaluating deficiencies on an annual and interim basis

33. Auditor's communication of deficiencies to the audit committee

34. Management's representation letter for deficiencies identified as part of management's assessment

35. Evaluating the significance of pervasive/information technology (IT) control deficiencies

36. Using internal auditors to assist in the audit of internal control

37. PCAOB's temporary transition rule for AS No. 2

38. Description of the top-down approach

39. Description of a risk-based audit

40. How assessment of risk affects audit procedures

41. Role of qualitative factors and risk in identifying significant accounts

42. Requirements for auditor testing of all management's key controls

43. How risk affects the auditor's nature, timing, and extent of control testing

44. Using information obtained in prior year's audit of internal control

45. Benchmarking strategy for testing automated application controls

46. Defining "alternating tests of controls"

47. Auditor evaluation of management's assessment

48. Auditor's use of self-assessment tests

49. Auditor evaluation of management's assessment on a control-by-control level

50. Testing periods for internal control audits

51. Auditor interim testing and roll-forward procedures

52. Auditor evaluation of internal control when there has been a key change to IT

53. Effectiveness of controls when there is no documentation or evidence

54. Obtaining the principal evidence supporting the audit opinion when the work of others has been used

55. Auditor testing for management's quarterly certifications on internal control

The PCAOB Staff Questions and Answers can be found at www.pcaob .org/Standards/Staff_Questions_and_Answers/index.aspx

Appendix E

SEC Office of the Chief Accountant Frequently Asked Questions Index

Twelve of the original FAQs were eliminated as a result of updates for the SEC's Guidance for Management issued in June 2007. Because they are no longer relevant, the 12 eliminated FAQs are not included here.

Date issued: October 6, 2004
FAQ
No. Topic

1. Legal rights to assess a consolidated entity's internal controls

2. Equity method investment's internal controls

3. Assessing internal control at acquired businesses

4. If registrants are current for Rule 144 when internal controls are ineffective

6. Disagreement between management and the auditor on internal controls

8. Attestation requirement when filing a transition report on Form 10-K/KSB

9. Disclosure of changes to controls in advance of first compliance date

14. The same auditors or different year-ends on SAS 70 reports

21. Consent to use auditor's report for 1933 Securities Act filing

22. Including management's and the auditor's report in annual reports to shareholders

23. Including required supplementary information in management's assessment

The SEC FAQ's issued on January 21, 2005, were all related to the exemptive order that extended the initial internal control reporting due date by 45 days for companies with year-ends between November 15, 2004 and February 28, 2005. Because they are no longer relevant, the 10 FAQs are not included here.

The SEC issued a revised version of its FAQs on September 24, 2007, to address new guidance and issues related to Section 404 compliance.

Date issued: September 24, 2007
FAQ
No./Topic

1. Legal rights to assess a consolidated entity's internal controls

2. Equity method investment's internal controls

3. Assessing internal control at acquired businesses

4. If registrants are current for Rule 144 when internal controls are ineffective

5. Disagreement between management and the auditor on internal controls

6. Attestation requirement when filing a transition report on Form 10-K/KSB

7. Disclosure of changes to controls in advance of first compliance date

8. The same auditors or different year-ends on SAS 70 reports

9. Consent to use auditor's report for 1933 Securities Act filing

10. Including management's and the auditor's report in annual reports to shareholders

11. Including required supplementary information in management's assessment

12. Foreign private issuer's evaluation of internal controls on its primary financial statements versus its reconciliation to U.S. generally accepted accounting principles (GAAP)

13. Evaluating the severity of deficiencies for foreign private issuers

14. Foreign private issuer's treatment of certain entities for purposes of evaluating internal controls

15. Foreign private issuer's treatment of certain entities on a proportionate consolidation basis for purposes of evaluating internal controls

The SEC Office of the Chief Accountant frequently asked questions can be found under the heading *Staff Guidance* at www.sec.gov/spotlight/soxcomp.htm.

Appendix F

Summary of Changes Made to Auditing Standard No. 2 and the Related New Guidance

Concept in AS No. 2	Paragraph	Concept in AS No. 5	Paragraph
Testing company-level controls alone is not sufficient for the purpose of expressing an opinion on the effectiveness of a company's internal control over financial reporting.	54	Omitted statement that "testing company-level controls alone is not sufficient."	N/A
"The auditor should not use the work of others to reduce the amount of work he or she performs on controls in the control environment."	113	Omits the specific restriction on using the work of others for testing controls in the control environment.	N/A
Requires auditors to opine on management's evaluation process.	40–46	Eliminates the requirement for auditors to evaluate management's evaluation process and requires auditors to express only one opinion on internal control.	N/A

(Continued)

Concept in AS No. 2	Paragraph	Concept in AS No. 5	Paragraph
Not discussed.	N/A	Describes ways for auditors to integrate their audits of internal control and the financial statements.	6–8 and B1–B9
Discusses management's risk assessment process only. Does not include auditor's risk assessment or risk assessment for planning purposes.	N/A	Emphasizes risk assessment at the top level and all the way down to the control level.	10–12 and 29–32
Size and complexity of company referred to only in terms of the form and extent of documentation used. Does not require auditors to evaluate size and complexity in planning their audit.	43	Advises auditors to consider the size and complexity of a company in planning and performing the audit.	9 and 13
Includes "principal evidence" provision, which requires auditors' own work to provide the principal evidence for their opinions on companies' internal control.	108	Auditors could determine how much of the work of others could be used by evaluating the competence and objectivity of those who performed the work.	16–19
Advises auditors to use the same conceptual definition of materiality that applies to financial reporting for internal control over financial reporting. References both quantitative and qualitative considerations and AU Section 312, *Audit Risk and Materiality in Conducting an Audit*.	23	Advises auditors to plan and perform their audits of internal control using the same materiality measures used to plan and perform the annual financial statement audits.	20
Gives examples for company-level controls.	53	Adds "controls over management override" to examples of entity-level controls.	24
Lists components that make up control environment but does not supply steps for evaluation.	53, 113–115	Supplies steps for auditor to assess the control environment.	25

Multilocation testing to cover a "large portion" of the company's operations.	B4–B11	Omits the provision requiring testing of controls over a "large portion" of the company. Multilocation testing focused on risk, not coverage.	B10–B16
"The auditor should perform at least one walk-through for each major class of transactions."	79	Focuses on the objectives that walk-throughs can accomplish but does not require the auditor to perform them.	37–38
"The auditor should perform the walk-throughs himself or herself because of the degree of judgment required in performing this work."	116	Omits requirement for auditors to perform the walk-throughs themselves.	N/A
"When the auditor identifies exceptions to the company's prescribed control procedures, he or she should determine, using professional skepticism, the effect of the exception on the nature and extent of additional testing that may be appropriate or necessary and on the operating effectiveness of the control being tested. A conclusion that an identified exception does not represent a control deficiency is appropriate only if evidence beyond what the auditor had initially planned and beyond inquiry supports that conclusion."	107	The new standard allows for more flexibility in finding exceptions. It states: "Because effective internal control over financial reporting cannot, and does not, provide absolute assurance of achieving the company's control objectives, an individual control does not necessarily have to operate without any deviation to be considered effective."	48
When testing at an interim date, auditors should determine what additional evidence to obtain concerning the operation of controls for the remaining period (through the "as of " date).	100–101	Allows for roll-forward procedures for testing controls based on risk.	55–56

(Continued)

Concept in AS No. 2	Paragraph	Concept in AS No. 5	Paragraph
"Each year's audit must stand on its own."	E120	Allows auditors the flexibility to reduce testing in some areas based on knowledge obtained in previous audits and allows this knowledge to affect auditors' assessment of risk.	57–61
Benchmarking is not precluded but not addressed.	E122	May use a benchmarking strategy for automated application controls in subsequent years' audits.	60 and B28–B33
In evaluating deficiencies, auditors should determine "the likelihood that a deficiency, or a combination of deficiencies, could result in a misstatement of an account balance or disclosure."	131	In evaluating deficiencies, auditors should determine "whether there is a reasonable possibility that the company's controls will fail to prevent or detect a misstatement of an account balance or disclosure."	63
The restatement of previously issued financial statements, an ineffective control environment, and uncorrected significant deficiencies from prior years were described as "circumstances that should be regarded as at least significant deficiencies and as strong indicators of a material weakness."	140, E94–E100	Removed the requirement to consider these circumstances as at least significant deficiencies. The language was changed to "Indicators of material weaknesses." It allows the auditor to conclude that a material weakness (or significant deficiency) exists but does not require the auditor to reach that conclusion.	69

Describes pervasive controls to address risk of fraud.	24–25	Describes different control-level processes to address the risk of fraud.	14–15
Material weakness defined as "a significant deficiency, or combination of significant deficiencies, that result in a more than remote likelihood that a material misstatement of the annual or interim financial statements will not be prevented or detected."	10	Material weakness defined as "a deficiency, or combination of deficiencies, in internal control over financial reporting, such that there is a reasonable possibility that a material misstatement of the company's annual or interim financial statements will not be prevented or detected on a timely basis."	A7
Significant deficiency defined as "a control deficiency, or combination of control deficiencies, that adversely affects the company's ability to initiate, authorize, record, process, or report external financial data reliably in accordance with generally accepted accounting principles such that there is more than a remote likelihood that a misstatement of the company's annual or interim financial statements that is more than inconsequential will not be prevented or detected."	9	Significant deficiency defined as "a deficiency, or combination of deficiencies, in internal control over financial reporting that is less severe than a material weakness, yet important enough to merit attention by those responsible for oversight of the company's financial reporting."	A11

Index